THE
VALLEY of VIRGINIA
IN THE
AMERICAN REVOLUTION

The Fairfax Coat of Arms
Made by the Zane Iron Works at Marlboro near
Winchester, Virginia, before the Revolution

THE

VALLEY *of* VIRGINIA

IN THE

AMERICAN REVOLUTION

1763-1789

By

Freeman H. Hart

NEW YORK / RUSSELL & RUSSELL

Preface

THE VALLEY OF VIRGINIA can rightly claim an important
place in the history of the American people, particularly
for the period of the American Revolution. There George
Washington began his manifold career, business, military,
and political; for it was in the Valley he surveyed for
Lord Fairfax, from there he led his regiment to the
French and Indian War, and there he entered politics as
a representative from Frederick County in the Virginia
House of Burgesses. He and his family owned broad
acres in the north Valley where two of his brothers established homes. Had it not been for his inheritance of
Mount Vernon, George himself would probably have settled in the Valley. He spent many of his adult years there
prior to the Revolution.

If we count Washington as one, the Valley furnished
four major generals to the American Revolution and not
less than three able and prominent brigadiers. Resolutions that presaged the Declaration of Independence came
from Frederick County as early as May, 1774. Other
Valley counties followed Frederick with similar resolutions very soon thereafter. Companies of riflemen from
this portion of the frontier were the first troops from the

South to join in the siege of Boston, and soldiers from these counties took part in nearly every engagement of consequence in the Revolution. The Virginia government fled to the Valley for refuge when Cornwallis invaded the state, and there, tradition says, Washington expected to make his stand had he been driven from the seaboard.

After the war, when the need came for a stronger government, the Valley again played a major role. At the critical time for the ratification of the new Constitution— since the sentiment in the Virginia Convention was evenly divided—the Valley delegates by casting a unanimous vote in favor of ratification assured the successful launching of the new venture. When the new federal government was being organized in 1789, Shepherdstown, in Berkeley County on the Potomac, was considered a possible seat for its capital.

John Sevier was born in the Valley of Virginia, and likewise John Breckinridge, Arthur and William Campbell, William Christian, Sam Houston, and many of the other leaders in the advance to the West and Southwest. Abraham Lincoln, grandfather of the president, was a militia captain in the Valley in the Revolutionary period. The ancestors of many prominent western leaders of a later day, such as Thomas Hart Benton, the Blairs of Missouri, William Jennings Bryan, and Champ Clark, had been pioneers in this portion of the Virginia frontier. At Staunton Woodrow Wilson was born in 1856 on the eve of the South's war for self-determination.

At Shepherdstown in the north Valley in 1788 Rumsey was experimenting with the steamboat and arousing Washington's enthusiasm for the possibilities of his invention. A little later in the south Valley McCormick and McGowan revolutionized American farming with their invention of the reaper; and one of their neighbors, Gibbs, was making his notable contribution toward perfecting the sewing machine. Ephraim McDowell, the pioneer in abdominal surgery, was still another to whom the Valley was a homeland.

For nearly two centuries the fertile lands of the Valley have appealed to those who looked for a better living or a granary for armed forces; and its scenic wonders, above and below the surface of the earth, have fascinated the traveler. Governor Spottswood's Golden Horseshoe Expedition to the Valley has become nearly classic. During the Revolution, Thomas Anburey, a young British officer and prisoner of war from Burgoyne's surrender at Saratoga, spoke for succeeding generations of travelers as he described in his diary his first impression of the Valley, from the top of the Blue Ridge Mountains: "When you reach the top you are suddenly surprised with an unbounded prospect, that strikes you with awe and amazement. At the foot of the mountain runs a beautiful river; beyond it a very extensive plain, interspersed with a variety of objects, to render the scene still more delightful; and about fifty miles distant are the lofty Alleghany Mountains, whose tops are buried in the clouds."[1]

This study of the Valley as a cross section of the frontier in the critical years of the American Revolution was started under the tutelage of Professor Frederick J. Turner, whose philosophy of the frontier has left a marked impression on the writing of American history. Its progress, in both research and composition, has been accompanied by the encouragement and constructive criticisms of three other former presidents of the American Historical Association, Professors Edward Channing, Charles H. McIlwain, and Evarts B. Greene and also by Dr. John H. Finley of the *New York Times*. Material for its

---

[1] Thomas Anburey, *Travels in America*, II, 415.

pages has been gathered from dozens of libraries, from numerous public and private collections of manuscripts and other papers, from countless pages of church records and minutes, from a score of Virginia courthouses, and from a close study of the geography of this fascinating portion of the Old Dominion.

It is the hope of the author that this description of the early Valley years will clearly demonstrate that this particular portion of the frontier did not fully match the pattern that has been drawn by the frontier philosophy of American history. During the Revolutionary period the Valley was an area of dissenters, of debt-ridden small farmers, and of a people made liberal in their political thinking by the necessity of shifting for themselves in the face of the constant menace of starvation and of warfare with dangerous Indian foes. Yet with all this the Valley people not only joined valiantly in the fight for civil and religious liberty, but likewise, and in contrast to most of the frontier areas, they supported the movement for stable government that followed the war and that was realized under the Constitution in 1789. The predominance in the Valley mind of a strong Calvinistic theology undoubtedly played its part in the struggle for freedom of religion as well as for the new Constitution.

In addition to the inspiration furnished by the historians mentioned above, the author has had constructive help from many colleagues and from those both within and without the Valley who are interested in the story of its early days. They have helped me to avoid many pitfalls and errors, but are responsible for none of those which remain in the pages that follow. Particular gratitude goes to Professor John A. Krout of Columbia University and his associates in American history, whose encouragement and invaluable criticisms have brought this

study to the point of publication. A final word of thanks
goes to Professor T. P. Abernethy of the University of
Virginia and to Director W. T. Couch and his associates
at the University of North Carolina Press for helping
polish some of the rougher edges.

Intimate personal gratitude is due a number of my
former students and student assistants, a few of whom are
Dr. W. Edwin Hemphill of Mary Washington College,
E. Lewis Lacy, Arthur M. Field, P. G. Cosby, and Philip
H. Ropp; and particularly to my wife, Jean Fraser Hart,
who was born and grew up in the Presbyterian manse
from which the Valley gave Woodrow Wilson to the
world.

CONTENTS

ILLUSTRATIONS

MAPS

THE
VALLEY of VIRGINIA
IN THE
AMERICAN REVOLUTION

On the Eve of the Revolution
1763-1775

BETWEEN the Blue Ridge and Alleghany Mountains lies that portion of Virginia which is known as the Valley. It extends from the Potomac River southward to the head-waters of the James. Not quite two hundred miles in length and varying in breadth from about ten to seventy miles, it comprises an area nearly equal to New Jersey.

The Shenandoah River, a tributary of the Potomac, drains the northern end of the Valley; and the head-waters of the James, the southern end. Numerous mineral springs are found in the watersheds, and as early as 1763 these—particularly the baths and sulphur springs[1] —were already arousing interest, even beyond the Valley. The girdle of mountains, the Blue Ridge and the Alleghany, as well as the mid-Valley Massanutten Range, add to the geographical interest of the region with its Natural Bridge, its numerous caverns, and its "Chimneys" (earlier known as "The Towers," more recently as the "Cyclopean Towers").

---

[1] These included Hot (or Warm) Springs and Yellow, Blue, Grey, Red, and Cold Sulphur Springs in Augusta County, and Bath and Warm Springs in Berkeley County.

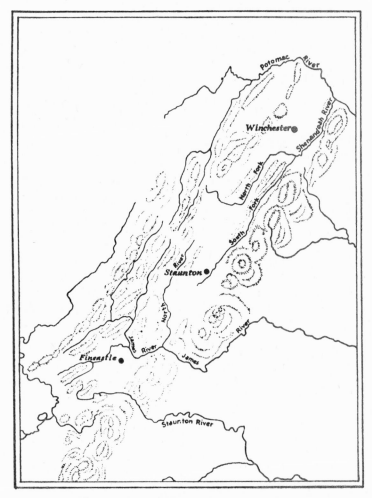

PHYSICAL MAP OF THE VALLEY OF VIRGINIA

The soil is primarily the stiff, red-clay limestone formation that readily lends itself to grain and grass production. Here in the Revolutionary era farmers reaped fine
crops of hemp, wheat, corn, flax, barley, oats, and rye;

and, since pasturage was abundant, they pocketed easy profits from raising cattle, sheep, horses, and hogs. The soil did not offer much promise for tobacco culture and that product found little favor in the Valley, a fact which was to create something of an economic problem later in the Revolutionary period.

In 1763 Augusta and Frederick counties embraced in their boundaries not only the Valley but also Trans-Alleghany Virginia, extending indefinitely toward the west.[2] By 1776 a part of Augusta had become the new county of Botetourt, while Frederick had been divided to form the two new counties of Berkeley and Dunmore.[3] Two additional counties, Rockbridge and Rockingham, carved largely from Augusta, were created in 1778.[4]

The Valley was settled chiefly by Palatinate Germans and Ulster Scots[5] who were a part of the large stream of these two races that moved west, south, and southwest from Pennsylvania in the eighteenth century. The Germans came first and occupied the more fertile areas of the north Valley; in the Revolutionary period they were predominant in Dunmore County (Shenandoah), Rockingham, and, to some degree, in Frederick. The Scots, who were almost entirely Ulstermen, followed closely behind, some stopping to occupy the somewhat less favored lands near the Potomac, others pushing on into the south Valley. Most of them settled in Berkeley County by the Potomac

[2] William W. Hening, *Statutes at Large*, V, 78; VI, 376 *et passim*.

[3] Hening, *Statutes*, VIII, 395; Botetourt, 1796, and Berkeley and Dunmore, 1772.

[4] *Ibid.*, IX, 421. Dr. R. B. Woodworth of Burlington, W. Va., makes a good case for including Hampshire as a Valley county. It undoubtedly is, or was in 1763-89, racially and politically one with the Valley if not topographically so. See also Jefferson, *Notes*, p. 193.

[5] The usual term is Scotch-Irish but they had little Irish blood. They were the Scots who had been settled in Ulster County, Ireland, a century before they began flocking to America. There were some pure Irish among the indentured servants in the Valley. These were termed "mere" Irish by the Ulster Scots.

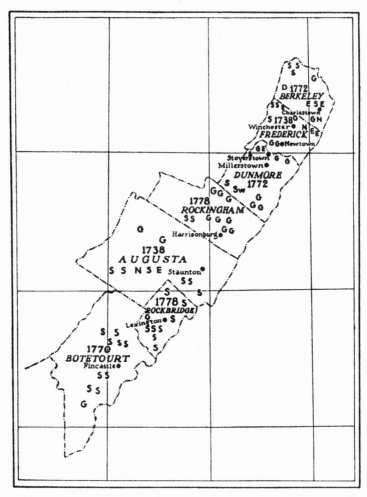

ANALYSIS OF POPULATION IN THE VALLEY OF VIRGINIA, 1776

Each letter represents approximately ten per cent of population
of the respective county.

G—German or Palatine   Sw—Swiss
E—English   D—Dutch
S—Scots or Ulstermen   N—Negro

(Date given on each county represents year county was established.)

and in Augusta, Rockbridge, and Botetourt.[6] In addition
to its German and Ulster Scot settlers the region had even
in these early years a considerable number of English
from eastern Virginia, some from Pennsylvania, and a
small number directly from England. A few Swiss,
Dutch, Swedes, and Welsh were also to be found. Likewise there were large numbers of indentured servants,
chiefly Irish it seems, who were rapidly becoming independent settlers as their indentures expired. James Ireland wondered at the numerous nationalities and sects but
saw them living together in a "common state of sociabil-
ity" when as a Baptist circuit rider he went to the Valley
to preach just before the Revolution.[7]

The most acceptable estimates for the population of the
Valley in 1763 show 20,000 whites and a thousand blacks;
by 1776 there were 48,000 whites and 5,000 blacks; and
in 1790, 71,000 whites and 12,000 blacks.[8] In so far as
these figures are correct there was a population density of
less than three to the square mile in 1763, a little over
seven in 1776, and about twelve in 1789. There were six
towns in the Valley in 1763: Winchester, Mecklenburg
(Shepherdstown), Staunton, Stephensburg, Strasburg,
and Woodstock. Five of them had been established within
the half-dozen years before 1763, partly on the theory

[6] The best indication of racial areas is to be found in the church records.
These show numerous Presbyterian churches in Berkeley, Augusta, Rock-
bridge, and Botetourt; German sects in Rockingham, Shenandoah, and
Frederick; and Anglican churches in Frederick, with some in Berkeley.

[7] See county court records, order and minute books, for the Valley
counties during the period; over forty naturalization certificates were
issued by the Augusta court, 1763-1776. See also James Ireland, *Autobiography*.

[8] Greene and Harrington, *American Population Before 1790*, pp. 152-
153; Stephen Papers for 1779, #132; Excerpt Amelia Order Book from
Va. Mag., XVIII, 81-82; Koontz, *Virginia Frontier*, pp. 167-168; Valley
Courts, Minute and Order Books, 1763-1776 *passim*, for the number of
tithables per the local levies; for 1776 see especially Miles S. Malone,
"The Distribution of Population on the Virginia Frontier in 1775"
(Princeton Thesis, 1935, unpublished); *Census of 1790*.

that the "erecting of towns" might aid the inhabitants in defending themselves against "the sudden incursions of the enemy"[9]—a reference to Indian raids. Two additional towns were established between 1763 and 1776, Fincastle in the south Valley and Martinsburg near the Potomac.[10] By 1789 eight more had been added: Bath, Lexington, Harrisonburg, Charlestown (named for the brother of George Washington who lived near by), Middletown, Front Royal, Pattonsburg, and Crowsville.[11] Thus the Valley grew and prospered in the Revolutionary period.

From the standpoint of a "money crop," hemp was the leading product of the Valley just before the Revolution. A half-century earlier Parliament, in an endeavor to make the Empire self-sufficient in the matter of naval supplies, had placed a bounty on hemp to encourage colonial production.[12] After continued prodding by Parliament, the Virginia Burgesses added their efforts to stimulate hemp planting.[13] Meanwhile the Valley was filling up with settlers and thus an area for hemp raising was provided.

The amount of hemp produced was remarkably large. In the year 1767 twenty-three Augusta growers each raised between 1,000 and 8,800 pounds.[14] For several years after 1770, Augusta averaged over 100,000 pounds

[9] Hening, *Statutes*, VII, 234, 406, 473, 598.
[10] *Ibid.*, 616-617; Berkeley Deed Book, I, 9.
[11] Hening, *Statutes*, IX, 247, 422; X, 293; XII, 370, 607, 672-674.
[12] *American Husbandry*, I, 258-259 (1775). The anonymous writer of this interesting contemporary treatise says that hemp was the "commodity of all others which we most want from our colonies," because the navy was dependent on it. He further suggests that there was an abundance of hemp land in the "back part" of Virginia. See also *Calendar of State Papers, America and the West Indies*, 1704-1705, p. 688.
[13] See Hening, *Statutes*, V, 357; Mercer, *Virginia Laws in 1758*; *Statutes at Large*, IX, 185, 4 Geo. III, ch. 26.
[14] Augusta Order Books, VIII-XVIII; Augusta Minutes, 1764-1775, *passim*. Nicholas Cresswell, in his *Diary*, reported hemp 14 feet high and equal to that of Riga. He saw no reason why the Valley should not rival Russia in producing it and supplant that country in supplying the English navy.

a year. The Frederick records show an annual output of 20,000 to 30,000 pounds.[15] Botetourt was one of the most prolific hemp centers in the Valley. In the county's first year, 1769, its hemp certificates represented 121,700 pounds, and the next year, 170,000 pounds.[16] The hemp bounty amounted to a substantial figure, and, since the price ranged from thirty to fifty shillings[17] the hundred-weight, depending on the year and place of marketing, the Valley realized goodly returns from this product. As the Revolution approached, bounty payments ceased, but production continued during the war. In the early years of the war the Scottish merchants on the James River established a ropewalk or factory which employed thirty men and depended on the south Valley to furnish the hemp.[18]

Some flax was raised, largely for domestic consumption. One ambitious Scot, Andrew Duncan, set up a fulling mill in Augusta County in 1767. He agreed to pay a fuller £20 a year and "vittles" for three years to teach him and his family the trade.[19] John Caldwell erected a mill for

---

[15] Frederick Order Book, XIV, *passim*.

[16] Botetourt Minute and Order Books, 1770-1776, *passim*. See L. C. Gray, *History of Agriculture in the South to 1860*, I, 182, for export data. He has Virginia exporting 388 tons in 1768, which could hardly have taken care of the Valley output, part of which undoubtedly went out through Philadelphia.

[17] English or colonial monetary terms are used here and in the succeeding pages. Money was rated by one contemporary Valley leader as follows: £ (Pound) equal to $2.68, shilling equal to .13½; and penny equal to .01⅛, per Gates Papers, Miscel., 1774. By another they were rated: £ (Pound) equal to $3.13⅓; shilling .16⅔; penny .01⅔, Breckinridge Papers, Miscel., 1770.

[18] In 1768 the price quoted in Augusta was 35 shillings per bale or bundle of 112 pounds. On the Philadelphia market, the price was 37 shillings in 1769 but went up to 50 in 1770 (Augusta Judgments, August, 1768; *Pennsylvania Gazette*, 1769-1772, *passim*). See Preston Papers, especially the correspondence between William Preston and his Scotch brother-in-law, Edward Johnson of Manchester (South Richmond), 1775-1779 *passim*, letters from Johnson dated July 2, 1778, and May 29, 1779.

[19] Augusta Judgments, Nov., 1767.

the manufacture of "linseed oyl," but it did not prosper, and his appeal for a state subsidy was denied by the Burgesses.[20] Governor Fauquier in 1766 reported an attempt to make hemp into osnaburgs.[21]

Wheat ranked next to hemp in production. Scores of flour mills had been erected by 1763, some with independent proprietors and others as adjuncts to the larger plantations.[22] By 1775 the north Valley was exporting large quantities of both flour and wheat, and the southern counties were not far behind. Wheat was raised easily, since it required little preparation of the soil, and even less cultivation. The amount produced per acre was about twelve bushels, a low yield as compared with the present day, but good when we consider the farming methods of the time.[23]

The colonial legislature showed an active interest in the production of flour, not by subsidizing it as in the case of hemp, but by providing for its inspection. This was done to protect the public and shippers from an inferior product,[24] as well as the producers from unscrupulous competition. In their bill of 1772, amending earlier inspection acts, the Burgesses noted that the production of flour had "of late very much increased in this Colony and become a very advantageous article for commerce."[25]

[20] Augusta Order Book, XIV, 104; *Journal, Burgesses,* June 6, 1775.

[21] A coarse fabric usually made of the roughest linen. Bancroft, *Virginia Papers,* I, 469.

[22] Court Records, Valley Counties, 1763-1776. See Gray, *op. cit.,* I, 164. See Revolutionary Claims, preserved in the form of certificates, which indicate Berkeley and Frederick were each producing over a million pounds of flour a year. See picture of mill, facing p. 42.

[23] See Cresswell, *Diary,* pp. 47, 49, 196; Stephen Papers, no. 138. The plowing was very shallow. The writer of *American Husbandry,* 1775, I, 263, claimed about 25 to 40 bushels per acre, but he seems to have known little of conditions on the frontier. Some efforts were made to get a larger yield per acre by introducing better seed. See Gates Papers (N. Y. P.), Evans letter, April 24, 1773.

[24] Hening, *Statutes,* V, 350; VIII, 143, 198; *Journal, Burgesses,* Dec. 16, 1766; Augusta Order Book, VIII, 382.

[25] Hening, *op. cit.,* VIII, 511-514; *Journal, Burgesses,* April 9, 1772.

Corn was another popular grain crop.[26] There was also an abundance of hay, some rye, oats, barley, and beans, as well as root crops. Most of these were produced for home or local consumption.[27] Largely because of the use of tobacco notes as legal tender, the Valley tried that crop, but without much success.[28] Thus while tobacco production was developing a stronghold in the Piedmont, as it had in the Tidewater, the Valley was laying the foundation for grain production both there and in the West.

Horses, cattle, and hogs rivaled wheat and flour as Valley products. In addition to their value in the raising of grain, horses had an especial appeal. They provided the frontiersman, ever interested in moving on when he heard of better lands elsewhere, with the necessary means of transportation. If raised for the market, horses were easily sold. Since such accessible and mobile property provided unusual temptation for the idle and vicious, the ready sale proved a bane as well as a blessing. As a result, horse stealing became the chief criminal problem of the

The barrels had to be labeled with the initials of the maker, be marked with "S.F." or "F." (i.e., superfine or fine), and have the weight stamped on. The range in price of flour and wheat during the period is not easily determined. About twenty-five shillings a barrel (flour ran about 220 lbs. to the barrel) was allowed to the French and Indian War claimants (*Journal, Burgesses*, Dec. 10, 1766). The price on the Philadelphia market, 1769-1772, varied from fifteen to twenty shillings (*Pennsylvania Gazette*, 1769-1772, *passim*). In 1775 General Gates was allowed ten and a half shillings a barrel at Alexandria (Gates Papers, N. Y. H. S., no. 198). The preceding year wheat sold for about three shillings a bushel in the Valley, but in Alexandria it brought as much as four and five shillings (Cresswell, *op. cit.*, pp. 47, 196).

[26] Corn sold locally at a shilling a bushel. Gates Papers (N. Y. H. S.), Misc., 1773.

[27] Cresswell, *op. cit.*, pp. 48, 198; Valley Court Records, 1763-1776, *passim*.

[28] *Journal, Burgesses*, Nov. 20, 1769. Some south Valley people joined with Bedford County in asking an inspection of tobacco at New London in that county. Washington had produced from twelve to fifteen hogsheads of tobacco on his Valley plantation in the period around 1760. *Diaries*, I, 166-167.

frontier. The colonial legislature offered ten pounds reward for the apprehension of such thieves.[29]

It was easier to raise cattle than horses; the expense was lower and there was less likelihood of theft.[30] Since there were several methods of marketing cattle, that problem was not so great as for some other Valley products. The animals were driven to market centers, or were slaughtered and prepared for shipment by one of three processes —drying, smoking, or salting—and then were packed in wooden casks.[31]

William Crow, a merchant of Staunton and later of Botetourt County, who dealt largely in cattle, usually drove his herds to such markets as Winchester, Philadelphia, and Fort Pitt, as well as to eastern Virginia.[32] Driving a large herd through such open country, in which there were more cattle than fences, without accumulation or loss was a difficult task—and Crow was sometimes charged with picking up cattle that were not his own. It was his custom to gather his herds, numbering from 150 to 200, as he moved north, and on one occasion when his herd grew from 131 to 141 within a few miles, the wife of a prominent settler remarked that "Crow's drove increased damnable."[33] To one of his complainants Crow is

[29] Hening, *Statutes*, V, 247. The frontiersmen developed a peculiar affection for their horses and gave considerable attention to the breeding and care of them. Was the Valley horse in some way the ancestor of the Kentucky thoroughbred? Horses were sold for good prices. Cresswell states that a horse, which could have been purchased in England for a fourth the amount, brought £40 in Berkeley County (Cresswell, *op. cit.*, p. 177). Allowing for probable exaggeration, the comparison still is interesting. The prices usually ranged from ten to fifteen pounds for yearling colts or old horses, and from twenty-five to forty pounds for the well-broken younger horses (Gates Papers—N. Y. H. S. Misc., 1773-1775, *passim*; Valley Will Books, 1763-1776, *passim*; Inventories of estates, sales).

[30] About 70 per cent of the people owned cattle of some sort.

[31] County Court Records, 1763-1776, *passim*.

[32] Augusta Judgments, March, 1764.

[33] *Ibid.*, August, 1767.

reported to have said, "You are like to make me a cattle thief." The reply was, "I never called you a thief but you took my cow." Because of this and other similar difficulties, he was haled into court and required to pay for the cattle that might or might not have voluntarily joined his herd.[34] Crow was a forerunner of the cattle herders of the Great West.

The by-products of cattle, such as butter, skins, and tallow, usually were kept for local consumption. We find, however, a shipment of twenty-nine casks of butter to Richmond, indicating an outside market for this particular product.[35]

Some progress had been made in manufacturing prior to 1776. There were distilleries and wineries,[36] at least four furnaces or iron works,[37] and one or more armories or gunneries. These industries were well known locally and evidently supplied all the frontier needs. Zane's Iron Works made several hundred tons of iron a year, and Bird

[34] In order to protect themselves from thievery as well as confusion of ownership, the more substantial cattle raisers recorded their markings in the county courts. See Augusta Order Book, IX, 375; XI, 236, 343, 504; XII, 275 for some of the more interesting ones, such as "A swallor fork in the right ear and an underkill in the left," "A slit in the right ear and a half penny on each side of the slit," and so on. There is no sure way of determining the amount of beef the Valley marketed annually. During the Revolution the section furnished the Continental armies with something over 500,000 pounds in one year (Revolutionary claims, Valley Counties, Virginia State Library. The assembly had voted that one-eighth of the cattle must be turned over to the armies). The marketable cattle of the time averaged in weight only about 350 pounds each (Revolutionary claims). The prices for cattle were from thirty shillings a head for good two-year-old cattle to two-and-a-half to four pounds a head for cows and older beeves (County Will Books, 1763-1776, inventories and sales). Beef was likewise comparatively cheap, ranging from a penny and a half to three pence a pound, regardless of cut, or age, or kind.—Gates Papers (N. Y. H. S.), Misc. Valley Court Records for period.

[35] Augusta Judgments, Feb., 1763.

[36] Augusta Order Book, X, 331; Augusta Judgments, Nov., 1762; Aug., 1768.

[37] The four were Zane's, Bird and Miller's, Vestal's, and the Bloomery. Valley Court Records, *passim;* Augusta Deed Book, XX, 352.

and Miller's works produced nearly as much. Zane made cooking utensils, stoves, ploughs and other implements. Adam Stephen's gunnery had a weekly output of ten to twelve muskets, which were reputed to be of good quality.[38]

The specie and paper money in use varied considerably, a fact which must have made no little trouble in business transactions. In addition to Virginia currency, the north Valley used Pennsylvania money and the south Valley that from both Pennsylvania and North Carolina.[39] Likewise there were tobacco notes, hemp certificates, bills of exchange, and even land bounty warrants.[40] Some of the specie was in English gold and silver pieces, but foreign coins were more frequent. When the Valley militia recovered two hundred pounds in gold taken from David Cloyd of Augusta by a marauding band of Indians in 1763, they found: "Double Loons, Loodores, Pistoles, Half Pistoles, Round Pistoles, Half Johannas, Dollars, and Guineas."[41] About one person in ten left some form of specie as part of his personal property. Nearly the same percentage left money scales—an important aid to a man doing business with various kinds of money. As in any frontier region, much of the business was done by the barter system, even wages being frequently paid in farm products. Such variety in the medium of exchange indicates extensive trade contacts.

[38] Jefferson, *Notes on Virginia*, p. 25; Zane Papers, 1771-1772; Pemberton Papers, XXIV, 28; Stephen Papers, 100a, 128.

[39] Gates Papers (N. Y. H. S.), Misc., 1773-1775; Stephen Papers, 1763-1776. The Pennsylvania currency usually passed at par, the Carolina at two thirds.

[40] Augusta Order Book, IX, 227; X, 290; Augusta Judgments, May, 1767; Valley Court Records, 1763 *et passim*. Virginia currency could be exchanged for sterling at twenty-five per cent discount.

[41] Augusta Order Book, 1764. Most of the coins are readily recognized. See also Augusta Judgments, Nov., 1764; Nov., 1766. William Allason, merchant of Falmouth, noted in 1774 the receipt of three hundred and seventy silver dollars at one time from one of his Valley customers.

The labor problem was a complicated one. There were at least four kinds of laborers: slaves, indentured servants, apprentices, and free laborers. There were two kinds of indentured servants: convicts and those who were working out passage money. The Valley pioneer also relied largely on the assistance of his wife and children.

The census of 1790 shows that the slave population of the Valley south from Shenandoah County was less than 10 per cent; in the more populous northern counties it was but 18 per cent, as compared with more than 50 per cent in the Piedmont and Tidewater. The proportion of slaves in the Valley before the Revolution was probably smaller than in 1790.[42] Isaac Zane, in 1771, had but one slave among his score of servants.[43] On the other hand, John Craig, the pioneer Presbyterian minister of the Valley, when he died in 1774 left behind five slaves. In 1767 echoes of a slave insurrection in Frederick County reached as far as Williamsburg. But the facts were that Colonel Adam Stephen, the county lieutenant, heard rumors of an uprising and ordered out a detachment of the militia, an "army" composed of thirteen men commanded by an ensign. They arrested a few slaves on suspicion and carried them before a justice, who finding no evidence of insurrection, discharged them. On two occasions Augusta County hanged slaves accused of murder and displayed their heads on poles by the roads leading into Staunton.[44]

Except for a few incidents of misbehavior, there is little evidence that the slaves were troublesome or that the

[42] *Census, 1790*, pp. 48-49. The northern counties had been settled longer and also had a larger percentage of eastern Virginians. According to the Blair Report to the Lords of Trade in 1756, less than five per cent of the Valley population was slave. Chalmers Papers, Virginia, I, 1756 report.

[43] Zane Papers, Inventory dated 1771.

[44] Augusta Will Book, VI, settlement recorded Dec. 20, 1785. *Journal, Burgesses*, Mar. 23, 1767; Nov. 14, 23, 1769; Augusta Order Book, VIII, 324; XIV, 362.

treatment of them was cruel. On the other hand we find John Anderson, the slave of John Craig, the Presbyterian minister noted above, suing his master for his freedom. He was allowed to go to eastern Virginia to secure evidence in support of his claim, whence he brought back a deposition that he was to be freed at twenty-one.[45] Since he had passed that age, the Augusta Court granted his suit and certified his freedom. In 1778 Mary Greenlee was summoned to court, on the petition of one of her slaves, to show cause why she held him in servitude. At the trial the court placed the burden of proof on the defendant, and, since her evidence in the form of a bill of sale was not reckoned sufficient, the slave was declared free.[46]

Indentured servants played an important part in the labor problems of the time. Augusta County had not less than a hundred and twenty-five cases of servant delinquency during a ten-year period. In the same period Frederick had nearly a hundred such cases, and the new county of Botetourt about fifty in three or four years.[47] Often the court dockets were almost entirely filled with such cases. One third of these defendants were women.

Not infrequently a master was haled into court on some charge of ill treatment. Usually, however, the defendant was a servant accused of some form of moral turpitude. From a third to a half of those on trial were runaways; but stealing was frequently the offense of both sexes. The

[45] Augusta Order Book, VII, 462; VIII, 122.
[46] Augusta Minute Book, Mar. 18, May 20, 1778. Local tradition makes Mary a most interesting character and something of a vixen. It also tells of the wandering bard who wrote her epitaph:

Old Mary Greenlee she died of late,
And straightway went to heaven's gate;
But the devil met her with a club,
And beat her back to Belzebub!

[47] Augusta Order Book, VII-XVI, *passim;* Frederick Order Book, XIV-XVI; Botetourt Minute Book, 1770-1775, *passim.*

punishment was thirty-nine lashes for the men and fifteen or twenty for the women. But the frugal Scot very often tempered mercy with profit by requiring the accused to serve additional time on his indenture. Added service was the usual sentence, if the delinquency had brought expense or loss of time to the master. Occasionally the servant volunteered extra service in return for being taught a trade, or for a wagon or tools to set up for himself, or for being allowed to marry.[48]

William Crow traded in servants as well as in cattle. One of his cases in court brought out the fact that he had bought and sold nine convicts—six men and three women.[49] Horatio Gates wanted Negroes for his field work but preferred a white servant for the household. He had some trouble, however, in getting the kind he wanted, but finally found a Dutch (German) girl who promised well.[50] William Allason sent servants to the Valley in October, 1765, representing the occupations an enterprising community would require—namely, a baker, a whitesmith—the contemporary term for tinsmith or silversmith—a weaver, a barber, a chair bottomer, a dyer, a brazier, and two gentleman's servants.[51] Allason received from fifteen to twenty-four pounds each for the various indentures, depending on the length of service and occupation.

[48] Valley County Order and Minute Books, 1763-1776. There is no way to determine what percentage of the white servants were convict, what passage-workers, and what apprentices. The fact that they were convicts was sometimes brought into the case to prove an indenture. Such evidence sometimes included the bill of conviction and the name of the ship on which they were brought.

[49] Augusta Judgments, March, 1768. Nicholas Cresswell planned to buy seven servants, two of whom should be women, and expected them to cost him an average of twenty pounds each (Cresswell, *Diary*, p. 195).

[50] Gates Papers (N. Y. P.), 1773, correspondence, *passim*. Isaac Zane owned fifteen servants in 1771, of whom four were women (Zane Papers, Inventory of 1771).

[51] The height of most of them reached only five feet, five inches, and their ages ranged from sixteen to forty. Their indentures ranged in time from four to seven years.

One Valley farmer paid for his purchase with wheat and butter.[52]

Edward Johnson, merchant on the James River, sent two lots, one of seven and the other of twenty-seven servants, to William Preston in April and May of 1774. They had cost him ten pounds each, but Preston was to get whatever he could for them.[53] Payment for several of these servants was made in hemp.[54] Meanwhile Preston wrote his brother-in-law, John Brown, the Presbyterian minister of Augusta, that he was entering the servant trade, and asked if there was any sale for them in those parts. Brown replied that there was no demand, for two reasons: first, the scarcity of money; and second, "Servants are plenty and everyone has as many as they want beside the County is sunk in debt by them already."[55] The next year Johnson sent a young doctor to be sold for the best price Preston could obtain. He was examined by another doctor, who found him "an Excellent Apothecary" and a "Tolerable Surgeon." His behavior was above reproach, and since he had four years to serve, Johnson thought he should be worth twenty-five pounds.[56]

In so far as names are dependable indications, the indentured servants in the Valley were chiefly Irish— "mere" Irish—and English, with some Scots and Germans.[57] At the end of their indentures they were assimilated by the other population, as was the case elsewhere. If they were courageous and resourceful, they pushed

[52] Allason Papers, paper in correspondence file. Oct., 1765.
[53] Preston Papers, Johnson to Preston, April 8, May 30, 1775.
[54] Ibid., July 17, 1775.
[55] U. B. Phillips, Documentary History of American Industrial Society, I, 374; John Brown to William Preston, Aug. 22, 1774.
[56] Preston Papers, Johnson to Preston, Sept. 5, 1775.
[57] Valley Court Records, 1763-1776, passim. One frequently finds the definitely Irish prefix "O," such as O'Brien and O'Connor, as well as such distinctive names as Cassidy, Murphy, and Callahan.

westward into the Indian country and in many cases eventually prospered.

The apprentice problem rivaled that of indentured servants, and was in some respects one with it. In accordance with the poor laws, children who had no support were bound out on somewhat the same terms as indentured servants. In the late colonial period Indian wars and depredations took a heavy toll of heads of families, and the county courts were kept busy providing apprenticeships for orphans. Not less than 150 were bound out by the Augusta Court in a period of ten years, and other counties had to provide for similarly large numbers. Frederick County Records show 220 orphans provided for in about the same ten-year period, while the Botetourt Court dealt with 55 apprentices and 32 orphans within six years from its establishment in 1770.[58] Few sections of colonial America felt this particular effect of Indian warfare as much as did the Valley.

The orphan was to be taught a trade, such as that of shoemaker, carpenter, wheelwright, wagonmaker, joiner, currier, or weaver, or, if a girl, spinning and weaving. Frequently he was to be taught to "read, write and cypher as far as the rule of three."[59] Now and then, in addition to freedom dues, he was to have specific gifts at the end of his apprenticeship. For a boy, the gift was usually a horse or saddle or wagon; for a girl, a cow or spinning wheel. The courts frequently called masters to account for failure to keep their agreements.

The wages of free labor were low as compared with present-day standards, but they were not out of line with

[58] Augusta Order Book, VIII-XVI, *passim*. See also Jernegan, *Laboring and Dependant Classes in Colonial America, 1607-1783* for an able treatment of this subject. He, of course, did not have access to the data on the somewhat peculiar Valley situation.

[59] Augusta Order Book, XV, 231, *et passim*.

those in other parts of the province. Horatio Gates paid
two and a half shillings a day, or two pounds a month, for
ordinary labor. Bearing in mind the prices, already noted,
of such commodities as flour and beef, the wages in pur-
chasing value were not as low as they seem. The two-and-
a-half shillings wage would have bought ten pounds of
steak or fifty pounds of flour; it amounted to 35-40 cents.
A wagon with two horses and a driver brought fifteen
shillings a day. Shoemaking brought nine and ten shillings a pair, wood-cutting two and a half shillings a cord,
and weaving two shillings a yard. Philip Fithian considered the Valley "a good place for labouring men."[60] In
Augusta County a storekeeper was paid fifteen to twenty-
four pounds a year and "keep," a fuller twenty pounds,
and a hunter fifteen to eighteen pounds.[61]

The chief problem of marketing lay in the mountain
barriers which blocked the way to seaport towns and made
trading difficult. As the people were bound to Pennsylvania by linguistic and religious ties, and since the products of the two regions were similar, Philadelphia became
an important market. Nevertheless the Valley was steadily turning its eyes toward the nearer eastern Virginia
market-places. The wagon haul and the cattle drive to
Philadelphia were so long that travelers were constantly
seeking better and shorter routes. During the pre-Revolutionary years, then, frontier merchants, as well as frontier planters, were bringing pressure to bear on the county
governments to build roads. They were also sending frequent petitions to the legislature, asking for highways
leading into and out of the Valley to strategic trade centers nearer home than Philadelphia.

In the decade 1763-1774, the county courts made pro-

---

[60] Philip V. Fithian, *Journal*, p. 147. He states that ordinary laborers
received two shillings a day, or half a crown at harvest time.
[61] Augusta Judgments, 1763-1776.

vision for hundreds of local roads leading from mills to
new highways or connecting areas of settlement with new
highways. The roads were usually opened by the labor of
tithable persons who lived on or near them; and there was
little expense involved, since road building meant little
more than clearing away trees and leveling the rougher
places.

The "Great Road," as it was termed by some of the
pioneers, crossed the Potomac at Mecklenburg, or Shepherdstown, then passed through Martinsburg, Winchester,
Strasburg, New Market, and Staunton, to Fincastle at the
lower end of the Valley. There it had three forks: the
south to the Carolinas, the center to the Southwest, which
meant also Tennessee and Kentucky, and the west to the
Trans-Alleghany region by way of the Greenbrier Valley.[62] This road has been termed the great highway of
commerce for the Valley in the colonial period as well as
later.

The interest in road building in 1763-76, however, was
not in the highway north and south but in the new routes
east and west. The petitions to the Assembly in those
years asked that a road be cleared through the Blue Ridge
Mountains at Rockfish Gap; that another be opened
through the same mountains at Swift Run Gap; and that
a road be made from Payne's Run in Augusta to Thur-
man's Run in Albemarle, in order considerably to "shorten
the distance" over which the petitioners were "obliged to
carry their commodities to market."[63] Others urged that
repairs be made on the roads from the mountains "to
Fredericksburg and Alexandria and other convenient
ports"; that a road be run through Craig's Gap between
Swift Run and Rockfish gaps in the Blue Ridge; that ade-

[62] Jefferson and Fry Map. One of the best authorities on early Valley
roads is Charles E. Kemper of Staunton, Virginia. See map, p. 153, below.
[63] Hening, *Statutes*, VIII, 549 ff.

quate repair be made of roads leading from the north Valley to Alexandria, which "by means of the great number of waggons which use the same are rendered almost impassible"; and that a road be extended over South Mountain, the southern end of the Blue Ridge, to shorten the road to the eastern markets by sixty miles.[64]

The keen interest in the commercial, as well as the medicinal, value of the mineral springs along the western boundary of the Valley has been noted. Crowds gathered at Bath[65] in Berkeley County, and promoters saw the possibilities of enhancing business through the development of the Hot and Warm Springs in Augusta County.[66] Accordingly these promoters petitioned the Burgesses for a new road that would connect these springs with eastern Virginia.[67] Their request likewise was granted by the Assembly, thus adding another link between the eastern and western parts of the state.[68]

The granting of ferry rights showed a similar tendency toward an East-West trade alignment. About the time that the Burgesses decided there was not enough business across the Potomac to allow both Thomas Shepherd and the widow of Thomas Swearingen to operate ferries at Shepherdstown, within a half mile of each other, petitions were sent to the Assembly by the Valley people, asking

[64] *Journal, Burgesses*, Jan. 14, Nov. 27, 1764; Mar. 27, 1767; Nov. 15, 17, 1769; Mar. 3, 4, 10, 1772. Nearly everything asked in these petitions was granted by the Assembly, which seemed ready to offer every encouragement toward turning Valley trade to the Virginia ports (Hening, *Statutes*, VIII, 16, 152, 252, 549, 552).

[65] Stephen letter in Etting Collection, Pa. Hist., IV, 71-72; Gates Papers (N. Y. H. S.), no. 197; Washington, *Diary*, July 31, 1769. Washington took his little stepdaughter, Patsy Custis, to the Springs in the hope that the water might help her. In September, 1775, Fithian reported 400 people at these springs, *Journal*, p. 125.

[66] *Virginia Gazette*, 1771; Fleming Papers, Dr. Meldrum to Fleming, Sept. 10, 1765.

[67] *Journal, Burgesses*, July 15, 1771; April 4, 1772. The plan included a public subsidy to make these places health centers.

[68] Hening, *Statutes*, VIII, 263, 546-549.

for three ferries across the Shenandoah, to connect with Alexandria and the roads of eastern Virginia.[69]

Other evidence that Valley trade with eastern Virginia and Potomac ports was steadily increasing can be found in the correspondence between Tidewater merchants and Valley planters.[70] The voluminous and well-preserved papers of William Allason, merchant of Falmouth on the Rappahannock River, show not only that he was doing business with hundreds of north Valley people but also that not less than a dozen merchants on the Tidewater rivers and in the Chesapeake Bay ports were competing with him for the Valley trade.[71] His brother operated a branch store in the Valley, and Allason himself frequently went there on business trips.[72]

Isaac Zane's wagons hauled iron by the shipload to Allason from Frederick County. Zane, however, found it difficult to balance his purchases, and at one time he was in Allason's debt about three hundred pounds. Allason had a regularly employed attorney in Winchester, in the person of Alexander White, who was kept busy collecting old debts for his client. Among Allason's patrons were most of the north Valley leaders, including Lord Fairfax of "Greenway Court." Allason's articles of trade with the

[69] See *Journal, Burgesses,* April 12, 1768; June 1, 1770; Mar. 21, 30, 1772; Mar. 10, 1773. The Potomac Canal scheme, another East-West trade project, also received legislative approval (Hening, *Statutes,* VIII, 570; Washington, *Diaries,* I). But since the plans for the Canal were unusually ambitious, the scheme was temporarily deferred, with the approach of the Revolution.

[70] See, for example, the growth of exports from Alexandria and Fredericksburg in Chalmers, *Virginia,* III, 58 ff. See also *Pennsylvania Gazette,* June 13, 1771; Cresswell, *Diary,* p. 47; Gates Papers (N. Y. H. S.), 1773-1775; Stephen Papers, 1763-1776.

[71] Allason Papers (Virginia State Library), consisting of correspondence, letter books, ledgers, day books, and so on, for the period from 1763 and before, until after the Revolution. The ledgers usually gave the county of the particular patron.

[72] Allason to Elsey, August 16, 1763.

Valley covered almost every conceivable item, both luxuries and necessities.

Edward Johnson of Manchester, at the falls of the
James River, did a flourishing business in the south Valley
in those pre-Revolutionary years. Nearly all the leading
planters there were Johnson's patrons, and most of them
were indebted to him. When Robert Breckinridge died
in 1773, his estate owed Johnson nearly 100 pounds, a
situation that was not considered unusual or alarming.[78]

The conditions under which the pre-Revolutionary
Valley settlers made their living were generally favorable
to a rapid economic expansion. Except for the great pat-
ents, such as those of Borden and Fairfax, there were few
estates that equaled in acreage the large Tidewater plantations. Nevertheless a number of landowners in the Valley during this period had tracts with acreages running
into the thousands, and after the manner of the Tidewater
and Piedmont sections, the large planter in the Valley felt
that he must have a name for his estate. Hence we find
Zane's "Marlboro," Fleming's "Belmont," Adam Steph-
en's "Bower," Jacob Hite's "Hopewell," John Hite's
"Springdale," Gates' "Traveler's Rest," William Preston's "Greenfield," Andrew Moore's "Cannicello," Samuel Washington's "Harewood," and many others. These
and similar designations usually meant well-established as
well as large plantations. For example, Isaac Zane had
25,000 acres; Peter Hogg, 9,000; Semple Manor, 7,000;
and Adam Stephen, 5,000.

In personal property there were a few who nearly
rivaled the Tidewater planters and were on a par with

[78] Allason Papers, 1763-1776, *passim*. The controversy of Jacob (son
of Joist) Hite with Adam Stephen in 1774, which nearly brought on a
minor civil war in the north Valley, arose largely from his having contracted a debt of over £1600 with a Fredericksburg merchant.—Berkeley
Minute Book, March-May, 1774; Frederick Order Book, XV, 409-410,
Sept. 3, 1772; Preston Papers, a large number of letters, Edward Johnson
to Colonel William Preston, especially for the years 1771-1780, *passim*.

those of the Piedmont. Some of them had livestock numbering more than a hundred head and from ten to twenty-five slaves or indentured servants. These, along with various items of plantation equipment, brought the personal property total in some cases to as much as two thousand pounds sterling.[74]

Isaac Zane's "Marlboro" in Frederick County had its mansion house, fountains, garden, bath house, fish pond, ice house, two orchards, three barns, houses and apartments for servants and slaves, forges, furnaces, still house, sawmill, smith's shop, storehouse, counting house, liquor house, spring house, and stables, most of them built of stone. In the mansion house one would have found a good library of about four hundred volumes, an eight-day clock, various kinds of silver, some walnut furniture and a few paintings.[75] Colonial America could have seen in the furnishings of Zane's place worthy rivalry for the best the colonies had to offer.

Not far from Isaac Zane lived James Nourse. When he died near the close of the Revolution, he left a personal estate valued at £1,037. The estate included a half-dozen slaves, a hundred and seventeen head of livestock, quantities of agricultural machinery and grain, a phaeton, and a well-furnished home. In the home were to be found mahogany and walnut furniture of various designs, books and book cases, paintings, silver, Venetian blinds, and even china jars for the mantlepiece—the latter evidently a unique bit of furnishing for the period.[76]

[74] Data gathered from inventories in the will books of the five Valley counties for the period, 1763-1776, *passim*, for such men as Andrew and Charles Lewis, Robert Breckinridge, Samuel Washington, Jacob and John Hite, Peter Hogg, and Gabriel Jones, not to mention Lord Fairfax and numerous others.

[75] Broadside in Zane Papers in Pennsylvania Historical Society Library; Zane inventory in Frederick Superior Court Will Book, I, 109-205; see also Zane Papers and Fithian, *Journal*, pp. 14-15.

[76] Berkeley Will Book, I, 382-384.

Mrs. Roger North of Staunton owned two hundred pounds' worth of mahogany furniture, china and silverware, books and paintings.[77] Both Thomas Lewis and William Fleming had good libraries for their time. In William Preston's "Greenfield," his Botetourt home, there were a number of the Latin classics, as well as excellent furniture and several paintings, among them one of his wife by Jeremiah Theus.[78] The better homes had some silverware as well as an occasional piece of unusual furniture, such as a bookcase, a great chair, or a bureau. There were also candlesticks, looking glasses, and a few rugs of various sorts, and sometimes "well furnished" feather beds. More than half the families had books, although in some cases this meant nothing more than a copy of the Bible.

There is, however, another side of the picture, and one that is not so cheerful. Not half the homes had kitchen utensils, only about a third had beds, and only one family in six had chairs or tables.[79] This, to be sure, did not signify destitution in the present-day sense but merely that most families prepared meals Indian fashion, slept on the floor or in bunks nailed up in corners of their log cabins, sat oriental fashion or on stools sawed from logs, and used, for tables, logs hewn on one side to make a level surface.

A few of these semi-frontiersmen evidenced a fondness

[77] Augusta Will Book, VI, 327.

[78] Preston Papers, Reproduction of Painting of Susannah Preston; see letter, Johnson to Preston, Aug. 7, 1776, referring to books ordered.

[79] These figures are based on inventories of estates and are thus more illustrative than accurate, though they are probably a fair sampling of contemporary personal property. Court Records, Valley Counties, *passim*. This description still is true of the Alleghany mountaineers in the coves and valleys leading off from the Great Valley. In this condition of home furnishing the Valley was definitely behind the Piedmont which could benefit from proximity to the Tidewater area. See Will Books, Buckingham, Prince Edward, Culpeper, Halifax, 1763-1776, *passim*.

for fine clothes, although buckskin and coarse cloth made up the usual attire. Mrs. Robert Breckinridge in 1769 purchased expensive red damask silk gowns for two of her nieces, Betty Brown and Sally Preston, paying for each dress four-and-a-half pounds.[80] Colonel William Preston had his merchant on the James send along with other goods some fine feathers for his daughter's hat.[81] In 1777, when two hats which the daughter had ordered could not be secured on the lower James, the merchant facetiously suggested that she "dress her hair nicely and go bareheaded."[82] Some jewelry was worn, usually shoe or knee buckles, with now and then a ring or brooch, and in rare cases a watch, at times described as a pinchback watch. An occasional pair of spectacles was to be seen. A few men wore greatcoats, and there were some who had several suits of broadcloth or other raiment, such as might have been reckoned fine for frontier life. One of the most prized possessions, however, was a "rifle gun." Sometimes it was just a plain gun. Even a tomahawk was cherished if one could not afford any sort of gun.[83]

In spite of the attractive names used for the homes in many cases, the landed gentry of the Valley were not yet erecting dwellings in keeping either with their acres or with their personal property. Even Isaac Zane's "Mansion House" at "Marlboro" was only twenty by forty feet.[84] Several of the colonial houses are still standing.[85]

[80] Breckinridge Papers, Accounts Robert Breckinridge, 1767-1769.
[81] Preston Papers, Johnson to Preston, 1776, no other date.
[82] Ibid., Johnson to Preston, June 5, 1777.
[83] Will Books, Valley Counties, 1763-1776, inventories. In so far as a sampling by means of the inventories is dependable, the average value of property in the Valley, most of which was livestock and farm equipment, was £132. The lowest average for a given area was in Dunmore (Shenandoah) County with £76, while the highest were in Berkeley with £168 and Botetourt with £151. These figures are based on the examination of over 200 inventories for those years.
[84] Zane Papers, Broadside on Iron Works.
[85] Such as that of John Lewis, the first settler of Augusta County; that

Most of these are one-storied and built of stone, all are well constructed, but not one of them is large or imposing. Contemporary descriptions or plans of homes, even among the better classes, indicate that they were comparatively small. Comfort and warmth, and sometimes protection against the Indians, seem to have been the chief considerations. Low cost and native frugality very likely were determining factors.[86] As in the Piedmont, the demand for more substantial homes was not yet popular.

It is difficult to ascertain the cultural resources of the Valley in those years. An interesting contemporary opinion, which gives one side of the picture, is to be found in a letter addressed to Horatio Gates from a Philadelphia friend. In trying to dissuade Gates from settling in the north Valley, the Philadelphian admitted that he knew little of the country, but volunteered the information that "the greater part of the inhabitants there have migrated from this Province and, to say no worse of them, they are not the politest kind of people."[87] James Ireland, one of the leading Baptist ministers of the period, describes them as "an uncultivated people," who were both "rude and illiterate," and who "constituted a compound of the barbarian and Indian." He found among them, however, "a number of respectable and well behaved people."[88] During his sojourn in the Valley in 1775-1776, Fithian frequently complained in his diary of the crudeness of life and manners he was compelled to endure.[89] A Hessian

of Horatio Gates who in 1773 built "Traveler's Rest" of stone, 24 x 40 feet, a story and a half (one estimate or bid for building it totals £383), Gates Papers (N. Y. H. S.), 1773; that of Charles Lee and others. See illustration facing p. 108.

[86] W. L. Stone, *Letters of Brunswick and the Hessian Officers During the American Revolution*, pp. 178-184. One of these officers writing from Staunton described the houses as comparable to the poorest in Germany. A prisoner of war could hardly have found much to arouse his enthusiasm.

[87] Gates Papers (N. Y. H. S.), no. 173.

[88] James Ireland, *Autobiography*.

[89] Fithian, *Journal*, 1775-1776, especially, p. 158.

officer, while a prisoner of war in Augusta County during the Revolution, wrote to his friends in Germany that he was in a remote corner of Virginia cut off from the rest of the world, and further stated: "We do not have good neighbors here, for there is hardly a *Gentleman* living within forty miles of Staunton."[90]

But these accounts do not complete the picture. Fithian himself found much to praise. He often relished the food placed before him and was grateful for Scottish and German methods of cooking. He frequently enjoyed good books in the Valley homes. There were some who "lived elegantly" or in "fulness and elegance."[91] To his surprise he found "Women of Taste born and educated in Augusta!"[92] And he grew eloquent over Miss Betsy Brown of the south Valley, who had "read many English Authors—several of the Latin Classicks—And you may be certain, though She has been born in this distant and unimproved Country, there are few young Women of her Rank and Education, who may be compared with her. . . ."[93]

There were a number of schools in the Valley in those years. Kemper found evidence for a total of seventeen in a relatively small area.[94] The Augusta court records show frequent suits brought by the journeymen schoolteachers of the time for breaches of contract. Undoubtedly others were successful in collecting their salaries outside the courts. Of the score of teachers noted in the court records none seems to have received more than eighteen pounds a year. The pay was often in wheat, or linen, and in one

[90] R. W. Pettengill, *Letters from America*, p. 149, letter from Staunton, June 1, 1779.

[91] Fithian, *Journal*, 1775-1776.   [92] *Ibid.*, p. 177.

[93] *Ibid.*, p. 141; Betsy was the daughter of John Brown, the Presbyterian minister and educator.

[94] Charles E. Kemper, "The Settlement of the Valley," in *The Virginia Magazine*, XXX, 179. See also Preston Papers for several references to schools in the south Valley.

instance it was a cravat.[95] Tuition was about two shillings
a month per child, and the number of children in a school
ranged from fifteen to thirty. The instruction was apparently considered effective. In one instance a father cherished the hope that his son would succeed the teacher at
the end of his third session!

The task of educating the pioneer youth obviously had
its difficulties. Charles Knight, schoolmaster, insisted that
his patrons must provide shelter in case of Indian alarms
or raids. Another teacher was accused of too frequent
"drunken frolics" with the patron at whose home he
boarded. A third had been promised additional pay for
"reading in Church," as well as for improving the land
on which he was a tenant.[96]

Children were sometimes sent to eastern Virginia
boarding schools, but only at considerable expense, as
compared with the cost of local schooling,[97] and occasionally parents moving to the "Western Waters" sent their
children back to the schools in the Valley.[98] These frontiersmen, both Scot and German, were evidently determined to have their children taught regardless of difficulties. The noted Baptist minister, John Leland, in an ap-
praisal of the Presbyterians of Virginia some years later,
said of them, "They indulge (perhaps) too much mirth
at their houses yet it may be said in truth, that they have
the best art of training up children in good manners of
any society in the state."[99]

One of the pioneer Presbyterian ministers of the Val-

[95] Augusta Judgments, 1763-1776, *passim;* Gates Papers (N. Y. H. S.),
misc., 1773-1776. The Gates schoolmaster made quills and drew faces on
water clocks for extra pay.
[96] Augusta Judgments, August, 1762; August, 1772; March, 1776.
Felix Gilbert's Account Book has record of payment to a schoolmaster.
[97] Augusta Judgments, November, 1772. Elizabeth Finley paid £10 per
session for such a privilege.
[98] *Ibid.,* November, 1768; Preston Papers, 1770-1776 *passim.*
[99] John Leland, *Virginia Chronicle,* p. 14.

ley, John Brown, a graduate of the College of New Jersey, took so seriously his avocation of teaching the youth of his congregation that even before 1763 he had established a more or less permanent school and called it Augusta Academy. Brown placed chief emphasis on the classics, and his students were reported to be "well grounded in the Latin and Greek Languages."[100] In 1770 there was a concerted effort toward making this school into a larger academy. It began with a resolution offered on the floor of the Presbytery of Hanover which expressed the need for higher education. After discussing the matter for several sessions the presbyters, in October of 1773, agreed "to fix the public Seminary for the liberal Education of Youth at Staunton in Augusta."[101] In April of 1775 the affairs of the academy were so far advanced that an announcement was made to the public, begging subscriptions and promising that the said Augusta Academy would "be established on the most catholic plan circumstances will permit."[102] The presbytery appointed twenty-five of the leading men in the south Valley to canvass that territory. Most of these were justices of the county courts or held other important offices in their respective counties.[108] By May of 1776 these men had raised about £125 for the new academy. But, since Graham had already spent £160 for equipment, they were asked to continue so-

[100] Minutes, Hanover Presbytery, April 14, 1775. Here he had educated a number of the Valley leaders, who were beginning to attract attention in the early years of the Revolution (*Washington and Lee Historical Papers*, II, 57, 70, 88, 91, 99), and when the movement started about 1770 to make the school into a full-fledged academy they came eagerly to its aid.

[101] Minutes, Hanover Presbytery, October 9, 1771; October 16, 1773.

[102] *Ibid.*, April 15, 1775.

[108] *Ibid.*, April, 1775. Among them were several colonels of militia: William Fleming, Andrew Lewis, William Preston, and William Christian; also Captains John Bowyer, Samuel McDowell, William McKee, and George Mathews, all of whom attained prominence in the Revolution.

liciting funds.[104] Meanwhile the presbytery created a
board of trustees to control the academy. A few days
before Virginia passed the Lee Resolution, calling for the
Declaration of Independence, the board named the academy Liberty Hall.[105] Like the Puritans of New England
the Valley dissenters were determined to have trained
leadership for the problems ahead.

[104] *Ibid.*, May 4, 1776.
[105] Washington and Lee University Records, I, May 13, 1775. Also
the academy was to be located at Timber Ridge rather than at Staunton.

≡☆≡ **2** ≡☆≡

A Haven for Religious Dissenters

To MOST OF THE early settlers of the Valley of Virginia, religion was as important as making a better living. The heavy price of conflict with the Indians was not too much to pay for a religious haven that also promised better economic prospects.

Although the colony of Virginia was reckoned loyal to the Church of England, from the beginning it had a varying number of dissenters. The laws of the colony required conformity to the doctrines and rites of the Anglican church as well as payment of fixed levies for its support, and from these laws the dissenters were not exempt.[1]

When the English Toleration Act of 1689 went into effect, however, the status of the Virginia dissenters was accordingly changed. The act allowed the dissenting congregations the right to worship according to their respective creeds, provided their places of worship were registered, and their preachers licensed to preach in them. The colonial government accepted the provisions as to worship in the Toleration Act, but other legal disabilities of the dissenters remained.[2] Dissenting ministers were not al-

[1] Hening, *Statutes*, I, 123, 144, 149, 155, 180, 268, 433, 532.
[2] *Ibid.*, III, 168 ff. The Virginia Act of 1699 authorized a five-shilling

lowed to profit from the public levies or to perform marriage ceremonies. Likewise, a dissenter could not hold office in the Virginia government unless he went through the motions of conforming to the Anglican Church. They did find ways to conform in order to hold office, hence the numerous Scottish Presbyterian elders who became vestrymen in the Church of England.

From its earliest settlement the Valley of Virginia had furnished a haven to dissenting religious groups, and its people were predominantly dissenters, even though the region continued to be under the control of the Anglican government at Williamsburg. Since these dissenters were a buffer against the Indians, they enjoyed a more favorable legal position than did other Virginia dissenters. Not less than six dissenting sects or denominations were active in the Valley in the Colonial period.[3]

By 1776 the Presbyterians had at least thirty churches or congregations in the Valley.[4] Ten of these churches were in the northern end of the Valley, most of them in Berkeley County. The other twenty were in the south Valley, chiefly in Augusta and Botetourt counties, that is,

---

fine for absence from worship for more than a two-month period but provided that attendance on a dissenter service would absolve one from the fine. The English Act of 1689 required swearing allegiance to the sovereign as the supreme head of the English Church, denial of transubstantiation, and a general assent to the doctrinal articles of the Established Church.

[3] They ranked about as follows: Presbyterians, Lutherans, German Reformed (there is an estimate of 25,000 German people in Virginia in 1775, about equally divided between Lutheran and Reformed in Kieffer, "Analysis of Population"), Baptists, Quakers, and Mennonites. Determining the strength of the Anglican Church is complicated by the fact that dissenters who conformed to the Established Church only for political purposes were frequently reckoned Anglicans.

[4] Minutes of Hanover and Donegal Presbyteries, 1763-1776, *passim*. The records of the (Associate) Reformed Presbyterian Church indicate also that there were congregations of that church in the Valley prior to 1763 (*Centennial History, The Associate Reformed Presbyterian Church*, pp. 538 ff.).

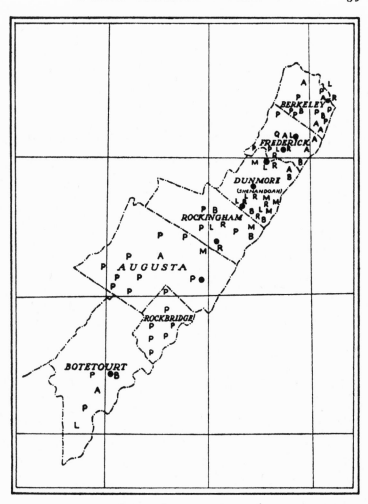

VALLEY CHURCHES IN 1776

Each letter represents a congregation or church:

A—Anglican   P—Presbyterian
B—Baptist   Q—Quaker
L—Lutheran   R—Reformed
M—Mennonite

that portion of Botetourt which later became a part of Rockbridge. The north Valley churches were Opequon or Opeckon, Tuscarora, Potomack or Shepherdstown, Cool Springs, Cedar Creek, Elk Branch, Bullskin, Back Creek, Falling Waters, very probably Round Hill, and one or two others. In the south Valley they were Stone Meeting House (Fort Defiance), Tinkling Spring, Brown's Meeting House (Hebron), North Mountain (Bethel), Cook's Creek, Peaked Mountain (Massanutten), New Providence, Timber Ridge, Hall's Meeting House (New Monmouth), Mossy Creek, Linville Creek, Pastures (Windy Cove), Forks of James, Cow Pasture, High Bridge, Oxford, Falling Springs, Jackson River, Roanoke, Fincastle, and several others of uncertain designation.[5]

The Anglican stronghold was in the north Valley, chiefly around Winchester, where Bishop Meade lists eight colonial churches. Meade's list includes Winchester, Shepherdstown, Charlestown, McCoy's, Morgan's, Cunningham's, North Branch of Shenandoah, and South Branch of Shenandoah. A petition from Frederick County in 1770, asking for a reorganization, stated that the parish had not less than seven churches and chapels, and argued that this made it impossible for the minister to perform the duties of his office in a proper manner and that the people could not "attend divine service so conveniently and frequently as they ought." There were two Anglican churches in the south Valley, one at Augusta Courthouse or Staunton, and the other at Botetourt Courthouse or Fincastle.[6]

[5] Minutes, Donegal and Hanover Presbyteries, 1763-1776, *passim*. The parentheses show the present-day names of some of these churches. The Presbyterians were almost entirely Ulster Scots. Very few of these at that time belonged to the Reformed branch of the church.

[6] In addition to Meade, *Old Churches and Families*, II, 71, references to the Anglican churches in the Valley may be found in Perry, *American*

Lutheran prestige centered primarily in the person of Peter Muhlenberg, son of the dominant Lutheran figure in colonial America, Henry Melchior ("Father") Muhlenberg. Although the younger Muhlenberg served only the Woodstock church, his widely heralded coming and his spectacular departure in command of a regiment of his fellow countrymen, marching to join Washington's army, undoubtedly increased Lutheran prestige among Valley dissenters.[7] Contemporary records show at least eight Lutheran churches prior to 1776.[8] These were chiefly in Dunmore (Shenandoah) County, with one each in Berkeley and Frederick counties. Like the Anglicans, the Lutherans usually established their churches in the courthouse towns or villages, or in the growing market centers. This preference for towns was different from the practice of the Presbyterians and most of the other dissenters, who built their meeting houses in sparsely settled areas.

The German Reformed churches, linguistically allied with the Lutherans but theologically akin to the Presbyterians, were strong numerically. However, the fact that they lacked an active ministry and spoke an alien tongue conspired to deny them the prestige they deserved in religious affairs. They had at least nine congregations, most of which were in Shenandoah County and in the region which later became Rockingham County.[9]

Colonial Church Documents, I, Virginia, 365, 413, 429, 432, 459; Gates Papers, 1763-1776, passim; Hening, Statutes, VIII, 425-428, 623-624; Journal, Burgesses, May 31, 1770.

[7] H. S. Muhlenberg, Life of Peter Muhlenberg.

[8] The churches were at Shepherdstown, Winchester, Stephens City, Woodstock, Mt. Jackson, New Market, Shenandoah, and Timberville, all established between 1735 and 1770. See Kieffer, Analysis of Colonial Enumerations, and Fortenbaugh, Inland Lutheran Migrations in Colonial Times, both from church records.

[9] Minutes and Letters, Coetus of Pennsylvania, 1763-1776, passim. The churches were: Winchester, Louis-Steffenstown (Stephen's City), Stauffer's-town (Strasburg), Muellerstown (Woodstock), Roeder's, Stony Creek, Schanador (Shenandoah), Messenutten (Massanutten), and Frieden's.

Among the smaller dissenting groups—mainly Baptists, Quakers, and Mennonites—the Baptists were the most aggressive. Under the able leadership of James Ireland and other preachers, itinerant and local, they steadily gained converts, particularly in the north Valley.[10] There was a large and growing Baptist church at Mill Creek in Berkeley County, and a half-dozen other congregations in that and adjoining counties, as well as two in Botetourt.

The Quaker stronghold was in Frederick County where the flourishing Hopewell Meeting House included several prominent leaders in its membership, among them Isaac Zane. When a number of wealthy and cultured Quakers were exiled from Philadelphia during the Revolution, they found no lack of kindred spirits in and around Winchester. In the face of almost continuous Indian warfare[11] the Quakers made themselves conspicuous by their objection to militia service.

The German Mennonites have left few records, but they were strongest in Dunmore (Shenandoah) County. They had a half-dozen congregations there and a few others farther south in Rockingham County.[12]

Most of the Valley dissenters were connected with the parent organization in Pennsylvania. The Presbyterians

[10] The Baptist churches were Mill Creek, Buck Marsh, Smith Creek, Linville Creek, Opeckon, Lower Shenandoah, Birch Creek, Botetourt, and South River. Some of these were probably branch churches. For the Baptist churches see: *Minutes*, Mill Creek Church, 1763-1776, *passim; Minutes*, Smith and Linville Creek, 1763-1776, *passim*; James Ireland, *Autobiography*; Records of the Church of Christ at Buck Marsh, 1786-1788, *passim*; Morgan Edwards, "Material towards a History of the Baptists in the Province of Virginia, 1772"; Asplund's *Register* (all in the Baptist Historical Society, University of Richmond, Virginia).

[11] For the Quaker strength in the Valley see Walker McC. Bond, ed., *Records of Hopewell Meeting House; Exiles in Virginia*, Thomas Gilpin, ed., pp. 158-226; Pemberton Papers, 1777-1778, *passim*; Chalmers Papers, IV, 5, return of Frederick militia 1772. Adam Stephen in 1772 reported that of two thousand men in Frederick County qualified for militia service a hundred and fifty were Quakers.

[12] J. W. Wayland, *Shenandoah County*, pp. 207, 423.

of the north Valley were in the Pennsylvania Presbytery
of Donegal, and the rest in the Virginia Presbytery of
Hanover, both of which presbyteries were subordinate to
the United Synod of New York and Philadelphia.[13] Few
Valley ministers attended the sessions of the New York
and Philadelphia governing body, although their congregations made appeals for ministers directly to the Synod.
The Synod in turn sent down instructions to the Presbyteries of Donegal and Hanover and to individuals and
congregations, but these instructions were largely ignored.[14] Distance and inconvenience of travel doubtless
accounted for this attitude, but probably the churches were
unconsciously joining with the Valley tradesmen in looking toward eastern Virginia rather than toward the more
distant Philadelphia.

The Lutherans likewise acknowledged allegiance to
the Ministerium of Pennsylvania, as did the Reformed
churches to their governing body, the Coetus of Pennsylvania.[15] The fact that the Valley Lutherans, for convenience of conformity to the Established Church in Virginia,
adopted the Swedish rather than the German attitude toward episcopacy, did not seem to affect their relationship
to the mother church in Philadelphia.[16] Since Muhlenberg, the leading Lutheran minister in Virginia, was the
son of the most influential Lutheran in Pennsylvania, the
continuance of such a relationship was to be expected.

One of the surprising things about the Valley clergy
was its relatively small personnel. The Presbyterians
seldom had more than half a dozen ministers at a given

[13] Minutes, Synod of New York and Philadelphia, 1763-1776, *passim*.
The Presbytery of Hanover, then, was composed of Valley and eastern
Virginia churches and met alternately east and west of the Blue Ridge.
[14] Minutes, Synod of New York and Philadelphia, 1763-1776, *passim*.
[15] Minutes, Ministerium of Pennsylvania; Minutes, *Coetus of Pennsylvania*, 1763-1776, *passim*.
[16] Muhlenberg, *Muhlenberg*, p. 33.

time; the Anglicans had three or four; the Lutherans
never more than two; the Baptists, four or five; the Reformed Church and lesser sects, except for local preachers,[17] often none at all. These figures refer, of course, to
the settled ministers. Most of the preaching was done for
the dissenting denominations by energetic itinerants. This
was particularly true of the Reformed Church, Baptists,
and Presbyterians. Even the settled dissenting ministers
were in a sense itinerants because of their widely scattered
congregations. Then, too, the neglected settlements[18] held
a peculiar fascination for this consecrated spiritual ancestor
of the heroic circuit rider of a later day who has earned
the praise of one of America's greatest historians.[19]

The salaries received by these men were small, if we
reckon in terms of services rendered. Even with compul-
sory tithes the Anglican clergy seldom received over a
hundred pounds a year.[20] John Jones contracted for the
Augusta parish at fifty pounds annually with twenty
pounds for maintenance and the use of the glebe buildings.[21] Adam Smyth probably expected a more bountiful

[17] The local preacher was a lay member of a congregation who con-
ducted services and sometimes preached in the absence of regular preachers.
[18] See Minutes, Hanover Presbytery, 1763-1776, for the constant provisions for the itinerancies of these settled ministers.
[19] The reference is to a tribute of Frederick J. Turner in the course of
a class lecture. See also his *Frontier in American History*, pp. 164-165.
[20] In 1735 when the Valley counties were established, the Burgesses provided that, in the payment of salaries of the clergy, tobacco could be
computed in money at three farthings a pound. In 1738 the Burgesses
allowed the clergy 16,000 pounds of tobacco, plus, per year. Then in
1753 a provision was made for salaries of a hundred pounds in currency
for the Valley clergy. By an act of 1768, the commutation for the tobacco
was raised to two pence a pound. Hening, *Statutes*, VIII, 267-268, 381-
385, 430-431; Perry, *op. cit.*, I, 459.
[21] Meade, *op. cit.*, II, 318. The Anglican clergy, of course, received
certain fees, particularly for marriages. At one time the vestry of Frederick, the Anglican stronghold, admired their rector to the point of asking
permission of the Burgesses to raise his salary to a hundred and fifty pounds
a year, but they repented and soon demanded that it be reduced to a
hundred. *Journal, Burgesses*, May 21, 1767; Nov. 29, 1769; Hening,
Statutes, VIII, 267, 430-431.

return than his fellow clergymen when he persuaded his Botetourt vestry to invest seven hundred pounds in glebe property consisting of five hundred acres on which was a grist mill with other improvements, but he was doomed to disappointment. His Scottish parishioners not only opposed vigorously the glebe purchase but later were alleged to have paid him less than a year's salary in three and a half years.[22]

The dissenting ministers, who depended on voluntary contributions, were much worse off than the Anglicans. Their salaries were usually raised by subscriptions, which, as in a later day, were never one hundred per cent good. When the comparatively strong congregations at New Providence and Timber Ridge called John Brown in 1754, they promised him, according to their subscription lists, about thirty and thirty-five pounds, respectively.[23] In 1775 when the Augusta congregations called John McKnight, they offered him a salary of a hundred pounds, Virginia currency.[24] In the north Valley the congregations of Tuscarora, Falling Waters, and Back Creek, when they were providing a salary for their pastor, Hugh Vance, in 1770, subscribed a total of a hundred and twelve pounds—four of the more liberal Scots each agreeing to pay three pounds a year—but Vance a few years later was finding difficulty in getting the salary.[25]

Most of the other dissenting groups except the Lutherans depended largely on local preachers who usually

[22] *Journal, Burgesses,* June 6, 1775; Virginia Petitions, Botetourt, no. 74, Nov. 11, 1776.

[23] Wm. H. Foote, *Sketches of Virginia,* 2nd Series, pp. 97-98; Johnston Papers. On the death of Parson Craig in 1774 his executor found that one of his churches owed him seventy-four pounds and the other ninety. See Augusta Will Book, VI, 505-506.

[24] Minutes, Donegal Presbytery, Oct. 11, 1775.

[25] Subscription list of Congregation of Tuscarora, etc., in 1770 (kindness of Mrs. Sarah Morgan Gordon, Gerrardstown, W. Va.). Other Presbyterian ministers of the day had similar difficulties (Minutes, Hanover and Donegal Presbyteries, 1763-1776, *passim*).

made their own living at some trade or other occupation. The dissenting ministers were, of course, unable to count on income from marriage fees, but occasionally received what might have been thought of as a voluntary fee for baptism.[26]

The Valley minister's time was not entirely taken up with preaching and reproving, and betimes with making a living. He also found spare moments for words and letters of consolation,[27] and for numerous baptismal rites for the frontier progeny. Parson Craig recorded over a nine-year period an average of nearly a hundred baptisms annually.[28] The Baptists, finding themselves handicapped by their opposition to infant baptism, adopted an interesting substitute to conciliate converts from other dissenting groups. They requested the members to bring their children to the church meeting, that the minister might "take them in his arms and beg a Blessing for them."[29]

The church buildings ranged from the Winchester Lutheran church with its "tall steeple" to rude log structures.[30] Because of the constant conflict with the Indians some of the Presbyterian congregations built their churches of stone to serve as forts as well as places of worship.[31] One of these is Fort Defiance, frequently mentioned in the Augusta Court Records as "the Stone

---

[26] *Minutes, Coetus of Pennsylvania,* 1769; see Peaked Mountain Church agreement of 1769 in Wayland, *Rockingham,* pp. 61-62, fees proposed for nonchurch members.

[27] Fleming Papers, 1774. Adam Smyth to Fleming after Point Pleasant.

[28] Craig's Diary, 1741-1749.

[29] Records, Linville Baptist Church, Sept., 1773. Morgan Edwards called this practice "devoting children." It was popularly termed "dry christening." It was perhaps the result of an earlier controversy on infant baptism, in which the eccentric Alexander Miller had gone into a Baptist meeting, taken over the pulpit, and denounced the Baptist doctrine of baptism (Minutes, Smith Creek, 1757-1758). Those who were persuaded by Miller were termed "Favourers of the Scriptureless Practice, Infant Sprinkling."

[30] Fithian, *Journal,* May 8, 1776.

[31] Foote, *Sketches, Virginia,* 2nd Series, pp. 32-33.

ABOVE: *The Stone Meeting House, near Staunton, Va., used as a fort and church by Presbyterian Scots in the late Colonial Period.*

BELOW: *The Charles Lee Mill, near Martinsburg, West Virginia, built by Joist or Jacob Hite in the middle eighteenth century.*

Meeting House." Another is at Timber Ridge in Rock-bridge. Prior to 1763 the Anglican vestry of Augusta contracted for the building of a substantial brick church at Staunton which was to cost about five hundred pounds.[32]

The attitude of the people toward the churches was generally favorable. The attendance was good for the most part,[33] even in churches without ministers.[34] Dissenting congregations usually had all-day religious exercises and sat through long sermons lasting two and three hours, morning and afternoon, with an intermission for a midday meal on the grounds.[35]

In sermonless periods the congregations of the dissenters were restless until the need was supplied by the itinerants of their own denomination, or, better still, by resident pastors. The minutes of the parent church organizations in Philadelphia show frequent and almost pathetic appeals for ministers. The Coetus of the Reformed Church, for example, in 1767, referred to "six or seven

[32] Augusta Parish Vestry Book, May, 1760. This church was on the site of Trinity Church of Staunton. It was used during the Revolution by the Virginia Legislature. Anglican churches for the most part, however, according to Meade, were like those of the dissenters, crude and temporary structures costing from forty to sixty pounds each. See *Journal, Burgesses,* Feb. 22, 1772; Hening, *Statutes,* VIII, 425-428; Meade, *op. cit.,* II, 281. One of those built in Frederick in 1764 was reported in 1772 as "likely soon to become ruinous." *Journal, Burgesses,* Feb. 22, 1772. In 1763 the Baptists of Smith Creek set about raising funds to build a meeting house. Their plan called for a subscription of twenty shillings each from the male members of the congregation and half that amount from the widows, but they could raise only a little over twelve pounds and so continued to meet in the homes of members (Minutes, Smith Creek, 1762-1763, *passim*). The Mill Creek Baptists evidently had a substantial place of worship.

[33] The Baptists at Linville Creek in July, 1774, complained that the "Inconstancy of the Members hath so much abounded that we are scarcely able to hold meeting."

[34] See, for instance, the interesting passage from Cresswell's *Diary,* pp. 125 ff., in which he describes a visit to the Nourses' where Mrs. Gates was a guest. She insisted on his going to church "ragged as I was." There was no parson, according to Cresswell, and his host Mr. Nourse read prayers.

[35] One of Craig's sermons is said to have had 55 heads. Christian, *Scotch-Irish,* p. 12.

deserted congregations in Virginia" which had "set forth their sad and shepherdless condition," and begged for "instant aid lest they should go to pieces altogether."[36] The congregations usually described their spiritual destitution and emphasized the need of resident ministers.[37] The Presbyterian Synod kept a steady stream of itinerants moving through Virginia. It also asked the stronger presbyteries in Pennsylvania and New Jersey to keep in mind the needs of the Valley congregations by encouraging young men to train themselves for service there.[38] The Valley itself was already sending itinerants into the Southwest, the vanguard of those who were to become the circuit riders of the Great West.

Church discipline was generally exacting. The dissenters were ever insistent that the moral code of the colony be enforced; hence there were recurrent indictments for breaking the Sabbath, for gaming, profanity, and drunkenness.[39] The churches set strict standards of behavior for their members and attempted enforcement, even amid frontier temptations. Nearly every session of the church courts dealt with cases of drunkenness, profanity, and irregularity in domestic relations.[40] In 1764 a day of prayer and fasting was appointed by the Virginia presbytery because of "the prevalence of vice and immorality and the decay of vital piety."[41] But fastings and resolutions evi-

[36] *Minutes, Coetus of Pennsylvania*, Sept. 6, 1767.
[37] Minutes, Synod of New York and Philadelphia, May 20, 1774.
[38] *Ibid.*, May 26, 1774.
[39] Valley Court Records, 1763-1776, *passim*.
[40] Parson Craig's Diary; Minutes, Hanover Presbytery, 1763-1776, *passim*, especially April 13, 1775; Minutes, Donegal Presbytery.
[41] Minutes, Hanover Presbytery, Oct. 3, 1764. A few years later the same body was asked to consider the use of "spirituous liquors and cakes at funerals." After some discussion the presbytery decided it was an improper custom and ought to be discontinued. Minutes, Hanover Presbytery, Oct. 16, 1772. See also settlement accounts, Valley Will Books, where charges were entered for whiskey for funerals, and sometimes in large quantities.

dently did not bring the desired results; in 1775 Caleb Wallace and Samuel Leake were appointed a committee to work out a plan for the better exercise of discipline in the churches.[42] The Baptists were even more uncompromising in their attitude toward delinquent brethren. There was the case of John Ray who was "censured in the highest degree next to excommunication," and a number of others received various degrees of suspension for waywardness.[43]

The first wave of the Great Awakening passed through the Valley before 1763, and the second did not come until after the Revolution. Individual congregations experienced awakenings that probably spread to neighboring churches of the same denomination, or even of other denominations.[44] The Baptists joined with their Tidewater brethren in a general revival for a time. About 1765 they were full of missionary zeal, and gathered converts of all classes in their part of the Valley, from "negro Joe" to Silas Hart, the latter noted as "a Person of Quality."[45] But this enthusiasm waned in a few years.

Both Ulster Scot and German were temperamentally conservative in religion, and hence were not easily stirred by a revival such as the Great Awakening. The earlier phase of it had few results, beyond the fact that John Brown, one of the half-dozen Presbyterian ministers in the Valley, had gone with the New Side, or liberal, Synod of New York, in the period when the church was split

[42] Minutes, Hanover Presbytery, April 13, 1775.

[43] Records, Linville Baptist Church, 1763-1776, passim; Minutes of Mill Creek Baptist Church. One of the grievances of the Valley Reformed Church against an erring pastor, Charles Lange, was his laxness toward delinquency in his congregation (Minutes, Coetus of Pennsylvania, September 21, 1769).

[44] Opecquon Church Records, 1763-1776, passim.

[45] Records, Linville Church, 1763-1776, passim, and especially June, 1765. One of the early Supreme Court cases grew out of Hart's will, which included a bequest to the Baptists for the education of ministers.

over the question of revivals.[46] The rest continued with
the Old Side or conservative Synod of Philadelphia.[47]
But Samuel Davies, the ablest of the New Side leaders,
left Virginia in 1759 to become the president of the College of New Jersey, obviously making easier the completion of the reconciliation of the two groups in the colony.
Such a reconciliation, coming as it did just before 1763,[48]
was accompanied by necessary compromises on the much
debated issue of revival methods. As a result, the zeal of
Valley New Siders was tempered, and the Old Siders
were aroused to the needs of revival in neglected frontier
areas, with consequent emphasis on itinerancies even of
settled ministers, including those in the Southwest and in
the Trans-Alleghany region.

Despite their conservative background, the Presbyterian itinerants were revivalists from necessity. Like the
Moravian missionaries of an earlier day, they had to
preach wherever they could get a hearing. The Valley
frontier was an area of various nationalities and creeds,
widely scattered abodes, and few fixed places of worship.
Although the circuit riders of other dissenting sects were,
like the Presbyterians, inclined to go first to those na-
tionally and doctrinally akin, they were also ready to minister to that ever-growing element, those unaffiliated with
any church. The size of this element prior to 1776 is
uncertain, but the minutes of church bodies indicate that it
was present.[49]

One of the most fascinating, and at the same time most

[46] Minutes, Synod of New York, 1755-1758, passim.
[47] Minutes, Synod of Philadelphia, 1755-1758, passim.
[48] The reconciliation had taken place in 1758, with the union of the
New Side Synod of New York and the Old Side Synod of Philadelphia into
the Synod of New York and Philadelphia.
[49] See Minutes, Hanover Presbytery, 1763-1776, passim; see also the
Peaked Mountain Church Agreement of 1769 in Wayland, Rockingham,
pp. 61-62.

difficult, problems in the Valley's religious history is the relation of the dissenters to the Anglican or Established Church in the colony. When, in 1738, Governor Gooch of Virginia, in answer to the petition of his fellow Scot, John Caldwell,[50] gave permission to Caldwell and his Ulster adventurers to settle in the back parts of the colony as a buffer between the old settlements and the Indians, he undoubtedly dealt a blow to the authority of the Anglican Church in Virginia.

As the dissenters proceeded to organize their local governments in the frontier counties, they found that a number of the local offices were closely tied up in name and theory with the Anglican Church, even though their functions were in varying degrees secular.[51] As the parish system operated in the Valley, there were: (1) the vestrymen, who laid the parish levy and from whose personnel the all-important local justices were usually appointed; (2) the church wardens, who were overseers of the poor, executors for needy orphans, and business managers for the parish property; and (3) the processioners, who made biennial checks of the boundary lines between plantations or holdings. Since these offices were filled by and from the freeholders, the Valley dissenters quietly took over most of them. The government at Williamsburg gave tacit consent, because it seemed the only solution of the local government problem for the dissenters.[52]

As the years passed and both Anglican and dissenter population grew, dissatisfaction arose over the workings of the system in the Valley. Accordingly, in 1769 the

[50] Grandfather of John Caldwell Calhoun.
[51] See Valley Court Records, 1745 et passim; see also Bruce, Institutional History of Virginia, I, 62-93. This book was written, however, of the period before the Valley was settled, when conditions were, of course, somewhat different. Also Bruce was describing conditions and institutions in eastern Virginia.
[52] Valley Court Records, 1745 et passim.

Burgesses passed an act declaring that, since in Augusta County the majority of the vestry were dissenters from the church of England, the said vestry was to be dissolved. The sheriff was instructed to call the freeholders together to elect a new vestry of men who had taken the "oath of abjuration, and repeated and subscribed the test, and also subscribed to be conformable to the doctrine and discipline of the Church of England."[53] Two years later the measure was reënacted, with the preliminary statement that, because of the "remoteness" of his county, the sheriff of Augusta had not heard of the act until its time limit had expired.[54] It evidently expired again, because the personnel of the Augusta vestry in 1772 was almost identical with that of 1769 and 1770.[55]

Some dissenting preachers likewise saw the advantages of a nominal conformity to the Church of England. The facility with which Muhlenberg and the Valley Lutherans fell into line with the idea has been noted. Their adherence to the theory of the Swedish branch in regard to episcopacy simplified matters for them. Conformity was not so easy for the Presbyterians, but at least two of them took orders in the Anglican Church—one, John Hindman, in the early days, and the other, Alexander Balmaine, on the eve of the Revolution. Hindman had been ordained[56] a Presbyterian and had served under that church for a time. Parson Craig's caustic remark concerning the matter is both characteristic and enlightening: "This day John Hindman attended having turned his coat and now appears in the quality of a Church of England parson."[57]

[53] Hening, *Statutes*, VIII, 432-443. Augusta Parish Vestry Book, 1769, cites three who refused to go through the procedure of conformity, to wit, Robert Breckinridge, Israel Christian, and John Buchanan, all prominent Valley leaders.

[54] Hening, *Statutes*, VIII, 504.

[55] Augusta Order Book, XIV, 102, 295, 335, 338, 409.

[56] Minutes, Synod of Philadelphia, May 26, 1743.

[57] Craig, *Diary*, April 5, 1747.

Hindman, of course, ceased to be regarded as a Presbyterian. There is no evidence that Balmaine was ordained a Presbyterian minister, although he was trained for that service. And since he retained much of the Presbyterian outlook, at least in his political philosophy, it seems that no Valley dissenter objected strenuously to his partial defection.[58]

The Valley dissenters, then, had only two possible grievances against the Established Church—the payment of the parish levy, and the denial to their ministers of the right to perform the marriage ceremony—and some of them found it rather easy to avoid both of these. They obviously had full freedom in the matter of worship and in most other ways.[59]

It is a matter of some interest that when the Baptist pleas for equal treatment with the other dissenters grew more insistent on the approach of the Revolution, the Presbytery of Hanover became alarmed lest a provision merely for *toleration* be incorporated in the colonial code. In 1775 therefore they sent a resolution or petition to the Burgesses, pointing out their objections to the proposed toleration act, "and praying that no Bill may pass into a law but such as will secure to the Petitioners equal liberties and advantages with their fellow subjects." This was one of the opening guns in the forthcoming struggle for full religious liberty.

Meanwhile, John Witherspoon, a Scotsman, was well established as the head of the College of New Jersey, and was already being thought of as the most distinguished leader of American Presbyterianism. One of his enthusiastic graduates, James Madison, was beginning to prepare

---

[58] Meade, *op. cit.*, II, 318 ff.

[59] *Journal, Burgesses*, June 1, 18, 1770; Feb. 12, 24, 25, March 17, 1772; May 12, 16, 1774; June 13, 1775; Minutes, Hanover Presbytery, Oct. 14-15, 1774; and especially *Journal, Burgesses*, June 5, 1775.

himself for the Virginia hustings, and at the same time was enunciating the Witherspoon tenets, such as freedom of conscience, the absolute separation of church and state, and the idea that a man's relation with his God is a natural right and not subject to legislation in any form.[60]

Ardently supporting Madison's ideas was a growing number of Witherspoon ministerial graduates, who were settling in the Valley or coming in as itinerants.[61] If Fithian was in any sense an example of these itinerants and resident ministers, they missed no opportunity to discuss politics and to put in their pleas for civil and religious liberty after the manner of their Princeton preceptor.[62]

On May 20, 1775, the Synod of New York and Philadelphia sent a broadcast to its churches in the form of a pastoral letter, presumably from the pen of Witherspoon, defending the patriot cause and making a plea for the liberty of conscience.[63] At about the same time the Presbyterian minister, Charles Cummings, a former Valley pastor now serving those of its people who had pushed just

[60] See Witherspoon, *Works*, especially III, 13-14, IV, 324, 330; Madison, *Works*, Hunt, ed., II, 24. Eckenrode's *Separation of Church and State in Virginia* is based largely on the petitions from the various dissenters but does not go far into other papers such as church minutes and correspondence of the leaders.

[61] Graduates of the College of New Jersey (Princeton) in the Valley who had been under Witherspoon were: John McKnight, William Graham, James McConnell, Samuel Leake, Samuel Doak, John Montgomery, Archibald Scott, James Templeton, John Duffield, and possibly several others. Some of them were just arriving as the Revolution began, but they were in sufficient time to make their voices heard. East of the Blue Ridge, but making more or less frequent trips to the Valley for presbytery meetings or for preaching to vacant churches, were Samuel Stanhope Smith, son-in-law of Witherspoon, John Blair Smith, brother to Samuel, Caleb Wallace, David Witherspoon, Nathaniel Irwin, Stephen Balch, and possibly others. The itinerants were Philip Vickers Fithian, John McMillan, Samuel Eusebius McCorkle, Robert Keith, Andrew Hunter, William Linn, Samuel Waugh, David Beard, and undoubtedly others—*Princeton Catalogue*, 1769-1776, *passim*; Fithian, *Journal*, 1775-1776, *passim*, see especially pp. 32-33.

[62] Fithian, *op. cit., passim*.

[63] Minutes, Synod of New York and Philadelphia, May 20, 1775.

beyond the southern rim of Botetourt, was penning vigorous resolutions against the English Parliament. The Presbyterian-Anglican Alexander Balmaine was pursuing the same course in Augusta with the ready support of the dissenters there. In the north Valley, under the tutelage of Muhlenberg and other prominent leaders, the dissenters were giving hearty acclaim to the protests of the Revolutionary patriots.

≡☆≡ **3** ≡☆≡

Valley Politics

WHEN, in the first half of the eighteenth century, the German and Ulster Scot migrated to the Valley, they found it to their advantage to adopt the forms of Virginia local government. Since a great majority of them were dissenters, they had to adjust themselves to a governmental system which was so closely associated with the Established Church that its officials, provincial and local, were expected to be Anglican communicants. As a result, non-Anglicans often became vestrymen and church wardens merely to fulfill the political duties involved.

As in other parts of Virginia, the chief local officers were the justices of the peace and the sheriffs. Each county listed a large number of justices. Augusta had as many as thirty-five or forty[1] in a given year, with Frederick and the other counties not far behind.[2] The caliber of these men may be judged from the fact that in the war period and in the movement for a stable government that

[1] Augusta Order Book, VIII, 113; XVI, 30, for example.
[2] Of these, from four to seven usually held the court. The appointments came from the Governor and Council at Williamsburg in the form of commissions of the peace. The justices, who were usually the leading men in the county in both property and ability, qualified by taking the oath of allegiance "to his Majesties Person and Government"—Augusta Minute Books, 1763-1776, *passim.*

followed it, many of them became leaders in the state. They served without salary, their only remuneration being the title "gentleman" or "esquire."[3]

From among the justices it was customary to select the sheriff and the county lieutenant, who were the chief administrative officers of the county.[4] The office of sheriff was an enviable one because of the dignity attached to it and because it usually offered ample financial return, including a percentage of all taxes and quitrents collected.[5] Appointment to this office generally came as a reward for serving acceptably as a justice. Deputy sheriffs, appointed by the justices for subdivisions of the county, shared both in the rewards and in the responsibilities of the office. The sheriff was heavily bonded, since he was personally responsible for the levies of his county. If he failed to collect any large part of the amount due, he might lose not only his own commission but his property as well.

Among the civil officers of the county who ranked close to the sheriff in prestige were the clerk of the court, the king's attorney or deputy attorney, the coroner, and the surveyor. The clerk and the coroner, as well as the sheriff, were appointed by the Governor and the Council on the recommendation of the justices. The attorney general of the colony appointed the deputy attorney, and the College of William and Mary was empowered by law to appoint the surveyor. Lesser administrative officers, such as the deputy clerk, constables, and road overseers, were appointed by the justices in court.[6]

In contrast with an earlier prejudice, lawyers were generally in good repute in the Valley. The leading member

[3] Valley Court Records, 1763-1776, *passim.* [4] *Ibid.*

[5] See Minute Books, Valley Counties; see also quitrent rolls, Chalmers Papers, Virginia. This rent collection was one of his chief duties. In so far as there was a tendency toward machine politics, the office went to the political leader of the county.

[6] Valley Court Records, 1763-1776.

of the bar was that picturesque dean of circuit-riding fron-
tier lawyers, old Gabriel Jones.[7] In the period from 1763
to 1775 fifteen lawyers were admitted to practice in the
Augusta Court alone. These included such later leaders
in the state as Patrick Henry (then recorded as Patrick
Henry, Jr.), Alexander White, Dabney Carr, Andrew
Moore, Charles Simms, William Christian, and John
Harvie, at least three of whom were non-residents.[8]

The chief organ of local government was the county
court composed of justices of the peace.[9] It was a legislative and administrative as well as judicial body. At times,
one gets the impression from its minutes that it was primarily a legislative body. Its most important work was
laying the annual levy or tax rate for the county,[10] but it
was also kept busy providing roads and bridges.[11] Likewise it fixed the prices for taverns, provided for the up-
keep of the county buildings,[12] supervised the workings
of the militia, made recommendations for officers under
the rank of colonel,[13] and performed other major functions of local government.[14]

[7] There is the classic incident preserved in the Augusta Court Records,
in which the court threatened to fine one Mr. Holmes, a young lawyer,
if he did not "stop annoying Mr. Jones and making him swear so." Tradition makes Jones the first law partner of Thomas Jefferson.

[8] Augusta Order Books, IX-XVI, passim. The process of licensing was
first, the granting by the court of a certificate "of probity, honesty and
good behavior." This was followed later—presumably after a course of
study in the office of some qualified lawyer—by an examination and the
subsequent granting of a license to practice.

[9] The courts met about six times a year, more frequently in March,
May, August, and November, seldom in January, February, July, September, and December. The sessions usually lasted about a week, sometimes
two weeks, each.

[10] Minute Books, Valley Counties, 1763-1776, passim.

[11] Order Books, Valley Counties, 1763-1776, passim.

[12] Minute Books, especially Augusta Minute Book, Mar. 22, 1775; see
also Augusta Order Book, XIV, 214; XV, 355.

[13] Two other functions of interest were markings for cattle and permis-
sions to build the numerous water-power mills, primarily for flour making.

[14] In that period of numerous apprentices and indentured servants the
court devoted much time to their regulations and the duties of their mas-

The courthouse, as the center of both political and social life, was a busy place. Litigation, as well as other court business, was stimulated by the desire for an excuse to go to the courthouse. The county seats were thronged when the court was in session, and the court docket was usually crowded. The trials, criminal as well as civil, reached a high-water mark around 1767-1768 and then gradually fell off until there was practically no litigation in 1776, when the Declaration of Independence came. In Augusta County, for example, the cases averaged about a hundred and fifty in 1768, thence falling off gradually but steadily until there were only sixteen in 1774, nine in 1775, and four in 1776.[15]

The wheels of justice did not always grind smoothly. A typical case is that of Israel Christian, a justice of the Augusta County Court, who cited John Graham for abusing him in the courtyard, while in the discharge of his duties, "by calling him a Rogue, a Cheat & a Rascal."[16] At another time three soldiers, Patrick Hara, Thomas Brannon, and John Hayes (perhaps Irish indentured servants who had gained prestige or freedom from service in the French and Indian War), swaggered into court with their hats on. To preserve decorum, the justices committed the offenders to jail during the pleasure of the court and until they had learned some manners.[17] In spite of these summary and sometimes drastic punishments for contempt, the court continued to have difficulties with those who would not recognize its dignity and authority.

ters. Order Books, Valley Counties, 1763-1776, *passim*. Sometimes this business ran into the hundreds in a single year.

[15] Augusta Order Books, IX-XVI. This decrease in court business was likely due to the growing antagonism to the royal government and the uncertainty as to whether the local justices would function.

[16] Augusta Minute Book, May 19, 1761. For this contempt of court Christian's fellow justices ordered Graham to pay £3 "to his Majesties use," and be held in jail until it was paid.

[17] Augusta Order Book, VII, 224.

There were frequent penalties for those who "misbehaved in the court yard in a riotous manner" or disturbed, or abused or insulted the court. One Daniel McAnare (McNair) was particularly rash, even "giving Gabriel Jones, Gent., Deputy Attorney for the King, the lie." Jones was the prosecutor of course. Sometimes the jury itself did not show proper respect for the court or for its own duties. In one instance the court held that the "jurors misbehaved themselves" in bringing in a certain verdict, which was therefore declared "idle and void" and a new jury was summoned.[18]

An outstanding example of the difficulties experienced in the functioning of local govenment was the controversy between Colonel Adam Stephen and Justice Jacob Hite.[19] Stephen, as sheriff of Berkeley County, executed a judgment of the Frederick Court against Hite[20] and sequestered in or near the county jail fifteen of Hite's Negroes and twenty-one of his horses,[21] which were to be sold at auction to satisfy the judgment. Hite vigorously resented the action. He wrote his neighbor and friend Horatio Gates, a justice of the county court, that the sale was to take place and threatened to stop it or sue any man who bought his property. The threat was accompanied by the more peaceful, though contradictory, suggestion that Gates and other friends buy the property at the sale, especially the Negroes and hold them until Hite could repay the purchase price.[22] Gates, however, used a more direct

[18] *Ibid.*, VIII, 38, 39, 132; IX, 213, 357; X, 148.
[19] His father, Joist Hite, was the chief rival of Lord Fairfax as a great landowner in the north Valley. Kercheval, *History of the Valley*, p. 46. Kercheval further states (p. 160) that there was bad blood between Stephen and Hite over the site for the courthouse of the new county of Berkeley, each wanting it on his own land.
[20] Frederick Order Book, XV, 402-410, Sept. 3, 1772. The case had started before Berkeley was created. Hite was the losing defendant in a debt case amounting to £1,641.
[21] Stephen Papers (Library of Congress), No. 86.
[22] Gates Papers (N. Y. P.), Hite to Gates, April 20, 1774.

way to aid his friend. Acting in his capacity as a magistrate, he authorized Hite to proceed against those persons who were "active in plundering him."[23] Another friend of Hite, who was a constable, assembled a posse consisting of Hite's son and several neighbors.[24] They went to the jail at Martinsburg and, threatening Stephen with violence if he interfered, recovered the Negroes and horses. Party spirit between the two factions ran high and bloodshed was imminent. But better counsel prevailed, and both principals, having employed able lawyers, returned to legal processes to attain their ends.[25] James Mercer, who was Stephen's counsel, wrote, "I shall only pity Major Gates from whose general good character I am surprised should authorize such a bare faced violence." Hite informed Gates that he was obtaining the opinion of the "Best Counsel can be had in this Colony."[26] The matter was carried to the General Court at Williamsburg, but action was postponed from time to time, because it was alleged that Gates' magisterial proceedings in the affair had been lost in transit.[27] Gates insisted that he had delivered the proceedings to the county clerk of Berkeley and that he, in turn, had sent them to Williamsburg. Mercer, Stephen's counsel, was threatening Gates with contempt proceedings. Tradition says that Gates and Stephen later became good friends in their mutual antagonism to Washington. The case was still pending when

[23] Gates Papers (N. Y. H. S.), Hite to Gates, May 2, 1774; also John Hite, Jr., to Gates, an undated letter to the same effect.

[24] *Ibid.* A letter from Hite's son thanks Gates for granting the warrant to his father and adds that he would "take it a particular favor if you will be kind enough to lend me a case of pistols for a few days & send them by the bearer." Stephen Papers, No. 86, is the warrant for the arrest of the jail breakers, as they are designated. It names twelve and adds "with many more."

[25] Stephen Papers, No. 84.

[26] Gates Papers (N. Y. P.), Letter, May 3, 1774.

[27] Gates Papers (N. Y. H. S.), No. 182, Gates to B. Waller at Williamsburg, Mar. 12, 1775.

some of the principals left to join the Revolutionary forces.[28]

The political leaders in the Valley during this period were chiefly Ulster Scots, but there were some Englishmen and Germans. The failure of the Germans to participate actively in the politics of the section was due in some measure to linguistic, racial, and religious differences.[29]

There were about a dozen outstanding leaders[30] in these pre-Revolutionary years and, in addition, there were several politically influential clerics.[31] These men not only furnished local leadership but it was to them that the Governor and Council looked for guidance in handling frontier problems, both in the Valley and in the Trans-Alleghany country. These leaders usually stood together and voted together in the colonial legislature.[32] Several of them were lawyers, at least two of whom, Gabriel Jones and Alexander White, had received their training in Great Britain. Two others, William Fleming and Adam Stephen, were physicians trained in Scottish universities. Nearly all were proprietors of large estates, and several were engaged in such enterprises as flour milling, iron manufacture, and gun making. Isaac Zane,

[28] Berkeley Will Book, I, 1777. John Hite's will states that not long afterward Hite moved to South Carolina, where in the early years of the war, he was killed by the Cherokee Indians.

[29] J. W. Wayland, *German Element of the Shenandoah Valley*, pp. 134-135.

[30] They may be listed as follows: George Washington, who spent much time there particularly in his earlier years; William Fleming, Adam Stephen, Andrew Lewis, Gabriel Jones, William Preston, Alexander White, John Wilson, Robert Rutherford, Isaac Zane, Charles Lewis, and James Wood. A less active group would include William Christian, Horatio Gates, Thomas Lewis, Abraham Byrd, Thomas Swearingen, John Bowyer, William Bowyer, Robert Breckinridge, Thomas Hite, Peter Hogg, Samuel McDowell, and the Madisons.

[31] These were John Craig, John Brown, Alexander Balmaine, Peter Muhlenberg, and Charles Mynn Thruston.

[32] *Journal, House of Burgesses*, 1763-1776, *passim*.

Adam Stephen, Thomas Lewis, and Gabriel Jones were comparatively wealthy men. Most of those from the Ulster Scot south Valley were closely related. The Christians, Flemings, and Bowyers had intermarried, as had the Prestons, Breckinridges, Browns, and McDowells. Thomas Lewis and Gabriel Jones were brothers-in-law. There were similar ties of kinship elsewhere in the Valley.

The legislator, or burgess, from the Valley, of greatest historic interest was, of course George Washington.[33] His political career began in Frederick County in the late fifties, when, under the tutelage of Gabriel Jones, he made an unsuccessful bid for a seat in the House of Burgesses. In this first campaign he received only forty votes out of approximately six hundred,[34] but in the next he was successful. After that Washington led the ticket, or was unopposed, until 1765, when he transferred his residence from Frederick to Fairfax.[35] He would probably have continued to live in the Valley but for his inheritance of Mount Vernon.

The number of burgesses increased from four in 1763 to ten in 1776. Their ability and experience, however, gave the section greater weight in the legislative councils of the colony than its number of representatives at any time warranted. This prestige became increasingly notice-

[33] *Ibid.*, 1758-1765. See list of members at the beginning of each session.
[34] Barton Papers (Winchester, Va.), election memorandum.
[35] *Journal, Burgesses,* 1776 *et passim.* In one of the Frederick elections, he was opposed by Adam Stephen, in a vigorous personal contest, but he easily defeated Stephen. Barton Papers; Washington, *Writings,* Fitzpatrick, ed., 1758-1765, *passim;* John Wilson of Augusta had the longest experience in the House of Burgesses and played a prominent part in the work of most of the standing committees of that body.—*Journal, Burgesses,* 1763-1772, *passim.* Others who rivaled him, in both length and quality of legislative service, were Robert Rutherford of Frederick, later Berkeley, James Wood, also of Frederick; Gabriel Jones and the Lewis family of Augusta, especially Charles and Andrew; the Hites, John and Thomas, of Berkeley; the Quaker ironmonger, Isaac Zane, of Frederick; and John Bowyer, of Botetourt.

able in the years 1774-76, especially in the work of the new standing Committee on Religion, which included nearly the entire delegation.[36] Somewhat the same was true of the Committee on Propositions and Grievances.[37]

Since the journal of the Burgesses failed to record individual votes, it is not possible to know just how this group of members voted on particular issues. It has been stated that the Valley vote assured the passage of the Stamp Act Resolutions, but definite evidence is lacking.[38] Three of the four members present in the House signed the non-importation association of 1770.[39] When the association of 1774 was voted, six members—Wood, Bowyer, Zane, Slaughter, Rutherford, and McDowell— signed.[40] The Lewis brothers, Charles and Andrew, were among the four who did not sign, but there is no record of any of the four having been present for that session, except Charles Lewis, who had probably returned home before the vote to help prepare the Point Pleasant expedition against the Ohio Valley Indians.

In the controversies between the Burgesses and Governor Dunmore during 1775, Valley members were again conspicuous. Wood and Zane were on the larger committees that represented the House in a quarrel over the governor's removal of the colony's powder from Williamsburg to a man-of-war, and in the inquiry concerning the "disturbances and commotions" that grew out of that quarrel.[41] They were also on a smaller committee, which

[36] *Journal, Burgesses,* 1774-1776, *passim.*   [37] *Ibid.*

[38] *Virginia Historical Collections,* Grigsby, "Virginia Convention of 1788," I, 10.

[39] *Journal, Burgesses,* 1769-1772, pp. xxvii *et passim.* Botetourt members had evidently not taken their seats. Gabriel Jones did not sign.

[40] *Journal, Burgesses,* 1773-1776, pp. xiv *et passim.* The association was formed at the end of the session, on May 27, by which time the Lewises were mobilizing their regiments for the approaching Point Pleasant campaign.

[41] *Ibid.,* June 8, 10, 1775. See also Eckenrode, "*Revolution in Virginia,*" pp. 49-52.

protested to Governor Dunmore against Lord North's proposals and against the Boston Port Bill.[42] At another time they joined actively in the pleas for conciliation, using the success of the Point Pleasant campaign as a basis for their hope that the difference between the Governor and the House might be removed and a happy relationship resumed. They kept the interest of the Valley in mind in their request that Dunmore procure a more adequate supply of arms and ammunition, since a tax bill for this purpose had been passed several years before. This supply was to be procured to meet a possible Indian invasion, the imminence of which Dunmore himself suggested.[43]

On June 19, 1775, the House received a spirited reply from Dunmore to an earlier address and also read his report to the Earl of Dartmouth, with its sharp indictment of the Virginia leaders. A committee of six was now appointed, with Wood and Zane as members, which drew up an exhaustive and caustic address to the governor.[44] Dunmore sent a reply of the same tenor as his earlier ones, to which the House, now joined by the Council, gave a vigorous answer, drafted by a committee of four including Andrew Lewis and William Christian.[45] Christian was a native of the Valley and was closely associated with it by kinship and politics. Now, however, he represented that group of Valley settlers who had moved into the Southwest, lately created the County of Fincastle.

On June 24, 1775, the House of Burgesses delivered its valedictory in a series of resolutions. One of these provided compensation for the Valley men at Point Pleasant, "those gallant officers and soldiers, who so nobly defended

[42] *Ibid.*, June 12, 1775.
[43] *Ibid.*, June 17, 1775.
[44] *Ibid.* This address covers about ten of the lengthy pages of the *Journal.*
[45] *Ibid.*, June 20, 21, 24, 1775.

this country against the incursions of the Indians." Another resolution called attention to the fact that Lord Dunmore had not concluded peace with the Indians as he had promised, expressed a fear of further conflict, and appointed six Valley leaders as commissioners to conclude such a peace if possible.

Before the Revolution the Valley people had little grievance against eastern Virginia. To be sure, when their militia joined Bouquet's expedition against the Ohio Indians, the House of Burgesses, which was controlled by eastern Virginia, disclaimed any responsibility or obligation. In assuming such an attitude the burgesses were largely on solid ground, but they compensated liberally just the same. Valley men frequently slew Indians with whom the government at Williamsburg and London had made peace. The home government stormed, the governor protested, and the burgesses passed vigorous and pointed resolutions against such "uncivilized" conduct, but no punishment was meted out by the colonial government.

In the matter of taxes the Valley had little specie and less tobacco with which to discharge its obligations, but the colonial government made liberal terms by which some commodity other than tobacco might be used. Ways were found to evade the parish levies for the Anglican Church. If taxes had to be paid in money, it was at the lowest possible rate of the tobacco levies.[46] At the same time a large amount was paid out to the Valley each year in the form of a bounty of four to six shillings a hundred-weight on hemp, which was raised there in great quantities.[47] Likewise the government provided a tax on slaves and wheel carriages, which was to be used to encourage and

[46] Taxes were levied in pounds of tobacco all over the state, but could be paid in money at the current price of tobacco in that part of the colony or as fixed by the legislature.

[47] Hening, *Statutes*, VII, 639 *et passim*.

protect settlers on the Western Waters. Eastern Virginia evidently paid the bulk of these taxes. Meanwhile benefits were provided in the numerous roads, which were ordered by the burgesses, to give the western counties outlets across the eastern mountains to the Tidewater, and across the Alleghanies to the "promised lands" on the Western Waters.

There were grievances, to be sure, but the impression remains that they were of minor importance. In 1766 the sheriff of Augusta was one of thirty who failed to return, properly executed, the writs of election to the House of Burgesses. He alone was sent for and brought before the bar of the House, where he was directed to make proper amends. He was then discharged, after being reimbursed for losses he had suffered.[48] Several years later John Madison, clerk of the Augusta court, was one of four who, having failed to send a list of tithables to Williamsburg as the law required, were compelled to pay the cost of a special messenger sent out to collect these lists.[49] Occasionally men complained of having to make the long trip to Williamsburg to testify at the General Court, especially if they failed to receive proper compensation. But the Burgesses usually provided compensation, if the case proved deserving.[50]

There was discrimination in the allowance for travel made to the burgesses, which worked to the disadvantage of the Valley because of its distance from Williamsburg. Some of its counties were required by law to allow ten shillings a day for twelve days of travel, others for sixteen days; this amount the county itself was expected to

[48] *Journal, Burgesses*, Nov. 10, 26, 1766.
[49] *Ibid.*, Feb. 28, 29, March 11, May 20, 1772.
[50] In 1774 the lawyers of the Valley unsuccessfully petitioned the Burgesses to have the days for holding court at various county seats arranged to meet the lawyer's convenience. *Journal, Burgesses*, May 23, 24, 1774; June 16, 1775.

pay.[51] It is difficult to find in this, however, a major grievance.[52]

Once the writs for the election of burgesses from Frederick failed to arrive in time for the election and the county was without representation, but in this case the government at Williamsburg was nowhere at fault. The writs had been given to Colonel William Preston of Augusta, whose chair broke down in Hanover on the way to Staunton. He turned them over to Thomas Bowyer, who was to give them to Gabriel Jones, since he frequently traveled to Frederick. Jones refused to take them and they fell into the hands of some irresponsible messenger.

The question of unequal representation, which became a burning one later, aroused little interest. During the colonial period, the Valley dissenter was not as vitally interested in the royal and Anglican government of Virginia as he was to become after he had helped to make it independent. There was not even united action in the proposed creation of new counties, a move which might partially have solved the problem of representation.[53] In 1773, after three new counties had been created in the Valley, Dunmore received a reprimand from the home government for permitting such action. In his defense the governor argued that it was necessary because of the tendency in the back country to "turbulent and refractory behavior," aggravated by their distances from the courts. He insisted that the creation of new counties and new courts was the only way to establish order.[54]

[51] Hening, Statutes, VIII, 314-315.

[52] Journal, Burgesses, Nov. 8, 10, 1766.

[53] Breckinridge Papers, William Preston to Robert Breckinridge, April 1, 1767. When the formation of Botetourt was being considered in 1767, Colonel Preston wrote Breckinridge from Williamsburg that there was so much confusion in petitions from the Valley for and against the new county that the House postponed action. He further suggested that the settlement of the matter was in the hands of the people themselves.

[54] Bancroft Transcripts, Virginia, II, 209-213, Dunmore to Secretary of State, May 25, 1773.

Thus in government as well as in religion the Valley was relatively happy as part of the body politic of the Old Dominion at the time when the breach was widening between Virginia and the mother country over the question of colonial policy. This portion of the frontier had served something of an apprenticeship in the matter of independence: economic, religious, and political.

Because of the mountain barrier between them and eastern Virginia and also because of their peculiar racial and religious status, these dissenter frontiersmen turned the local governmental units into almost independent states. Perhaps most interesting, we find this pre-Revolutionary Virginia frontier setting the stage for the drama of American democracy as it was to be enacted for the next century and a half. Here was a melting pot where Scot, German, English, Swiss, Dutch, and Irish were to blend into a democratic community of interest; where even the indentured servant could aspire to full equality if he should prove deserving. It is not surprising then to find these frontiersmen taking the lead in passing resolutions against British oppression, and threatening revolt two years and more before America was ready to declare herself independent.

≡☆≡ **4** ≡☆≡

"The Long Knives" versus "The Cornstalk" and His Indian Allies

FROM THE BEGINNING the Valley frontiersmen proved to be almost as excellent woodsmen as the Indians, winning from their Shawnee foes the name "Long Knives." The consequent rivalry, together with the fact that theirs was a buffer colony, developed in the Scot-German pioneers a distrust of their Indian neighbors. While no Indians lived in the Valley in the settlement period, they were keenly interested in it. The Senecas made it one of their highways, as the Seneca trail of popular tradition indicates. Cherokees, Tuscaroras, and Catawbas were constantly passing through it, while Delawares and Shawnees, particularly the latter, seem to have regarded it as their own peculiar game preserve.

Relations were generally peaceful, until the English and French began their struggle for the Ohio Valley. From that time the Valley of Virginia and its adjacent coves suffered frequent Indian raids. The Shawnees, under their great chief Cornstalk,[1] evidently saw in the war an opportunity for revenge against the trespassers. What-

---

[1] At the time nearly always referred to as "the Cornstalk."

ever the cause, they proceeded to make "Shawnee" and "Cornstalk" words of household dread and hatred.[2] Valley men under George Washington, Adam Stephen, Andrew Lewis, and others of their own leaders, had a part in most of the campaigns of the French and Indian War, including Braddock's expedition, for the possession of the Forks of the Ohio.

Therefore, with the terror and destruction of Indian warfare this pre-Revolutionary period was ushered in and came to its close. During the intervening years the two races were ostensibly at peace, but no year passed without its raids, stealings, burnings, and murders or massacres. Meanwhile the white man was constantly pushing his surveyor's lines and clearings into cherished hunting grounds; hatred grew more intense, and reconciliation more difficult.

When the Ohio Valley Indians were drawn into Pontiac's league, an appeal was made to Virginia to join Colonel Bouquet's expedition against them.[3] Since Governor Fauquier had been denied the power to raise troops even for the defense of the Valley frontier, much less for such an expedition as this, he could do nothing in the matter. However, he referred Bouquet's letter to the lieutenants of the frontier counties.[4] In the south Valley, Colonel Andrew Lewis gave every encouragement to the expedi-

---

[2] See Augusta Court Martial Record Book for the period; also Adam Stephen Papers; Washington, *Writings*, Fitzpatrick edition, I-II, *passim*. In the 1758 campaign of Forbes and Bouquet against Duquesne Colonel Washington ordered that "the dress of the officers and soldiers" of Major Andrew Lewis's contingent from Augusta County should be the guide for the other provincials in the matter of uniform—obviously a compliment to the spirit of these frontier soldiers. During the campaign they proved worthy of the young colonel's confidence. Washington, *Writings*, Fitzpatrick, ed., II, 240, to Adam Stephen, July 16, 1758. See also the Augusta County Court Martial Record Book, 1756-1763, *passim*.

[3] *Historical Account of the Bouquet Expedition in 1764*, pp. 33-35.

[4] *Journal, Burgesses*, Dec. 15, 1764.

tion, and two or three hundred men were soon raised.[5] A large detachment was likewise assembled in the north Valley. These two corps, as Bouquet designated them, were used as the van and rearguard of the expedition on its successful march from Fort Pitt toward the Indian towns in the Ohio Valley.[6]

When Bouquet had made a temporary peace, the Valley troops helped to escort to their homes the nearly three hundred captives (part of an accumulation of ten years) surrendered by the Indians. Many of these captives were kinsmen of the Valley men on the expedition. This probably accounted for the readiness of many to volunteer. A great many of the captives were not returned. The next spring some of the Valley officers, on behalf of their men and themselves, petitioned for pay for the expedition, as having been "in his Majesty's service." The petition was accompanied by letters of glowing commendation from General Gage and Colonel Bouquet. However, the colonial legislators rejected the petition with the terse phrase, "They have no claim against this Colony." A year and a half later the Burgesses relented and granted each of the officers of the expedition £40, "not as pay . . . they not being entitled thereto as they were not appointed to the said service by the Direction of the General Assembly," but "as an acknowledgment of their Merit and extraordinary service they rendered to this Colony by their gallant Behavior on the said Expedition."

But the real issue—which neither a treaty in Paris nor a Bouquet expedition nor a Virginia government could settle—was whether the eastern tributaries of the Ohio River were to furnish hunting grounds for the red men or homesteads for land-hungry pioneers. The period,

[5] Thwaites and Kellogg, *Dunmore's War*, pp. 426-427.
[6] *Bouquet Expedition*, pp. 40-43; *Journal, Burgesses*, May 10, 1765; Dec. 11, 1766.

1763-1776, saw the tide of Valley settlement move steadily through the passes of the Alleghanies to the Ohio Valley. The "Long Knives" were ignoring the "no trespassing" orders of Cornstalk and his Shawnees.

The conflict gained momentum through the impatience
and bad temper caused by the vacillating and seemingly
unfair land policy of the English government.[7] Wild
rumors spread over the frontier to the effect that those on
the land would be denied what seemed to them their natural right to occupy. Just as the French war was coming
to an end, Governor Fauquier of Virginia wrote to the
home government, "I much fear we shall not be able to
live upon the same terms with the Indians as the French
did, unless this enthusiasm of running backwards to hunt
for fresh lands can be stopped."[8] He recommended that
the London government establish strict regulations for
the granting of lands.[9] But such regulations were already
in the making in the settlement provisions of the Proclamation of 1763. These forbade the granting of lands in
the area west of the sources of rivers flowing into the
Atlantic Ocean, and further reserved that area as hunting
grounds for the Indians.[10]

Soon after Lord Dunmore's appointment to the Virginia governorship, he reported that the Proclamation had
not in the least prevented the occupying of the forbidden
lands by "People who are Continually in search of New

[7] See Alvord, *Mississippi Valley in British Politics*, 2 vols., for a thorough and able discussion of the English proclamation of 1763 and its
consequent development of frontier or land policy. He carries the reader
through a maze of English party politics and policy making and emerges
with a large measure of success in clarifying the workings and inadequa-
cies of such policy making. The question from the Valley side, however,
is not a part of his study.

[8] Bancroft, Virginia Papers, I, 193-195, Fauquier to Board of Trade,
July 8, 1763.

[9] *Ibid.*, pp. 197-199, Fauquier to Egremont.

[10] MacDonald, *Documentary Source Book of American History*, p. 116.

Lands."[11] Two years later he presented a similar argument in his often quoted statement that these frontiersmen were not to be restrained by the Proclamation of 1763 or anything that followed it, that "they do and will remove as their avidity and restlessness incite them," that "they acquire no attachment to place, but wandering about seems engrafted in their nature," and that they "forever imagine the lands further off are still better than those upon which they are already settled."[12]

It was a case of Canute commanding the wave—the Valley frontiersman stood on the boundary of what to him was a promised land, and London was a long distance away. The working out of a land policy was further complicated by the fact that 200,000 acres lying within the disputed territory had already been granted to numerous frontier or Valley leaders as bounties for their services in the French war, which had ended in 1763. It was made still more difficult, as far as the frontier was concerned, by grants, or proposed grants, to several land companies such as the Ohio and Transylvania companies. These grants not only seemed to jeopardize the bounty lands, but, particularly to the back counties, they appeared an evidence of unwarranted favoritism on the part of the home government.

Nevertheless, the constant peril of prolonged conflict with the red man tended to retard the westward movement. There is no lack of evidence that during the French war the inhabitants of the Valley had sought safety in the Carolinas and other more peaceful places. Parson

[11] Bancroft, Virginia Papers, II, 199; Dunmore to the Secretary of State, Oct. 3, 1771 and Nov. 16, 1772. It is argued, of course, that Dunmore had an axe to grind in his own interest in the lands.

[12] Bancroft, Virginia Papers, II, 399. These statements are in a large measure corroborated by the records of the Valley counties in their picture of a restless and constantly roving land-hungry population (Valley Court Records, especially Order and Minute Books, 1763-1776, *passim*, and particularly a petition to the Augusta court, loose leaf in Order Book XI).

Craig's diary reveals this tendency to flee for refuge, and how he urged his own people to build convenient forts for protection.[13] Among his congregation, he tells us, "Some of the Richer sort that could take some money with them to live upon, were for flying to a safer part of the country. My advice was then called for, which I gave, opposing that scheme as a scandal to our nation, falling below our brave ancestors, making ourselves a reproach among Virginians, a dishonor to our friends at home, and evidence of cowardice, want of faith and a noble Christian dependence on God, as able to save and deliver from the heathen; it would be a lasting blot on our posterity." The Fort Defiance congregation, according to Craig, preferred to remain in the Valley.[14]

The advance toward the Indian country, however, was much greater than any tendency to retreat.[15] Following the fortunes of prominent families of the Valley, we find their course steadily toward the west and southwest. The Washingtons, the Hites, the Crawfords, the Zanes, the Breckinridges, the Campbells, the Lewises, the Prestons, the Moores, the Buchanans, the Christians, and others were starting on the road that was to lead to better fortunes on the Western Waters.[16] A particularly interesting

[13] Washington, *Writings*, Ford ed., I, 234-235, 264-265, 360-361, 377-381; *Virginia Magazine*, XIX, 293; Bancroft, *op. cit.*, I, 27-29, 193, 197; Parson Craig's Diary as copied in Foote, *Sketches of Virginia*, 2nd Series, p. 32. Craig was the first Presbyterian minister to settle in the Valley.

[14] Foote, *op. cit.*, p. 33. The county records for the period indicate a movement toward the Carolinas but by individuals rather than *en masse*. See Valley Court Records, especially Minute Books and Judgments, 1763-1775, *passim*.

[15] See especially, extra leaf, Augusta Order Book, XI, 1768; also Bancroft, Virginia Papers, I and II, *passim*; Chalmers Papers, Virginia, III; Gates Papers, 1772-1774; Stephen Papers, 1763-1776; as well as the *Journal of Burgesses* and Hening, *Statutes*, for the period, to note the westward trend.

[16] Augusta County Records, 1763-1776, *passim*; Chalmers Papers, Virginia, IV, 7 ff.; Gates Papers, 1773-1775, *passim*; Glass Papers. Augusta Order Book, XI, 90, has a petition for a road to the "Western Waters"

example is the family of Israel Christian who lived in or near Staunton about 1763. By 1776 his son, Colonel William Christian, was a prominent leader of Fincastle County in the Southwest, and three of his daughters had married Colonel William Fleming, Caleb Wallace, and Colonel William Trigg, respectively, also of the same county. Within another ten years they had all moved to Kentucky, with the exception of Colonel Fleming, who was several times on the point of migrating to that land of promise.[17] Andrew Lewis, William Preston, Adam Stephen, several Washingtons, William Christian, Peter Hogg, Alexander White, William Fleming, Zachariah Johnston, William Crawford, and Robert Rutherford are representative leaders from Valley counties, who were busy surveying and seating claims for land on the "Western Waters," apparently with scant attention to Indian claims or English land policy, not to mention the constant menace of hostile savages. Between 1774 and 1776 nearly four hundred surveys, ranging from thirty acres to six thousand, were made in the new frontier county of Fincastle, which bordered the Valley to the southwest.[18]

This migration to the west and southwest was also obvious from the petitions that flowed into the House of Burgesses.[19] The petitioners frankly asked for legal titles to the new lands that were being taken up, and for the organization of new counties or local government units, regardless of Indian claims.[20]

---

signed largely by these families; Washington, *Diary*, Fitzpatrick, ed., 1763-1775, *passim*.

[17] See Preston, Stephen, Washington, Fleming, and Johnston Papers for the period, also Valley Court Records and Virginia Land Office Records.

[18] Summers' *Annals of Southwest Virginia* has a list of these surveys, pp. 652-665.

[19] To the House of Delegates, of course, after 1776.

[20] *Journal, Burgesses*, 1763-1776, especially May 25, 1763; Nov. 8, 15, 1764; Mar. 30, April 1, 1767; April 2, 1768; May 10, Nov. 27, 28,

In 1769 the Presbyterians of Virginia sent Reverend John Craig of Augusta to make a religious survey, presumably of their denomination, in southwest Virginia.[21] He reported eight communities with enough people in each to organize a church, that is, from thirty-six to seventy-five families. His report took no account of smaller groups and isolated homes.[22]

The paths of the surveyor of new abodes and new counties and the trails of the Presbyterian circuit riders thus corroborate the evidence implied in family names. These pioneers were moving steadily westward, in spite of Indian opposition. They were taking possession not only of adjacent coves but also of the New and Holston River areas and the regions which later became Tennessee, Kentucky, and West Virginia. The Prestons and Campbells of the Valley became the dominant leaders of southwest Virginia, and representatives of their neighboring Valley families were likewise prominent in other new settlements. Among these were the Seviers of Tennessee, the Breckinridges of Kentucky, the Crawfords, the Zanes, the Van Meters, and the Lewises of the Trans-Alleghany country (West Virginia).[23] The early Valley settlers were hardy souls, inured to danger and led on by the prospect of better things somewhere in the West. Their pioneer philos-

Dec. 12, 1769; June 2, 9, 1770; Feb. 19, Mar. 21, 26, April 8, 1772; June 3, 1775; Virginia Petitions, Botetourt, No. 138.

[21] Southwest Virginia is that area extending southwest from Roanoke toward Cumberland Gap and composed of the numerous beautiful valleys of the New River and its branches, as well as those of the Clinch and Holston rivers, all upper tributaries of the Ohio.

[22] Minutes, Hanover Presbytery, April 13, 1769.

[23] From the safety of the Virginia tidewater, a kinsman took Colonel William Preston to task for pushing forward into the Indian country, with such complaints as: "I can't understand why you give up Safety and Satysfaction for risk and disquiet"; "you will get part of your family or yourself butchered," and "I wouldn't live at Smithfield (Preston's new place in the Southwest) for all you possess."—Preston Papers, Johnson to Preston from Manchester, Virginia, July 2, 1778.

ophy assured them that the Indian must continue to surrender his hunting grounds, upon the demands of British
farmers, and that there was no better title to lands than
"natural rights."[24] The presumption was that such "natural rights" were more strongly inherent in "Long Knife"
farming than in Shawnee hunting.[25]

A friend of Horatio Gates, discussing the problems arising from Parliamentary interference, commented: "What
is that to us here! (says you) we have the Banks of the
Mississippi to Settle which to us is better than all the
kingdoms of the World and the Glory of them." In similar vein, at about the same time, the Reverend John
Brown, who is regarded as the founder of Washington and
Lee University in Virginia, wrote, "What a Buzzel is
amongst People about Kentuck? to hear people speak of
it one would think it was a new found Paradise and I
doubt not if it is such a place as represented. Ministers
will have thin congregations but why need I fear that?
Ministers are moveable goods as well as others and stand
in need of good land as any do for they are bad farmers."[26]

Possession of land which was equally promising to Indian hunter and Valley farmer was therefore the major
cause of the bloody strife between Cornstalk's Indian
warriors and the Virginia frontiersmen. It is doubtful
whether the attitude of the government at Williamsburg
affected the conflict much either way. The same may be
said of whatever there was of policy or of bungling on
the part of the home government, in the matter of Indian
boundaries. The actual happenings of those perilous years
were much more important to the Ulster Scot and the

[24] Virginia Petitions, Botetourt, No. 138, Nov. 5, 1778. This presages,
of course, Revolutionary philosophy.

[25] Gates Papers (N. Y. P.), John Cary to Gates, Aug. 30, 1773.

[26] Thwaites and Kellogg, *Revolution on the Upper Ohio*, p. 10. The
Brown family did join the westward trek.

German of that time than any number of plausible theories that might have explained them. They probably knew that a peace had been made in Paris in 1763, but their feelings, outraged by the carrying off of their women and children, could not be appeased by European diplomats. Massacre and retaliation for massacre continued.[27]

From 1764 to 1766 there were a number of destructive Indian raids throughout the Valley. The worst of these, on Kerr's Creek in Rockbridge County, was led by Cornstalk who took a heavy toll of scalps and prisoners. Some reports listed the number of victims as high as a hundred or more. Evidently this was an exaggeration, but it is indicative of the horror that the raid brought.[28] Just prior to this raid the same Shawnees, though pretending friendship, almost wiped out one or more settlements on the Greenbrier River in the Trans-Alleghany region just west of Augusta. These settlers were for the most part close kinsmen of the Augusta people. At the other end of the Valley John Rhodes (Roads), a Mennonite minister, and his family of ten children were likewise killed by the Indians. In keeping with the tenets of his faith, he had continually preached against the use of force and pleaded for kindness in the treatment of his Indian neighbors.[29] Again in the south Valley, Indian raiders attacked a schoolhouse in Augusta, killed the teacher, and carried off the children.[30] In 1769 George Washington, while enjoying a vacation at the Bath in Frederick County, wrote a friend

[27] Withers, *Chronicle of Border Warfare*, Thwaites, ed., especially pp. 125-135; Kercheval, *History of the Valley*, pp. 96-108; Valley Court Records, 1764-1774, *passim*.
[28] Thwaites and Kellogg, *Dunmore War*, pp. 432-433; Peyton, *Augusta County*, pp. 139-142, per old chronicle; Waddell, *Annals of Augusta*, p. 122.
[29] Kercheval, *History of the Valley*, pp. 101-103.
[30] This incident is from a chronicle of Indian warfare in Waddell, *Annals of Augusta County*, p. 121.

that an Indian scare had very much alarmed the "Female Visitors of these Waters."[31]

In court records as well as in contemporary correspondence[32] and chronicles, we find the same story of Indian outrages, exaggerated undoubtedly, but none the less effective in creating a frenzied state of mind. This meant a virtual reign of terror on the frontier and brought a demand for war to the death against the Indian enemies. To those pioneers of the Valley, Indians were murderous "heathen" who killed even the missionaries sent among them,[33] whose smell was the smell of a "varmint,"[34] who were "without any kind of sensibility or Sense of Honor,"[35] and who were "little removed from the brute creation."[36]

Meanwhile the white settlers were not passive in this tragic drama. The series of forts on the eastern ridges of the Alleghanies were manned, and new ones were built at strategic points.[37] Thirty captains of militia were appointed in Augusta County alone during this period, with numerous other officers, military and administrative.[38] The new frontier county of Botetourt, organized in 1769,

[31] Washington, *Writings*, Fitzpatrick, ed., II, 522, to Colonel Armstrong. The Presbyterians appointed a day of prayer and fasting because of the "dangerous situation" arising from the constant Indian warfare. See Minutes, Hanover Presbytery, Oct. 3, 1764. Fithian, who traveled through the Valley counties in 1775, heard the sad story of the widow of a victim in a massacre, herself a captive for thirteen years. He added, "It is not a wonder that these Inhabitants are filled with high Indignation against those Savage Heathen." Fithian, *Diary*, Dec. 27, 1775.
[32] See letter of Joseph Neavill (Neville) in Allason Papers, Letter No. 316, June 17, 1774; *Journal, Burgesses*, Oct. 30, 1764 and so on.
[33] Virginia Petitions, Augusta, No. 326; see also sketch of McFerrin in *Virginia Convention of 1788* by Grigsby, II, 37-39.
[34] Graham, *Presbyterianism*, on Colonel William Darke, p. 33.
[35] Preston Papers, Johnson to Preston, Nov. 24, 1774.
[36] Bancroft, Virginia Transcripts, II, 391, Dunmore to Secretary of State, Dec. 24, 1774.
[37] Koontz, *The Virginia Frontier*, pp. 111-148; Chalmers Papers, Virginia, IV, 5; *Journal, Burgesses*, 1763 et *passim*; Augusta County Order Books, VIII-XIV, *passim*.
[38] Augusta County Order Book, 1763-1775, *passim*.

devoted a large part of its court business to defense, and in a few years had set up eighteen captains of militia.[39] In 1772 a militia return of Colonel Adam Stephen of Frederick County showed nearly twenty-two hundred men under arms and ready to repel invasion.[40] In addition to these regular militiamen, patrollers and rangers were kept on the alert to prevent surprise attacks by bands of Indians.[41] The pressure for men was so insistent that the Valley dissenters who were conscientious objectors, such as the Quakers and Mennonites, were frequently petitioning the House of Burgesses for relief.[42]

In his retaliation program the Valley settler held to the frontier tenet that the only good Indian was a dead Indian. It is not surprising then to find hunters, who passed through Winchester in 1765, exhibiting Indian scalps after the manner of trophies from the chase.[43] Other contemporaries tell of reprisals in which whites and Indians vied in savage cruelty.[44] The tomahawk was an important part of the equipment of the Valley militiaman.[45] The Indian name for these frontiersmen, "Long Knives," is in itself significant. White traders aggravated the situation by making liquor one of their chief items of commerce with the Indians. The colonial government protested vigorously against the practice but in vain.[46]

[39] Botetourt Minute Books, 1770-1774, *passim*.

[40] Chalmers Papers, Virginia, IV, Dunmore Report, 1772.

[41] Valley Court Records, 1763-1775, *passim*; Allason Papers, White to Allason, June 25, 1774, concerning Daniel Morgan as a ranger.

[42] *Journal, Burgesses*, March 28, 1767; Nov. 14, 1769; March 23, 1772; June 12, 1775; Hening, *Statutes*, VIII, 503, 534; Augusta Court Martial Record Book, Oct. 16, 1776. Exemption was granted only on the condition that they furnish substitutes or a money payment of £10. See Hening, *Statutes*, VIII, 241.

[43] Letter in Peyton, *Augusta County*, p. 143.

[44] Young, "Chronicle of the Battle of Back Creek," 1764, in Peyton, *Augusta County*, p. 150.

[45] *Journal, Burgesses*, Dec. 3, 1766, claim for furnishing tomahawks to Valley militiamen. See also Augusta Court Martial Record Book.

[46] Report of Nelson, acting governor, to Secretary of State in 1771, in Bancroft, Virginia Transcripts, II, 159. Nelson despaired of any attempts

Settlers were frequently charged with killing allegedly friendly Indians passing through the Valley. Early in 1765 Colonel Andrew Lewis, county lieutenant of Augusta, reported such a case to Governor Fauquier. The governor in turn wrote the Lords of Trade that "hot headed frontier inhabitants" who were "villainous bloody minded rascals" had killed five Cherokees near Staunton as they passed through.[47] A few weeks later Fauquier informed the home government that the conduct of the people of Augusta was worse than at first reported. The governor's council concluded that, since the colonial government was not able to enforce obedience to the laws, it was better to pursue prudent than vigorous measures. Furthermore, the governor gave credence to a rumor that the "Paxton Boys" of Pennsylvania had promised the Valley settlers "that if they are not strong enough to rescue any of their party who may be apprehended they will come to their assistance, for they say no man shall suffer for the murder of a savage."[48]

to stop the trade. "When I consider how bewitching the passion for strong drink is among the lower and unthinking part of mankind, insomuch that it is one of the greatest evils, I am told in England, which cannot be suppressed by all the wisdom of the wisest legislature in the world," how could he hope to stop it on the frontier of Virginia?

[47] *Journal, Burgesses*, May 13, 1765; Bancroft, *op. cit.*, I, 279.

[48] In 1767 Fauquier wrote Secretary Shelburne of the British government, "Your Lordship seems surprised and indeed, my lord, very well you may be that no offender can be brought to justice for the murder of an Indian," the people of the frontier "secrete and screen these miscreants." He then told of one Ryan who had killed a chief warrior of the Delawares, for whose apprehension he had offered a reward, not because he had any hope of catching the man but to show the Indians that the government at Williamsburg was trying to bring the murderers of their people to justice. According to Fauquier, even if the man could be brought to trial, the local justices would refuse to punish him; if he were sent to Williamsburg for trial, the jury, which must be brought from his own county, would acquit him. It was useless to send the militia, he argued, because that would show the weakness of the government, as well as stir up the frontiersmen, who would to a man "take part with the murderer" (Bancroft, *op. cit.*, I, 333-335, Fauquier to Board of Trade, June 14, 1765). The "Paxton

The governor was perhaps unduly alarmed, for the county authorities, whenever possible, apprehended the whites who were the aggressors. Yet in at least two cases the frontier inhabitants were so far unwilling to have any man punished for killing an Indian that they broke open the jails and released the offenders.[49] When the governor submitted to the House of Burgesses the report of Colonel Adam Stephen censuring this lawlessness, the House passed vigorous resolutions condemning the killing of Indians as "atrocious and inhuman," "contrary to law and order," and "a violation of a sacred treaty," and denouncing the jail deliveries as an "insult to the government." They promised the governor to bring the offenders to "condign punishment," but nothing was done.[50]

Indian relations continued to grow worse, until the government at Williamsburg was drawn definitely into the conflict. During the midsummer of 1774 both parties made ready for war, the Indians by attempting a great confederation of all the Ohio tribes, and the whites by calling out the frontier militia and by starting two divisions on the march toward the Ohio. The north Valley division, commanded by Governor Dunmore himself, was to advance by way of Fort Pitt, and the division from the south Valley, commanded by General Andrew Lewis, was to go by way of the Great Kanawha Valley.[51]

Boys" of Pennsylvania were a band of frontiersmen in that state, who had grown restless under the do-nothing Indian policy of the Pennsylvania government and had somewhat ruthlessly taken matters into their own hands. (See Bancroft, *op. cit.*, pp. 485-489, Fauquier to Shelburne, May 24, 1767.)

[49] Withers, *Chronicles of Border Warfare*, pp. 135-136. Kercheval, *History of the Valley*, 3rd ed., pp. 104-105. Kercheval says that one of these prisoners later fought as a captain of the militia at Point Pleasant.

[50] *Journal, Burgesses*, Nov. 10, 1769. In 1771 Acting Governor Nelson was still promising the home government that he would bring justice to the perpetrators of violence and murder on the neighboring Indians.— Bancroft, *op. cit.*, II, 161.

[51] See Thwaites and Kellogg, *Dunmore's War*, pp. 68-202, *passim*, 315-

The south Valley made thorough preparations, and most of the militiamen eagerly fell into line.[52] Colonel William Fleming of Botetourt commanded one regiment of the southern division and Colonel Charles Lewis, brother of Andrew, the other. The division lost little time in getting to Point Pleasant at the junction of the Ohio and Great Kanawha rivers. There they unexpectedly met the Indians in force, under Cornstalk, and after an all-day battle, with great losses on both sides, including a heavy toll of Valley officers, the Indians retreated across the Ohio. The Shawnees and the "Long Knives" had finally met in force and fought one of the most decisive battles in the annals of Indian warfare. The Proclamation line of 1763 was thus swept aside by the onrush of Valley pioneers.

333, 413-425; Fleming Papers, 1774; Stephen Papers, 1774; Preston Papers, 1774-1775; Chalmers Papers, Virginia, IV; Withers, *Chronicles*, as the best sources for the Dunmore War. See especially the accounts by participants, as given in the Thwaites and Kellogg collection. An interesting figure of this period was the Grenadier Squaw, sister of the Shawnee chief, "the Cornstalk." She seems to have been a loyal friend of the whites throughout the period and acted as their emissary in negotiations with the Indians. Several additional Valley units were engaged in the conflict, notably a battalion of Frederick militia commanded by Major Angus McDonald. See Morgan Papers for Daniel's part; see also Frederick County Minutes, 1773-1780, p. 75. Dunmore ordered Colonel Horatio Gates to command a part of the former contingent, but that newly established country gentleman declined (Emmet Collection, Stephen to Gates, August 24, 1774). Colonel Adam Stephen wished to attend the meeting of the Continental Congress in Philadelphia, but Dunmore insisted that he go along as second in command (Stephen Papers, Stephen to R. H. Lee, August 27, 1774).

[52] See letter of Reverend John Brown to Colonel William Preston in regard to Augusta volunteers in Thwaites and Kellogg, *Dunmore's War*, pp. 159-161. According to Thwaites (note p. 164, Wither's, *Chronicle*), they took with them four hundred pack horses carrying 54,000 pounds of flour and drove along over one hundred head of beef cattle as a source of supply. There were twenty-five to thirty companies of militia in the expedition, perhaps more, with a total of 1500-3000 men. Governor Dunmore reported to the Burgesses, June 5, 1775, that General Lewis had 3000 men. See company rolls in Thwaites and Kellogg, *Dunmore's War*. The Piedmont, as well as southwest Virginia, was represented by small contingents.

After various conflicting orders from Dunmore, Lewis continued the pursuit of the Indians to their towns north of the Ohio, where Dunmore's division joined him. Within a short time, however, Dunmore ordered Lewis' division to return to the Valley, on the ground that its presence might embarrass the negotiations for peace.[53] This action aroused the indignation of the Valley troops and set the stage for later misunderstandings.

An important result of the Dunmore War was the renewal of the struggle between Virginia and Pennsylvania for the Fort Pitt area. Valley interest in the region had been revealed earlier by the moves to improve the old Braddock Road and to open a water route by way of the Potomac and Monongahela rivers.[54] Dunmore visited the region early in 1774, and reported that he had found 10,000 settlers.[55] According to his report to London, 600 petitioners asked him to establish a government there to protect them from the Indians. This he did by appointing his close friend, Dr. John Connolly, a justice of the peace of Augusta County, of which the Fort Pitt area was counted a part.[56] The sheriff and magistrates of Augusta

[53] Thwaites and Kellogg, op. cit., pp. 302-303; Withers, op. cit., pp. 175-176. The governor's attempt at peace was unsuccessful but later the Assembly, after it had broken with Dunmore, sent a peace commission of its own, composed almost entirely of Valley men, including Andrew Lewis, Adam Stephen, James Wood, and Thomas Walker (Chalmers Papers, Virginia, IV, 24-25; Journal, Burgesses, June 24, 1775; Thwaites and Kellogg, Revolution on the Upper Ohio, pp. 25-127; Fleming Papers, 1774. George Washington was appointed to the Commission but was, of course, in Boston). The commissioners in turn sent Wood to the Indian towns to invite them to a conference at Fort Dunmore (Fort Pitt). Wood, however, met with little response, and the conference, which was also attended by representatives of the Continental Congress, proved unsatisfactory. The Indian problem of the Valley was still unsettled when the Revolution began.

[54] Gates Papers (N. Y. H. S.), No. 137, Stephen to Gates, Nov. 24, 1772.

[55] Bancroft, op. cit., II, 231-233. Dunmore to Dartmouth.

[56] Ibid., II, 261-271, 301-311, 449-461. In a letter to Dartmouth, Nov. 12, 1774, Dunmore said that Virginia's claim was based on both the Jefferson and Fry Map of 1751, and the Henry Map of 1770.

were to support Connolly at all times, and its deputy attorney was instructed to prosecute his cases. Connolly built a new fort and renamed the place Fort Dunmore.[57] These moves by Dunmore and Connolly brought from Pennsylvania a vigorous denial of the Virginia claims, and the ensuing controversy between Penn and Dunmore before the Lords of Trade became extremely bitter.[58] The question of the Fort Pitt boundary was left to plague the Continental Congress.

These dozen years of strife between the Valley people and their Indian neighbors, then, came from land hunger and from attempts at vengeance that grew out of wrongs, real and imagined. Land meant primarily a living to these frontiersmen, and, as they saw it, the fullness of that living was dependent on the breadth and fertility of the acres they possessed. Knowing even less ethnology than Latin, and not much geography, they could not understand how wandering bands of savages had better claims than they to tillable lands. Scots and Germans refused to heed the "no trespassing" sign of a king on the English throne three thousand miles away. They would permit nothing to bar their way across mountain passes that led to fertile fields on the Western Waters, where there was so much promise of better things for themselves and for their numerous progeny.

[57] *Ibid.*, II, 307-309, Dunmore to Connolly, April 25, 1774.

[58] *Ibid.*, II, 261-271, 275-301, 355, 449-461. Dunmore to Dartmouth, Penn to Dartmouth, and so on. Dunmore apparently had the worst of the argument, until the success of the Point Pleasant campaign increased his prestige and emboldened him and Connolly to assert their claims more vigorously. Bancroft, *op. cit.*, II, 391-539, *passim*. Most important from the Valley point of view, in 1775 the Augusta County Court was ordered to meet at Fort Dunmore (Pitt) in alternate months; and it did so for nearly two years, dealing with the usual court business but with a different set of justices from those who sat at Staunton (Augusta County Order Book, 1775, *passim*). For the minutes of the Augusta County Court that functioned at Pittsburgh for nearly two years, see *Annals of the Carnegie Museum* (1901-1902), Boyd Crumrine, ed., pp. 525-568.

≡☆≡ **5** ≡☆≡

The Valley and the Appeal
to Arms

No FRONTIER AREA of Colonial America surpassed the Valley in its zeal for the Revolutionary movement. Along with this, one important fact must be kept in mind: for a generation prior to the outbreak of the War for Independence the patience of its agriculturally-minded people had been tried by almost continuous Indian warfare. Although an important victory was won over the Indians at Point Pleasant in October, 1774, any hope for a lasting peace was dispelled when it was found that neither Governor Dunmore nor the Valley's own commissioners had succeeded in making an effective treaty with the savages.[1] If a hostile English government continued to stir up Indian troubles, Valley settlers could resume their peaceful occupations only after a twofold victory—over hostile Indians and English alike.

On the eve of the War for Independence, then, and for most of its duration, Valley leaders were faced with the dual problem of furnishing soldiers for Washington's armies and of protecting their homes from frequently re-

[1] Fithian, *Diary*, Nov. 28, 1775.

curring Indian raids.[2] The Valley was an armed camp
from the beginning of the war. Numerous militia companies constantly mustered and drilled and were ready to
march on almost a moment's notice to the west, north,
south, or east, wherever pressure was greatest. Near the
end of the war the Indian menace was checked, but not
removed, by the spectacular expedition of George Rogers
Clark to the Northwest. The danger was sufficiently les-
sened, however, to enable the Valley to throw most of its
manpower and food supply toward the greater menace of
the British invasion of Virginia in 1780-81, thus making
an important contribution to the successful Yorktown campaign.

Its zeal and inurement to war gave the Valley strength
for the conflict. Almost immediately on receipt of the
news that the port of Boston had been closed by the
British Parliament, the Valley people began to assemble
and pass resolutions. On June 8, 1774, less than two
months after the Port Act was passed, the "freeholders
and other inhabitants of the county of Frederick and gentlemen practicing at the bar," met at Winchester and were
presided over by Charles Mynn Thruston, rector of Frederick parish. Resolutions, unanimously adopted, asserted
the rights of the American colonists, provided for an
agreement against importing English goods, particularly
East India tea, and designated a committee of correspondence. The most significant statement, however, was that
the attempt on the part of the English government to enforce the Boston Port Act would "have a necessary tendency to raise a civil war, thereby dissolving that union
which has so long happily subsisted between the mother
country and her colonies."[3] These resolutions came more

[2] See correspondence of William Fleming, 1775-1781, *passim.* Fleming
was county lieutenant of Botetourt. See also *Journal, Burgesses,* June 14,
1775.
[3] The members of the committee were Charles Mynn Thruston, chair-

than two years before the Declaration of Independence.

A few months later Adam Stephen voiced his philosophy of liberty to the effect that, "for my part before I would submit my life, liberty, and property to the arbitrary disposal of a corrupt, venal aristocracy, the wanton and effeminate tools of power, I would set myself down with a few hundred friends upon some rich and healthy spot, six hundred miles to the westward, and there form a settlement, which, in a.short time would command attention and respect."[4]

In February of 1775 the south Valley counties were also voting resolutions.[5] At Staunton the Augusta freeholders, presided over by the Anglican rector, Alexander Balmaine, an Edinburgh Scot, reasserted their loyalty to King George but insisted that "his title to the imperial crown rests on the liberty and his glory on the happiness of his subjects."[6] They dispelled any doubts of the seri-

---

man of the meeting, Isaac Zane, Angus McDonald, Samuel Beall 3rd, Alexander White, and George Rootes. The people of the neighboring County of Dunmore, in a meeting presided over by the Lutheran leader, Peter Muhlenberg, who was also an Anglican clergyman, passed the same resolutions a week later, likewise unanimously.—*American Archives,* 4th Series, I, 392-393, 417-418.

[4] *American Archives,* 4th Series, I, 1244, Stephen to R. H. Lee.

[6] Along with those additional resolutions from Valley patriots at that time, we find the people of Augusta alert and sympathetic. They sent 137 barrels of flour as an indication of their regard for the patriots of Boston. Bancroft, *History of the U. S.,* 1876 ed., IV, 352. In Waddell, *Annals of Augusta County,* p. 134, the statement is made that Jacob Bumgardner of the Valley took part in the Boston Tea Party. In those same days of 1774 Horatio Gates wrote his friend Charles Lee urging him to settle in the Valley. Discussing politics, Gates added, "I am ready to risque my Life to preserve the Liberty of the Western World." Lee Papers (in *New York Historical Collections,* IV-VII), I, 126. Gates ended his letter with this rhyme:

In this condition would I build my Fame,
And emulate the Greek and Roman name;
Think Freedom's rights bought cheaply with my blood—
And die with pleasure for my country's good.

American Archives, 4th Series, I, 1253-1255. See also in this connec-

ousness of their purpose in the statement: "Many of us and our forefathers left their native land, and explored this once savage wilderness, to enjoy the free exercise of the rights of conscience and of human nature. These rights we are fully resolved, with our lives and fortunes, inviolably to preserve."[7] The resolutions further suggested that the Convention of the Colony, which was to meet in the following month, should put a bounty on the manufacture of salt, steel, wool-cards, paper, and gunpowder. It was a good suggestion from those thrifty Scots, especially since the list included things in which they themselves were keenly interested commercially. They also proposed a day of prayer for providential guidance through their difficulties. In Botetourt County the freeholders, echoing the Augusta sentiment that they would "part with liberty only with our lives," asserted that they were ready for any contingency, and called attention to the need of watching carefully the frontier because of its "alarmed conditions."

Describing the general attitude toward the approaching struggle, Fithian, in June of 1775, observed:

Mars, the great God of Battle is honored in every Part of this spacious Colony, but here every Presence is warlike, every sound is martial! Drums beating, Fifes and Bag-pipes playing and only sonorous and heroic Tunes.

He further described the Valley patriots as uniformed in

tion Augusta Court Records, Document file for August, 1780, which has the call for the Augusta Convention signed by Thomas Lewis, Sampson Mathews, William Lewis, Alexander McClenachan, and Michael Bowyer, dated February 2, 1775.

[7] Ibid., p. 1255. The committee on resolutions, in addition to its chairman, Balmaine, was composed of Sampson Mathews, Alexander McClenachan, Michael Bowyer, William Lewis, and George Mathews. Thomas Lewis and Samuel McDowell were elected delegates to the colonial convention of March, 1775.

hunting shirts, cockades, and "Bucks Tales," and representing themselves as "hardy, resolute and invincible Na-
tives of the Woods of America."[8]

A little later, however, Fithian's idealism and enthusiasm for the cause of liberty received a shock, when he
saw the stern reality of the frontier philosophy at work.
At a muster of companies from the Alleghany border of
Augusta he saw at close hand these sons of the forest,
Ulster Scots of the second generation whose conflict with
Chief Cornstalk and his Shawnee warriors had produced
what Burke termed a "fierce spirit of liberty." As Fithian
describes the scene:

Instead of military Exercises, Drinking and Horse-Rac-
ing—Hollowing, Carousing—but most thirsty for News—O
have you heard from poor Boston? Afflicted Sons of Freedom there, in what manner shall we best contribute to their
Relief?

To the last "Half-Bitt" of our Substance; and with every
Precious Drop of our Blood, we are ready to help them.

False, or at best visionary, are such Pretensions with so
base a Conduct—talk of supporting Freedom by meeting
and practicing Bacchanalian Revels—preposterous and vain
are all such Pretensions.

Allowing for Fithian's tendency to exaggerate, he undoubtedly has furnished us a realistic picture of war fever
in the frontier area. In this way he has done at least something toward vivifying our impressions of the working of
the frontier mind, at its worst as well as at its best, in
those crucial years of the nation's history.

In June, 1775, Thomas Lewis, a leading figure in Valley politics for a number of years, wrote William Preston,
for his "private ear," a bitter denunciation of Lord Dunmore and the English government. He particularly de-

---

[8] Fithian, *Journal*, June 6, 1775.

nounced the English land policy because of the hardship it brought upon the people of the frontier.[9]

Such statements, coming as they did from organized groups, from leading individuals, from the writings of intelligent though sometimes biased contemporaries, tend to show a frontier area not far behind Boston and Williamsburg in both a grasp of the issues and a determination to find for those issues a successful conclusion. However, here as elsewhere high ideals and lofty sentiments were often marred by selfishness and by frontier realism.

In keeping with its sentiments, the Valley entered the approaching struggle for liberty most seriously. The best talent was assembled for both civil and military affairs. To the various conventions of the colony it sent such men as Thomas and Andrew Lewis, Adam Stephen, Charles Mynn Thruston, Peter Muhlenberg, Isaac Zane, Robert Rutherford, Samuel McDowell, John Bowyer, and James Wood.[10] An able personnel from the section continued to serve in the state assemblies during the war period.[11] In

[9] It seemed to Lewis that, just as the "Fool has said in his Heart there is no God," so "our Rulers seem to talk in the same Stile and Deny there is any such thing as Faith and Justice." He was sure that "King ministry and Parliament are bent on our Ruin," and was thrilled at the report that "1000 Troops of Tyrrany" had been killed in New England. He expected much of the "prowise of frontier soldier," garbed in his hunting shirt, with his trusted weapons, the "Rifle and Tomahawk."—Thomas Lewis to William Preston, June 19, 1775 (in University of Virginia Manuscripts). He was a brother of General Andrew Lewis.

[10] For Journals of Conventions see *American Archives*.

[11] Swem and Williams, *Register General Assembly, Virginia*, 1776-1783, *passim*. These included in addition to those already noted, men of the caliber of William Fleming, James Nourse, Moses Hunter, William McKee, Zachariah Johnston, Silas Hart, Thomas Madison (brother of Bishop Madison), Joseph Holmes, Andrew Moore, John Breckinridge, Taverner Beale, Alexander White, and Archibald Stuart, all of whom would have been useful and able members of any legislative body in America at the time or at any other period. Andrew Lewis and William Fleming each served on the State Council. For a time in 1781, when the legislature was in full flight and the state government thoroughly demoralized, Fleming served as governor, in which office he merited a vote of thanks from the

the critical days of invasion the state government made Staunton its capital. Flight further west was stopped when the Augusta militia rushed to the defense of the Blue Ridge passes against Tarleton's advance in that direction.[12]

In the matter of local government, the Revolution simply meant an easy transfer of allegiance from the crown of Great Britain to the Commonwealth of Virginia. The personnel, justices of the peace and other local officials, changed but little. There were, however, a few examples of hesitancy and one or two of actual defection.[13]

The Valley's participation in the field has particular interest in its array of generals, as well as in a number of regimental commanders whose records in action were highly creditable. At the head of the list of generals, with a measure of right to the claim, it could place George Washington. The north Valley had been the scene of most of his activities from boyhood until about 1765; afterwards he made frequent visits to his large plantation there.

Next in importance to Washington was the eccentric Charles Lee, who, when the war broke out, had just bought a large estate in Berkeley County. Lee's near neighbor there, Horatio Gates, settled in the north Valley in 1773, where he built a stone house of some pretensions for the time.[14] At another corner of a three-mile triangle

---

Assembly.—*Virginia Gazette*, May 31, 1780. *Journal, House of Delegates*, June 3-19, 1781.

[12] Breckinridge Papers (Library of Congress), John Breckinridge in a letter to his mother, June 7, 1781, describes the flight to Staunton and the service of the militia.

[13] Augusta County Minute Book, July 16, 1776. See also Frederick Minute Book for August, 1776.

[14] He called it "Traveler's Rest." Thence he went to Boston in 1775 to become Washington's adjutant general and later a ranking major general. His subsequent service is well known—his brilliant victory over Burgoyne at Saratoga, and his equally disastrous defeat at Camden, when

from the homes of Lee and Gates lived Adam Stephen, one of the earliest settlers of the north Valley and for years one of its outstanding military and political leaders. He too was in the army soon after hostilities began, and rendered able service, especially at Trenton and Princeton. In 1777 he was commissioned a major general by Congress and was placed in command of one of Washington's divisions.[15]

Though of slightly lower rank, Andrew Lewis of the south Valley played a prominent part in the first years of the war. Because of his long military career, and particularly because of his victory over the Indians at Point Pleasant in 1774, he was, according to one contemporary, considered for the post of commander-in-chief of the Continental Army.[16] Lewis was placed in command of the Virginia troops as a brigadier general in 1776. Supported by officers and soldiers from the Valley in an even larger proportion than by those from eastern Virginia, his first service was in driving Governor Dunmore from the colony.[17]

---

his green militia were rushed headlong into Cornwallis' trap. Tradition says that when Gates stopped in Berkeley on his way south, Charles Lee suggested that he must have a care lest his Northern laurels turn to Southern (weeping) willows. Gates had served in the Braddock expedition as a British regular. He had risen to the rank of major in the British army. See life in *Dictionary of American Biography*.

[15] At Germantown the combination of a foggy morning and a brain alleged to have been foggy from indulgence in intoxicants prevented his carrying out an important assignment. As a result, he too was court-martialed and returned to his numerous industries and interests in the Valley. For a brief account of the court-martial, see Washington, *Writings*, Fitzpatrick, ed., X, 89, 153. For Stephen's defense of his conduct, see his letter to Robert Carter Nicholas, December 25, 1777, in the Gratz Collection (Pennsylvania Historical Society).

[16] *Magazine of American History*, 1877, p. 743. The statement is on the authority of Captain, later Colonel, John Stuart of Greenbrier County, a nephew-in-law of Lewis.

[17] See General Lewis' *Orderly Book*, printed at Richmond by Charles Campbell, 1860.

The governor had gathered a force of several hundred men, including soldiers, loyalists, and Negroes, on Gwynn's Island near the mouth of the Rappahannock. With a fleet estimated at from fifty to a hundred small craft and three or four larger vessels of ten to forty-four guns, Dunmore was evidently planning to establish himself there until reinforcements arrived from England. On July 8, General Lewis opened fire on both the fleet and the island. Dunmore's gunners attempted to return the fire, but the fleet was driven off after losing one vessel, the *Dunmore*, described as "a very fine schooner." Lewis then ordered one of his Valley regiments under Colonel McClenachan to storm the island. The command was carried out by means of small boats and canoes. Dunmore, after receiving a slight wound, hastily made off to the mouth of the Potomac. Lewis' army captured supplies— mostly cannon, ships, and cattle—to the value of £1,200 to £1,500.[18]

Another striking personage in this group of leaders was General Daniel Morgan who had lived in the north Valley for a number of years. He had devoted much of his time to military or Indian service and in the Dunmore campaign on the Ohio in 1774 he had commanded a Valley company. In the following year, when the Frederick County Committee decided to send a company of a hundred expert riflemen to the defense of Boston, in response to the appeal of the Continental Congress, Morgan was placed in command.[19] His riflemen made a record-break-

[18] *American Archives*, Force ed., 5th Series, I, 149-153, 213-215, 341-342, 362, in the form of reports of the battle, a letter of John Page, President of the Virginia Council, and other letters. A list of Dunmore's ships is given on pp. 152-153. See also Andrew Lewis, *Orderly Book*.

[19] They resolved that, "This Committee reposing a Special Trust in the Courage, Conduct and reverence for Liberty under the spirit of the British Constitution, of Daniel Morgan Esq. do hereby Certify that we have unanimously appointed him to Command a Virginia Company of Riflemen to march from this County." With such a commission Morgan could not

ing march to Boston and there rendered excellent service.[20] Later, under Arnold and Montgomery, Morgan
led his riflemen through the New England woods to
Quebec, where again they performed admirably, even
though in defeat. Since Morgan's men had shown the
value of this type of soldiery to the Continental Army,
Washington and Congress proceeded to recruit and organize a larger unit of them, made Morgan a colonel, and
called the unit Morgan's Rifle Corps.[21]

When Burgoyne's Indian allies began to weaken the
morale of Gates's army, Washington readily saw the possibilities of Morgan's Corps in this kind of warfare, and
reluctantly transferred them to Gates's defense. When he
was himself hard pressed by Howe a few weeks later, he
requested Gates to return them, if they could be spared.
Gates replied, "Your Excellency would not wish me to
part with the Corps the Army of General Burgoyne are
most afraid of." Burgoyne surrendered on October 17,
and the next day Morgan's Corps started down the Hud-
son on a forced march to join Washington, but, of course,
arrived too late, since Germantown had been fought two
weeks before.[22]

---

have done other than great things! See Cowpens Papers of Myers Collection (N. Y. P.), no. 1081. The paper is dated June 22, 1775.
[20] Washington, *Writings*, Fitzpatrick ed., September 28, 1776.
[21] *Ibid.*, June 13, 1777. Hugh Stephenson who was slated for this position had died the preceding year. He had commanded the Berkeley riflemen.
[22] Washington, *Writings*, Fitzpatrick ed., September 24, October 5, November 2, 1777. High compliment to the prowess of Morgan's riflemen
came also, indirectly to be sure, from their foes. A young British officer,
in describing the death of a gallant comrade in the Burgoyne Campaign,
says of the manner of his fatal wound, that he, "in all probability fell
a victim to the great disadvantages we experience peculiar to this unfortunate contest, those of the riflemen."—Anburey, *Travels*, I, 290,
364-365. In an attempt at explaining military tactics to one of his
subordinates, General Charles Lee, who usually held provincial soldiers
in contempt, likewise paid tribute to the type of soldier Morgan commanded, to the effect that, "It is a certain truth that the enemy entertain

Morgan's outstanding triumph came in the Southern campaign, where he had gone in answer to the personal appeal of General Gates.[23] There, by his victory at Cowpens, he did much toward restoring to the Southern armies and people the morale that had suffered severely at Camden.

Still another Valley brigadier, whose career matched that of Morgan in dramatic quality, was Peter Muhlenberg of Dunmore (Shenandoah). He was an enthusiastic participant in the Virginia conventions of the first year of the Revolution.[24] Then came the spectacular day on which, according to persistent tradition, after his preaching service he threw off his clerical robes, which had covered the regimentals of a patriot officer, and recruited his congregation for the cause of liberty. Whether the tradition is authentic or not, the fact remains that very early in the war he led his German regiment, the Eighth Virginia, to the defense of eastern Virginia against Dunmore. Later he was sent with this regiment to join Washington's army, where he was soon promoted to the rank of general. He continued to serve with distinction until the end of the war.[25]

In addition to the seven generals whose services have been cited the Valley furnished several notable officers of lesser rank. Berkeley County gave the army Colonel

---

a most fortunate apprehension of American Riflemen."—Lee to Colonel Thompson in *American Archives*, 5th Series, I, 99-100.
    [23] Cowpens Papers (Meyers Collection, N. Y. P.), two letters, Gates to Morgan, 1781.
    [24] *American Archives*, 4th Series, II, 165; IV, 75.
    [25] Andrew Lewis, *Orderly Book*, *passim*; Preston Papers, Muhlenberg to Preston, March 24, 1776. Muhlenberg was then on the James with his regiment. See Schuricht, *German Element in Virginia*, I, 129, for the pulpit incident. See Court Records, Valley Counties; *American Archives*, 5th Series, *passim*; Dandridge, Shepherdstown; and Augusta Court Martial Record Book, for the services of these men. See also Saffell's *Records*; McAllister, *Virginia Militia*.

Hugh Stephenson, the first commandant (he was slated for the rôle later played by Morgan) of the Continental Army riflemen, whose untimely death in 1776 undoubtedly cut short a brilliant career, and Colonel William Darke, who did valiant service at Yorktown. Dunmore County furnished Colonel Abraham Bowman, who succeeded to the command of the German regiment. From Frederick County came Colonel Charles Mynn Thruston, another fighting parson from the Anglican church, and Colonel James Wood, later governor of Virginia. Augusta County gave four regimental commanders: George Moffett, who played a prominent part at Cowpens, George Mathews, captured at Germantown, Alexander McClenachan, whose regiment under Andrew Lewis helped drive Dunmore from Virginia, and William Bowyer, captured at Jamestown. Rockbridge County contributed Colonel John Bowyer, who was active in the early phase of the Yorktown campaign.

The rank and file of Valley soldiers in the Revolution can be known only in a fragmentary way, since very few muster rolls have been preserved.[26] However, it is evident that the Valley was an armed camp throughout the Revolution, with men constantly going out by companies, by battalions, and by regiments:[27] to Boston to join Washington, to the Tidewater against Dunmore, to the southwest against the Cherokees, to the west against the Shawnees or other Ohio tribes for both field and garrison duty,

[26] The extent of their service must be gleaned from county records. One of the most remarkable of these is a letter written by a Rockbridge soldier to his sweetheart, which is recorded as a will.—Rockbridge Will Book, I, 61. Two other records of a different nature concern a soldier's robbery of a comrade at the battle of Guilford Court House and another stealing a pinchback watch from a French sergeant at Yorktown. Both were sent to the General Court for trial. See Rockbridge Order Book, I, June 27, 1781 and March 27, 1782.

[27] *Virginia Gazette*, February 19, 1780, shows that half the rendezvous places for troops were in or near the Valley, that is, at Winchester, Staunton, and New London.

to Trenton, to Brandywine and Germantown, to King's Mountain, to Cowpens, to Guilford, to the defense of the Virginia Assembly, to the west with George Rogers Clark, and finally to the Yorktown campaign. Thus Valley soldiery fought from Quebec to Georgia, often valiantly.[28] The very incomplete records show about five hundred officers commissioned in the Valley from 1776 to 1781. Of these over two hundred were captains. The Augusta Court Martial Record Book alone shows as many as thirty-eight companies active at a given period, and these did not include units then in the Continental Army.[29]

When Daniel Morgan led his riflemen on the forced march to Boston in the summer of 1775, he was followed closely by Hugh Stephenson, in command of another rifle company from Berkeley.[30] A large number of Valley units were in the eight regiments which General Andrew Lewis used in the summer of 1776 to guard Virginia from Lord Dunmore's wrath and from a possible British expeditionary force.[31] There were sixty-five Valley companies in service against the Indians at various periods, nineteen at the Battle of Guilford Court House, and sixty-three in the Yorktown campaign.[32] In a petition to the state Assembly from the staff officers of two regiments of Augusta militia in December, 1780, the claim was made

[28] But they did not always submit to discipline with the best grace. See letter, Washington to Morgan, October 4, 1775, insisting that Morgan's as well as the other rifle companies be amenable to discipline on the Quebec campaign, in *American Archives*, 5th Series, III, 946.

[29] Augusta Court Martial Record Book, especially pages 74-84. One of these companies had as its captain Abraham Linkhorn (Lincoln).

[30] See Diary of Henry Bedinger in Dandridge, *Shepherdstown*, pp. 105-144, *passim*.

[31] Andrew Lewis, *Orderly Book*, *passim*; "Stubblefield Orderly Book" in *Virginia Historical Collections*, VI, 143-149.

[32] These statistics were gleaned from depositions in the records of the Valley courts during and after the Revolution. Some of it is collected in McAllister, *Virginia Militia in the Revolution*. See also Cowpens Papers (N. Y. P.), pp. 25-27 *et passim*, for Morgan's account of units at Cowpens.

that there were four hundred militia from the county in active service at that time.[33]

As we have seen, the Indian phase of the Valley's participation in the war stemmed not only from previous conflicts but also from the fact that Indian animosity was believed to be instigated by British officers in the northwest. Such cases were undoubtedly exaggerated in the minds of the Valley people, but the effect on the Indian phase of the war was the same, regardless of the amount of exaggeration. In September, 1775, Governor Dunmore wrote the home government that the Ohio Indians had sent a message to him with the assurance that whatever the Virginians might say to them, unless it came through him (Dunmore), they "would receive it at one ear and let it out at the other," and, further, that they were ready to obey his orders.[34]

The Valley counties were constantly forced to line up units of militia for the Indian frontier from Fort Pitt to Point Pleasant, two hundred men here, a hundred there, and lesser numbers at less vulnerable points, until one official wrote that his county was "drained of men" and that it was difficult to raise the quotas called for.[35] An additional hardship arose from the scarcity of supplies, particularly of small arms and ammunition. The lack of salt and the increasing demand for cattle threatened a shortage

[33] Virginia Petitions, Augusta, no. 601, December 12, 1780. Botetourt County seems to have kept twenty to thirty companies of militia active from 1777-1781, Minute Book, Botetourt, 1777-1781, *passim*.

[34] Bancroft Transcripts (N. Y. P.), III, 205 *et passim*; Dunmore to Secretary of State, September 24, 1775. A month later Dunmore gave instructions to raise a regiment of Indians, composed chiefly of Shawnees and Delawares. It was to be known as "Lord Dunmore's Own Regiment of Indians" and was to be marched to Norfolk to help the governor hold Virginia in line. *Ibid.*, IV, 14, paper dated November, 1775; Thwaites and Kellogg, *Revolution on the Upper Ohio*, pp. 136-142.

[35] Fleming Papers (Washington and Lee University); Augusta Court Martial Record Book, August 29, 1777, also 1775-1781, *passim*.

of the kind of food supplies necessary in warfare against rapidly moving Indian units.[36]

Indian troubles were further aggravated in the autumn of 1777 by the murder of Cornstalk, noted Shawnee chieftain. In the years 1759 and 1763 he had led his tribesmen in two bloody massacres against the people of Kerr's Creek in Rockbridge County. During the early days of the war there was a company of Rockbridge soldiers under Captain John Hall on garrison duty at Point Pleasant.[37] During their tour of duty, Cornstalk and some of his people were brought to the fort as hostages. Not long afterward one of the soldiers, who was also a neighbor and kinsman of Hall, was killed by some Indians while hunting near the fort. Thereupon Hall and several members of his company, it was alleged, lost their heads and proceeded to wreak vengeance on Cornstalk and the other Indian hostages for this and earlier outrages.[38]

Colonel William Fleming, county lieutenant of Botetourt, exerted every effort to prevent retaliation by the Indians. His partial success in the negotiations evidently was due in no small measure to the efforts of Cornstalk's sister, the Grenadier Squaw, one of the most picturesque

[36] The state legislature was meanwhile making provision for replenishing the supply of clothing, food, and transportation by a series of acts that empowered commissioners to raise quotas from the various counties including the Valley. See Hening, *Statutes*, X, 338-342, 377, 393, 462, 482-483.

[37] Thwaites and Kellogg, *Frontier Defense*, pp. 157-158, 168-169.

[38] Thwaites and Kellogg, *Frontier Defense*, p. 159. The affair was generally condemned as murder by Valley leaders and by Governor Patrick Henry. *Ibid.*, pp. 168-169, 175-177, 240-241; Preston Papers, February 19, March 27, 1778. Captain Hall and three of his men were haled before the court of the newly created Rockbridge County, but no witnesses would appear against them and the matter was dropped. Rockbridge Order Book, I, April 18, 28, May 5, 19, July 7, December 2, 1778. The three men were Hugh Galbraith, Malcolm McCoun, and William Rowan. The trials, or proposed trials, evidently created much feeling and interest. Thus ingloriously ended the career of the great Shawnee whose name had bred terror in that region for so many years.

of the frontier figures of those years. This remarkable woman, who constantly appears in the extant records of warfare on the Virginia frontier in the Revolutionary period, is said to have received her nickname from her unusual height and stately bearing. Her Indian name was Nonhelema. She seems to have been a baptized tribeswoman, which fact might account for her friendliness to the whites. We find her serving the whites almost as a minister plenipotentiary in their negotiations with the Indians. Probably to her more than to any other person can be attributed whatever there was of peace between the Valley and the Indians during the period of the war.[39]

The Valley watched eagerly the George Rogers Clark expedition to the Illinois country. Colonel Fleming of Botetourt was busy with possible schemes for such a campaign, and, when the news of Clark's success arrived, one of his friends wrote him gleefully hoping "that the savages will not have the same confidence in the present commanding officer at Detroit as in Governor Hamilton and consequently will not so considerably distress our Frontiers this season."[40] Nevertheless, the conflict with the Indians by no means ceased, either with the campaigns of Clark or following the surrender at Yorktown. Although Valley people were flocking to Kentucky and other parts of the Trans-Alleghany country, the menace of Indian raids and massacres continued for nearly another decade, and militia companies from the various Valley counties were constantly on the march.[41]

The Valley, however, did not devote all of its energies to patriotic meetings, or to furnishing leaders, or to cam-

[39] See Fleming Papers (Washington and Lee University), 1776-1781, *passim;* Withers, *Chronicles,* pp. 176, 242; Thwaites and Kellogg, *Frontier Defense,* pp. 26 note, 186, 195, 209, 225, 261.

[40] Fleming Papers, Colonel William Russell to Fleming, May 21, 1779.

[41] Augusta Court Martial Record Book, 1782, *passim; Calendar of Virginia State Papers,* I, 597; II, 117, 294-295; III, 87-88.

paigns against the "worst of kings," or yet to fighting
Indians. Its participation in the War for Independence
included providing supplies as well. Beginning with a
hundred and thirty barrels of flour to the unfortunate
Bostonians in 1774, it continued to furnish a large quantity of this important commodity to the patriot forces. In
the period of the Yorktown campaign four of the seven
counties furnished nearly 200,000 pounds of flour and
about 10,000 bushels of wheat to the Continental armies.
In this they were much ahead of the eastern Virginia
counties. During the same period, six of the counties supplied 500,000 pounds of dressed beef and great numbers
of cattle in which service they rivaled the Piedmont and
surpassed the Tidewater.[42] They kept a steady stream of
privately owned wagons moving with supplies for their
own militia regiments on the James River, as well as for
the regular forces.[43] In addition to flour and beef, these
wagons carried such provisions as bacon, corn, hay, rye,
oats, butter, mutton, beverages, and cheese, the amounts
from a given county running into hundreds of pounds.
Valley wagon trains had, in the first years of the war,
hauled bacon as far north as New York and New Jersey.[44]

[42] Hening, *Statutes*, X, 338, for the legislature's provision for these supplies. Revolutionary Claims, or Revolutionary Claims and Taxes, 1779-
1781. These claims are in the form of thousands of individual papers
listing the kind and amount of the given commodity furnished, the name
of the person furnishing, and are signed by the county commissioner. They
are numerous for each of the Valley counties. The record is not complete
for all of these counties, hence the incomplete statistics. Six eastern Virginia counties furnished 170,000 pounds of flour and 3,000 bushels of
wheat, but the same six sent 560,000 pounds of beef. The eastern Virginia counties used were Brunswick, Charlotte, Prince Edward, Southamp-
ton, Spottsylvania, and Westmoreland, representative counties.
[43] In Berkeley Claims and Taxes we find not less than thirty to forty
wagons in a given year engaged in army transport.
[44] McAllister, *Virginia Militia*, p. 119. During the Yorktown campaign,
as well as in earlier years, the Valley people continually furnished supplies
for the militia that was being mobilized in the various counties, for units
of the Continental Army passing through, for the families of indigent

Along with the various kinds of quartermaster stores and supplying prisoners of war, the Valley also contributed money through the six per cent loan program of the state government.[45] Augusta seems to have been particularly generous in this connection.[46] In ten months of 1779 Augusta and one or two neighboring counties furnished the prisoners at Staunton 40,000 pounds of flour and meal, 33,000 pounds of beef, 3,350 pounds of bacon, and smaller quantities of other supplies. In the same area during eight months of 1781 there were collected for "Colonel White's Regiment of Light Dragoons, prisoners of war," and for troops rendezvousing at Staunton supplies as follows: 10,000 pounds of flour, 150 bushels of wheat, 5,100 pounds of bacon, 29,000 pounds of beef, 214 head of cattle, 6,000 pounds of butter, 300 gallons of whiskey, 20 pounds of "Shuger," 20 bushels of "Tators," 66 pounds of venison, 84,000 pounds of hay, and several other items of provender for man and horse.[47]

Various proposals for the manufacture of certain supplies were made by residents in the section. One man planned a powder mill on his lands, which were "mixed and impregnated with saltpetre." Another wanted to start a factory for the manufacture and bleaching of linen. One Peter Light offered to make nails. Two brothers were ready to start a gun factory, if given a little encouragement and exemption from military service. Sampson Mathews and Alexander Sinclair were appointed by the state assembly "to superintend the making of Sail Duck in the

soldiers, and especially for the great number of prisoners of war who were interned at Staunton and Winchester.

[45] Augusta Revolutionary Claims, February to November, 1779.

[46] Virginia Petitions, Augusta, nos. 513, 603, June 12, December 12, 1780. One Smyth Tandy, the messenger, allegedly lost £4376 of this money.

[47] Revolutionary Claims and Specific Tax Records, Augusta, 1781.

town of Staunton."[48]   The Council of State allowed Thomas Rutherford £250 to start a gun factory at Mecklenberg (Shepherdstown).[49]

Isaac Zane had a miniature munitions plant at his Marlboro Furnaces near Winchester. Throughout the war he was busy making various kinds of ordnance for the Continental armies. This included six- and four-pounder cannon, along with numerous shot and shell of various weights and descriptions.[50] Sixty-five wagons were required to move one order from Zane's works in Frederick to Falmouth on the Rappahannock River. Zane was also making grape shot, langrages, swivel balls, camp kettles, and the all-important pans for making salt.[51]

Generally speaking, the Valley presented a united front for the cause of American liberty, and the three dominant groups there, Ulster Scot, German, and English, served side by side with little discord and many sacrifices. As a reward their way of life was to be more peaceful with the menace of hostile Indians as well as hostile Englishmen in some measure removed.

[48] Virginia Petitions, Berkeley, nos. 46, 58; Augusta, nos. 61, 111; Botetourt, no. 576. Mathews and Sinclair had difficulty with high wages and suggested that Negroes be bought and trained for this work.

[49] Journal, Council of State, I, 286.

[50] One order alone covered 10,308 shot from four to twenty-four pounds, described as round shot, double-headed shot, sliding shot, and chain shot.

[51] Zane Papers, 1776-1779, passim; Letters, Governor of Virginia, I, 40, 74, 113; III, 182; Journal, Council of State, I, 394, records an order to Zane for 1500 shot and mortar. Ibid., II, 32, shows that he was paid £2000 for casting cannon. Langrage, or chain shot, consisted of scrap iron and nails placed in a canister, the whole to be fired at ships to destroy the sails and riggings. In Berkeley County General Adam Stephen's armory was turning out muskets and bayonets at the rate of ten to twelve a week, which he was selling the government in lots of a hundred or more. Stephen Papers (Library of Congress), nos. 101a, 128, Letter from Noble, November 14, 1776. Botetourt County was making gunpowder in large quantities, and was furnishing saltpeter for other manufactures of it. The same section was also furnishing flints for the revolutionary muskets. Fleming Papers (W. & L.), 1776-1781, passim; Breckinridge Papers (Library of Congress), Preston to Mrs. Breckinridge, June, 1777.

≡☆≡ **6** ≡☆≡

Opposition to the War

IN THE MIDST of this life-and-death struggle for frontier
security and for independence, there were those who opposed a break with the old order. Some can be readily
designated as Tories or loyalists; others were no more
than disaffected, although the distinction between a Tory
or loyalist and a disaffected person is not easy to make. If
a Tory is defined as one who rendered active assistance
to the British government, the number of Tories was not
large, and their efforts were rarely organized. If, however, the term includes all those who, at the beginning
of the war or at any time during its course, found themselves out of sympathy with its leaders or objectives, the
number is considerably larger.

Probably the most conspicuous Tory was Alexander
Miller, the outspoken Ulster Scot who came to the Valley
as a Presbyterian minister[1] in October, 1775. Miller
charged the Augusta committee with being seditious persons and traitors, but the committee took notice of his
charges only to the extent of recommending that the people have nothing to do with him.[2] Later, however, when

[1] Minutes, Hanover Presbytery, p. 176, *passim;* Augusta Order Book,
XI, 388; Augusta Records, March, 1771.
[2] He insisted that their opposition to the English government was a

the new state Assembly had passed an act against disloyalty, Miller did not fare so well with the Augusta leaders,
now organized as a county court. In a letter addressed to
a newly elected delegate to the state legislature from Augusta, he tried to persuade the member to use his efforts
to undo the work of the revolutionists. He argued that the
Revolution was wrong because it deprived Great Britain
of her rightful property, and because of the evils which
grew out of it: trade was stopped; taxes were increased;
oaths of allegiance were violated. Miller was thereupon
haled into the Augusta court where he was found guilty of
endeavoring by "words and sentences" to "support, main-
tain, and defend the power and authority" of the "King
of Great Britain." The court placed him under heavy
bond and confined him to his estate for the duration of the
war. Two months later Miller was again before the court.
This time he was fined £100 and given two years in
prison. The last record of the case is a petition of his
wife in 1778, asking that he be transferred to the jail of
the new County of Rockingham. The plea was rejected
for an unstated reason.[3]

In Rockingham County, among the first items of business for the court, newly created in 1778, was the trial on

---

scheme to get public money, that they might live at ease; they were, he
said, using the money collected for the purchase of ammunition "to the
making gentlemen of themselves." *American Archives*, 4th Series, III, 939-
940.

[3] Augusta Court Records, July, 1777. To John Poage, the delegate in
question, Miller quoted a verse from the Book of Esther, "Who knowest
but that thou are come to the kingdom for such a time as this." Virginia
Petitions, Augusta, no. 224a, October 23, 1778. The wife claimed it was
inconvenient to supply Miller with the "necessaries of life" in the Staunton
jail. Two Cryders, Martin and John, presumably brothers or kinsmen,
and perhaps reckoned as accomplices of Miller, were tried and convicted
at the same time and for the same offense. In 1780 the jailor of Augusta
claimed that his jail was a "Common Place for the Reception of persons
Inimical to Government." See Virginia Petitions, Augusta, no. 563, November 16, 1780. By his own statement, however, he had only two Tories
at the time.

a charge of treason of a leading merchant, Felix Gilbert, who was a near neighbor and intimate friend of Gabriel Jones, the noted frontier lawyer. Gilbert was convicted and placed under a heavy bond for "speaking Treasonable words that tend to encourage sedition on the Western Waters."[4] This was not the only difficulty Rockingham had with Tories. In a two-year period not less than a dozen indictments were brought by the county court against persons charged with such treasonable offenses, as "speaking disrespectful and disgraceful words of the Congress and words tending to depreciate the Continental Currency," "propagating some News tending to raise Tumult and Sedition in the state," "Swearing to join a company of black boys," "conspiring and consulting the Destruction of the Commonwealth," "speaking disrespectfully of the Commonwealth," trying "to rouse Tumult and Disorder in the state," and sometimes just plain "treason." Some of the persons indicted were fined and imprisoned, and others were placed under heavy bonds.[5]

Meanwhile, beginning in December, 1775, the Virginia legislature had passed a series of acts against disaffection

[4] Rockingham Minute Book, May 25, 1779.
[5] Rockingham Minute Books, March 22, 23, July 26, August 23, 1779; March 27, June 9, 1780. In Frederick County in 1778 ninety-three persons were summoned to court for "refusing to give in an Account of their Taxable Property" and were thereby reckoned as opposing the new state government. Frederick Order Book, XVII, 89, September 2, 1778. There is no record of the punishment inflicted for this particular kind of treason. Berkeley County at present has a place called Torytown, with the shadowy but persistent tradition that there James Morgan, while on leave from the Continental Army, was called from his home one night and shot down by a neighboring band of Tories. The tale is made more lurid by the circumstances of the killing, in that he is said to have been required to hold a lighted candle in front of his heart to aid his executioners. Hardesty, *History of Berkeley County; Morgan Monument Commission Report*, pp. 65-68. While the incident may be authentic, its value lies in its being illustrative of a state of mind. The antagonism to Toryism in those parts was evidently both aggravated and persistent. The tale itself has evidently not yielded to research, and even the Morgan family records are against it.

or disloyalty. At the core of these acts was one requiring an oath of allegiance to the Virginia government. Punishment for disaffection and for failure to take the oath varied from fines, imprisonment, and double taxes to the confiscation of property and even the death penalty, if the disloyalty extended to helping the enemy make war.[6]

The first Tory brought to trial in Rockbridge was Mary Walker who was charged in 1778 with supporting "the power of the King and Parliament of Great Britain over the United States contrary to the Act of the Assembly."[7] She was found guilty, assessed the costs of the trial (amounting to fifteen pounds), and ordered to be confined to "close gaol four days." Three Whitleys—Moses, Jonathan, and Solomon, probably brothers—also were reported to be disloyal and were haled into the Rockbridge court on various charges of treason. One was reported to the court as having "joined the King of Great Britain," and his property, consisting of three slaves, was seized. The second was kept in jail for most of the war, and the third was placed under bond. Thomas Vance was placed under a heavy bond for "Declaring himself a Tory, publishing false news and speaking words to terrify the people." In the same county, also, Samuel Jack was given a small fine and a day in jail for consigning the Continental Army to the regions of the damned, in what he considered appropriate language.[8]

As has already been suggested, there was almost no armed opposition in the Valley. The military records refer to an expedition made up of two companies of militia against a body of Tories who had assembled near Peaked Mountain (Massanutten), presumably in Rockingham

[6] Hening, *Statutes*, IX, 101, 130-132, 168, 170-173, 281-283, 349, 547.
[7] Rockbridge Order Book, May 14, October 6, 1778.
[8] *Ibid.*, February 2, 1779; September 5, 6, October 3, 4, December 5, 1780.

County. The Tory leaders were reported to have been
jailed and their followers dispersed.[9]

Among those who were suspected of loyalist inclina-
tions, some interesting figures are to be found. The best
known was probably Thomas (Lord) Fairfax, proprietor
of the Northern Neck and country gentleman of "Greenway Court" in Frederick County. One of Fairfax's biog-
raphers insists that this great friend and benefactor of
George Washington was not a Tory.[10] It must not be forgotten, however, that Fairfax refused to continue to serve
as a justice in the Frederick County court, and also that he
actually gave no encouragement to the cause of independence.[11]

One of the most picturesque of this particular group of
actors in the Revolutionary drama was the circuit-riding
lawyer, Gabriel Jones, who was one of the two executors
designated by Lord Fairfax in his will dated in 1777.[12]
The only possible indication of any disaffection on the part
of Jones is a negative one, and lies in his inactivity during
the period of the war. Although he had been active in
public affairs for many years prior to 1776, having held
various offices in nearly every Valley county, he seldom
appears in the records for the years immediately following
that date. In December, 1776, the Augusta court ordered
the sheriff not to pay Gabriel Jones's salary as attorney
until he said whether he intended "to act in that appointment in the future."[13] In 1778, however, he qualified as
deputy attorney of Rockingham County.[14] So great was

[9] McAllister, *Virginia Militia*, p. 123.
[10] See article on Fairfax by Fairfax Harrison in *Dictionary of American Biography*.
[11] Frederick Minute Book, August, 1776 *et passim*.
[12] Frederick Land Book, 1758-1828, p. 179 *et passim*. Jones was to receive a fee of £500 Virginia Currency, which was changed to sterling of Great Britain in a codicil to the will.
[13] Augusta Minute Book, December 17, 1776.
[14] Rockingham Minute Book, 1779, especially May 25. He was given £40 a year salary.

the confidence of his fellow Virginians in Jones that he continued to be appointed to office, even to a judgeship on the new highest court of the state, an appointment which he declined. On one occasion he was haled into court for threatening to shoot a man for taking one of his horses for militia service under a captain's orders. The case against him was, nevertheless, dismissed.[15] Evidently an apparent lack of enthusiasm for the cause of independence did not materially affect Jones's prestige in the Valley.

The above examples do not, of course, include all Toryism or quasi-Toryism in the Valley. The court records give other instances of leaders, including justices of the peace, who were summoned to appear before their respective courts and to take the oath of office under the new government, or give reasons for not doing so. One gathers the impression, however, that there were few rather than many actual Tories. In the fall of 1775 Fithian wrote: "No Tories are permitted to vent their sentiments. The name of Whig has the Post of Majesty."[16]

The tide of disaffection ebbs and flows during the course of any extended war, and the Valley in the Revolution was no exception. Here the opposition took various

---

[15] Rockingham Minute Book, April 26, 1779. Some years after the Revolution, Alexander White of Frederick County, in the heat of the contest over ratification of the new Federal Constitution, was accused of lack of sympathy for the Revolution during the war years. Since he was active in helping to pass the Frederick Resolves of 1774 and subsequently served on the committee of safety of that county, the charge of disaffection seems in a large measure unfounded. He had, during the war, defended a group of refugee Quakers from Philadelphia, who had been interned at Winchester because of their alleged Tory leanings. This probably had something to do with the charge against White himself. See *Winchester Advertiser*, February 15, 1778. He was accused of being a "slacker." *American Archives*, 4th Series, I, 392-393; *Exiles in Virginia*, Gilpin, ed., pp. 194-200.

[16] Fithian, *Journal*, November 20, 1775.

forms, from mild criticism of the conduct of the war to refusals to serve, and even, on one occasion, to a draft riot.

Leading the list of those in the Valley who at one time or another opposed the war were the three major generals whom we have already met. Each achieved both fame and misfortune during the years of the conflict, and then returned to his Valley home: Adam Stephen participated in a triumph at Princeton and Trenton and a fiasco at Germantown; Charles Lee won the plaudits of those who would have made him commander-in-chief and the invectives of his fellow officers because of his retreat at Monmouth; and Horatio Gates triumphed at Saratoga and met disaster at Camden. While all three of these men nursed a grievance with some intensity, Lee was the most bitter.[17] Stephen seems to have forgiven and forgotten readily, and was soon lending every encouragement toward good government, even in the trying year of 1781. Gates eventually returned to the army and to more difficulties in the matter of the Newburgh addresses, but after the war he too coöperated heartily in the movement for preserving the fruits of the Revolution.

Charles Lee, peculiarly pathetic in his bitterness, could not bring himself to forgive but vented his spleen against his supposed enemies on every occasion. Very often he found willing ears, even among those to whom the country accorded honors which it denied him.[18] There were times when the censure of former friends caused him to express a vigorous, and sometimes able, defense of the

[17] Local tradition preserves a story that the three generals met frequently at Gates's home, "Traveler's Rest," for dinner and for a discussion of their grievances, at which meetings Lee would propose the solemn toast, "To you, General Stephen, who were drunk when you ought to have been sober; to you, General Gates, who advanced when you should have retreated; and to you, General Lee, who retreated when you should have advanced."

[18] See *Lee Papers* (New York Historical Collection, IV-VII), especially Vol. III, of the *Papers*.

ABOVE: *General Charles Lee House, near Martinsburg, West Virginia, bought from Jacob Hite, 1772-73.*

BELOW: *Traveler's Rest, near Martinsburg, West Virginia, built by General Horatio Gates, 1773.*

loyalists. He seems for some unknown reason to have developed a particular antipathy toward the Valley and its leaders. His description of them is characteristic: "We in Virginia live (if it can be called living) neither under Monarchy, Aristocracy nor Democracy—if it deserved any name it is a Macocracy, that is, a Banditti of Scotch-Irish Servants or their immediate descendants (whose names generally begin with Mac) are our Lords and Rulers."[19] Lee's eccentric will is preserved in the Berkeley County Court House at Martinsburg (now West Virginia). Among its concluding paragraphs is the following: "I desire most earnestly, that I may not be buried in any church, or church-yard, or within a mile of any Presbyterian or Anabaptist meeting house; for since I have resided in this country, I have kept so much bad company when living that I do not chuse to continue it when dead."

If Revolutionary generals experienced all the moods from enthusiasm to despair, entire constancy to the cause of independence is hardly to be expected among the rank and file. It is, then, not a question of the presence of disaffection among the soldiery of the Valley, but rather the relative amount of such disaffection. Even in the midst of the enthusiasm for war, during the spring and summer of 1775, lukewarmness toward military service was already developing.[20] Fithian tells of a local militiaman who failed to appear for drill, whereupon a guard was sent for him and he was brought with fear and trembling. His fears increased greatly when he heard his fellow townsmen talk of tar and feathers. Fithian noted, "These mortifying Weapons, with their necessary Appendages, Scoff and Shame, are popular Terrors, and of great influence." It is chiefly remarkable that the militiaman had the hardihood to run counter to popular pressure.

The next year General Charles Lee, in command of the

[19] *Lee Papers*, III, 457-458.   [20] Fithian, *Journal*, June 8, 1775.

Southern Department, complained of difficulties with Muhlenberg's German regiment, the Eighth Virginia, from Dunmore (Shenandoah) County. Although imbued early with the enthusiasm of their fighting parson, they had evidently lost some of it in the trials of campaigning. Lee reported them as "Disorderly mutinous and dangerous" in disposition, and warned that "The spirit of desertion in these back country troops is so alarmingly great" that something must be done at once to stop it.[21] Lee took care that this spirit of disaffection would not be attributed to a racial weakness of the German soldiery by explaining that the officers of the German companies had injudiciously filled up the ranks to the proper quotas by enlisting "old countrymen, particularly the Irish," who had contaminated the rest of the regiment.

Captain William McKee's south Valley Scots, on garrison duty at Point Pleasant, threatened mutiny on one occasion because of an order from General Hand reducing their ration. They were quieted only by the rescinding of the order.[22]

The court-martial records also show numerous examples of dereliction, such as failure to report for drill or muster; the culprits included even captains—and on one occasion a colonel—who were fined ten pounds each.[23] There were attempts to evade service by feigning physical disability; refusing to respond when called for designated services or campaigns; desertions; and armed resistance,

[21] *Lee Papers*, II, 34.
[22] McAllister, *Virginia Militia*, nos. 61 and 69.
[23] Augusta Court Martial Record Book, April 13-17, 1779. Disaffection was also implied in failure to appear at rendezvous; appearing improperly armed or accoutred, for example, John Woods, who was fined "for Appearing Without a Tomahawk" (*ibid.*, March, 1780, p. 168) and conscientious objection, in which cases certificates were required from churches whose "Articles of Religion" forbade the carrying of arms (*ibid.*, October, 1776. Quakers and Mennonites were exempted by act of the Assembly, Hening, *Statutes*, X, 261, 314, 417).

one instance of which was "opposing by force of arms" a
lieutenant and guard, thus violating the "Law Military
and the Good Faith and Alaigence that He Owes this
State as a Subject thereof." One deserter from both British and Valley forces petitioned to be allowed to serve
against the Indians; and his petition was granted.[24]

A perusal of the petitions to the State Assembly from
the Valley, between 1779 and 1781, adds to the impression that discontent added spice to Valley patriotism. The
petitioners complained of "a load of Taxes which we cannot Discharge but at the Expense of the Greatest Distress," of depreciated currency fast becoming worthless,
of the burden of military service, of draft laws, of "Confusion and Disorder," of discrimination in calling militia
companies into service too often and field officers too seldom, of too long periods of service, of loss of horses in
service and the failure of the state government to com-
pensate for them, of the arbitrary seizure of property for
war purposes, and of the "Great number of Prisoners and
Soldiers constantly stationed amongst us."[25] One group
threatened a new revolt and a new government.[26] Captain
Abraham Lincoln and his neighbors of Rockingham complained of dire poverty brought on them by drought, by
large families, and especially by taxation, and concluded
with the plea, "We have herein stated the poor man's
case."[27]

[24] See Augusta Court Martial Record Book, October, 1778 to October,
1780, *passim*, for the entries noted in the above paragraph, especially
October 22, 1778.

[25] Virginia Petitions, Valley Counties, nos. 332, 434a, 468, 476, 565,
601, 630a, 652, 673a, 678, 758, dated 1779 to 1782.

[26] *Ibid.*, Frederick, no. 652, November 22, 1781.

[27] *Ibid.*, Rockingham, no. 434a, November 9, 1779. He was the grandfather of President Lincoln. Two hundred and fifty Rockbridge farmers
likewise pleaded poverty, and explained that they got sustenance for themselves and their families "by their own hands and one day's Labor is
necessary for the next day's support." *Ibid.*, Rockbridge, nos. 631a, and
631b, March 10, June 14, 1781. Their chief demand was for a three

Disaffection in the Valley during the Revolution may be thought of as reaching a crisis in the draft riots of Augusta County in 1781. The Augusta people had petitioned the Assembly against the unfairness of the draft law of 1777,[28] and the answer was a further cause of resentment in the passing of a more stringent act. Sometime later one Thomas Hughes reported to the Assembly that "an opposition in arms had been made in Augusta" to a law passed by the last Assembly,[29] and, further, that Zachariah Johnston, a delegate for that county, had been the principal instigator of it.[30] An inquiry was voted, which was duly made by the Committee on Elections, and on June 14, 1781, its findings were reported by Patrick Henry to the House of Delegates. The report dealt primarily with the charges against Johnston, as follows: "It appears to your committee, from the testimony of various witnesses, that Zachariah Johnston hath uniformly recommended to the people of the county of Augusta an obedience to the law for recruiting this state's quota of troops to serve in the Continental Army; and did by no means instigate them to an opposition to said law." The committee resolved further, "That the said information is groundless."[31]

---

months' tour as riflemen rather than eighteen months as regulars. They concluded their petition with the reassuring note: "We hope these requests will not be construed into disloyalty, for should you think them incompatable with the safety, and dignity of the Commonwealth, we revoke them forever, and cheerfully offer our Lives and fortunes, for the support of our Liberties and Independence."

[28] Johnston Papers (in possession of Johnston family at Lexington, Virginia) have a copy of the petition.

[29] Hening, *Statutes*, X, 257-262.

[30] *Journal, House of Delegates*, May 31, 1781.

[31] *Ibid.*, June 14, 1781. The Assembly had been sitting at Staunton in Augusta County during this period of inquiry. Meanwhile the opposition to the draft law was easily put down, and the leaders, Ward and Baker, were brought to trial in the Augusta Court of June, 1781. Augusta Order Book, XVII, 348, June 14, 1781. They were found guilty of treason and held for a further trial, which does not seem to have been held, or if so, the records have been destroyed. Nothing of importance resulted from

Early in the war any tendency to disaffection was aided by a considerable rise in the prices of certain necessities, especially salt, which could be secured only with great difficulty. Moreover, the scarcity came at a time when salt was most needed for an important Valley industry, the curing of meats. Along with the rise of prices came the breakdown in the market for Valley products. Wheat was only three shillings a bushel, other grains were still lower, and no price at all was offered for country produce. The merchants, meanwhile, had resolved to go strictly upon a cash basis: "No merchant will book a Shilling Value to the best Men."[82]

---

the movement, and little further was heard of it. The Augusta Court Martial Record Book as well as the Augusta Court Records are all but silent on this affair. See Hening, *Statutes*, X, 413-416.

[82] Fithian, *op. cit.*, November 27, 1775.

Post-War Economic Troubles

In keeping with the aspirations of Americans generally, the Valley pioneer expected certain economic advantages from a successful war for independence. His taxation burden had never been heavy, but the "fierce spirit of liberty," with which Edmund Burke credited him and his compatriots, was economic as well as political in its background. He cherished the right to live as happily and as abundantly as he could, on lands of his own choice, with as little interference as possible from the government at home or abroad, except in facilitating his getting a better living. Early in the war a group of Valley petitioners, after explaining to the Legislature how lands were expected to increase in value as a result of the trend of affairs, closed with the statement, "Your Petitioners would wish to reap all the advantages and enjoy all the sweets of the desirable and glorious change."[1]

Like other Americans to whom peace brought economic adversity, the Valley settlers experienced their portion of the trials as well as "the sweets" of victory. Taxation became more burdensome and was made irksome by

[1] Virginia Petitions, Berkeley, no. 89, May 14, 1777.

the growing consciousness of unfair representation in the state legislature. This consciousness of unfairness came, of course, from the more rapid growth of population in the Valley as well as from the fact that the section had developed the feeling that it was a definite part of the new state whose independence it had helped to win. The breakdown of markets left Valley products stranded. There was little specie but many debts—and debtors. Debt seemed to accumulate in various ways. Part of the burden which it placed on the Valley, as elsewhere, arose from accounts due to British merchants. During the war most of these accounts had been confiscated by the new state government, and this act created further complications when the treaty of peace indirectly provided for their collection.

A survey of the items of Virginia taxation leaves the impression that, although the levies were higher than before the war, even with the parish levy abolished, they were fairly distributed.[2] For example, the specific tax on a slave was ten shillings; on a horse, two shillings, and on cattle, three pence each.[3] The inventories of the period show that these taxes were proportionate to the values.[4] However, the post-war productive value of the slave was higher and that of the horse lower than in earlier times. The majority of the slaves were in eastern Virginia, while horses and cattle were more numerous in the Valley. The

[2] Post-war taxation in Virginia took the form of a specific tax on personal property, and on some services, as well as an *ad valorem* tax on land and on exports and imports. As the people grew restless under the burden of internal taxes, the tendency developed to shift to the external or export and import duties. Hening, *Statutes*, X-XII, *passim*.

[3] *Ibid.*, XI, 93, 113, 418; XII, 413.

[4] See County Will Books, 1785-1787, *passim*, for inventories. Carriages were five to six shillings a wheel, with a later provision for graduation according to the nature of the vehicle, but billiard tables were fifteen pounds each. Such items were seldom found in the Valley. Hening, *Statutes*, XI, 93, 113; XII, 283.

slave, of course, was used primarily for tobacco cultivation and the horse for grain. Tobacco markets and prices were better in this period than those for grain. While the production tax tended to be heavier on the Valley, the luxury tax bore more heavily on eastern Virginia.

On the surface, the same general fairness appears in the land levy. In 1782 the Legislature created a special land commission to equalize land assessments. It recommended that eastern Virginia lands should be assessed at seven to ten shillings per acre and the supposedly more fertile Valley lands at five to seven shillings,[5] which appeared to be an advantage to the Valley. But when we further find that Valley lands were, for the time being, far below those of eastern Virginia in the production of marketable goods we are more ready to appreciate the complaint of inequality. Then, too, at the very time the market for Valley products had broken down, the eastern Virginia product, tobacco, found its market augmented and insured, as it were, by being legislated into chief favor as a commutable[6] for taxes. This does not mean that the tobacco planter was free from troubles but that an attempt was made to bring relief to him more than to the Valley farmer. The attempts of Valley farmers to change from

[5] The commission divided the lands of the state into four classes according to location:

First class: 10 shillings per acre for 41 counties, mostly in the Tidewater.

Second class: 7 shillings, 6 pence per acre for 18 counties, mostly in the Piedmont, but including two Valley counties, Berkeley and Frederick.

Third class: 5 shillings, 6 pence per acre for 8 counties, the five remaining Valley counties and three in the Trans-Alleghany country.

Fourth class: 3 shillings per acre for the 8 other Trans-Alleghany counties, including the Southwest and Kentucky.

See *Journal, House of Delegates*, October, 1782; Hening, *Statutes*, XII, 283. See also Ripley, *Financial History of Virginia*. However, Ripley is based primarily on Hening, *Statutes* and secondary material and does not deal with the Valley as such in any sense.

[6] Synonymous contemporary terms were *specifics, commodities,* and *taxes in kind* but *commutables* was the popular one.

grain to tobacco, and their early realization of the folly of such attempts, supported the contention that the land levies were unfair.[7]

Then, as the collection of internal taxes grew more difficult, and the demand for reduction more insistent, the legislators tried to find a way out by shifting to duties on imports.[8] Here again the Valley counties, especially the northern ones, felt the pinch of discrimination. Winchester was eager for a larger share in the trade of the people on "the Western Waters,"[9] and, while this traffic was developing, her merchants were busily working toward a more definite trade connection with Alexandria—which promised mutual advantage. But interstate duties, levied by both Virginia and Maryland, were interfering not only with the Winchester western trade but also with the improvement of Potomac navigation, which was the key to Alexandria's commercial development. The Potomac route west must cross the corner of Pennsylvania by way of the Monongahela River thus adding Pennsylvania duties to those of Maryland and Virginia. The Winchester trade as well as navigation improvement would find this an added handicap. The people of the north Valley were thus persuaded to join with the merchants of Winchester and Alexandria in petitions against interstate duties, which gave Maryland a trade advantage since she controlled the Potomac.[10] North Valley newspapers, correspondence, and petitions emphasized the prospect of better days for the economic development of that region, when interstate duties should be entirely eliminated.

[7] See petitions from Valley Counties, 1784-1787, *passim*, in Archives Department, State Library, Richmond, Virginia.
[8] *Journal, House of Delegates*, Jan. 8, 9, 1788, for instance.
[9] See *Winchester Advertiser*, 1787, *passim*.
[10] *Ibid.*, 1787-1788; Virginia Petitions, especially nos. 1569a, 1576, 1602a, 1774, 1905; Stephen Papers, 1786-1788, *passim*.

The method of payment was the problem of Virginia taxation which provoked a feeling of discrimination as well as intense legislative conflict. Along with the breakdown of the market for Valley products, the demand for luxuries and the absence of a state or national coinage caused a scarcity of specie. Taxes were usually paid in tobacco or other commutables. Tobacco had been a commutable in eastern Virginia for a long time, and since there had never been much specie or tobacco in the Valley, other forms of commutables had been allowed in that section, particularly during the Revolution.[11] Some of these were bacon, deerskins, hemp, wheat, and flour. When the war was over, however, the eastern controlled legislature refused to allow more than a limited and temporary right of commutation in any product except tobacco. Consequently, the Valley farmers had to find specie for tax payments; but, as early as 1780, Zachariah Johnston of Augusta feared that the continental and state paper money would drive all the specie in his county out of circulation.[12] A few years later Archibald Stuart, another Valley legislator, appealing to his constituents to pay up their tax arrears, told them that he knew and sympathized with them in the fact that there was "little specie and few opportunities for sale." Shortly afterward, Stuart wrote Jefferson that specie had "wholly disappeared" from his section, but he scratched out "wholly" and substituted "almost."[13]

[11] See *Journal, House of Burgesses*, 1769-1775; *Journal, House of Delegates*, 1778-1781. See also Rockbridge County Will Book, I, 163 ff., an unusual place for a tax record, of course.
[12] Johnston Papers, 1780.
[13] Jefferson Papers (Library of Congress), Oct. 17, 1785. In 1783 Rockingham petitioners complained of hard times and no money with which to pay their taxes, and a year later the sheriff of the county corroborated their claim of specie scarcity, in a petition which stated that he could collect no taxes except deerskins and hemp certificates. Virginia

In the winter of 1786-1787, five Valley counties petitioned the Assembly to lighten the unusually heavy tax
burden that had developed from the specie shortage there.
These petitions frequently used such phrases as "great
scarcity of specie," "no specie in the county," "extreme
scarcity of specie," and "absolute want of specie." One
of them stated that the horses and cattle in that county, on
the sale of which the people depended for specie, could
not be sold even for the amount of tax assessed on them.
When we remember that the tax on horses was only two
shillings, and on cattle only three pence, such a statement
seems highly improbable, but it illustrates the seriousness
of the situation.[14]

Two of the remedies for tax ills which appealed to the
Valley people were a better representative system in the
state Assembly and the elimination of interstate duties.
The first could be accomplished by a change in the state
constitution and the second by a reform in the federal
government.

In order to understand more fully the Valley's grievance of unequal representation, it is necessary to note the
extent of the inequality during the period of the Confederation, as illustrated by the statistics of representation.
These statistics indicate that the Valley had by far the
poorest representation of the seven sections of the state, in

Broadsides, no. 179 (Library of Congress). The acute scarcity of specie in
the Valley was recognized in the legislative act of 1784, which remitted one
half of the taxes for the next year. This act not only emphasized "the
scarcity of specie in the frontier parts of this commonwealth" but in addition made a special provision because of it for the counties "westward of
the Blue Ridge."—Hening, Statutes, XI, 543. Madison, Writings (ed.,
Hunt), II, 109, felt that good crops and better prices would save the day
especially for the tobacco planter, but this had little comfort for a Valley
farmer.
    [14] Virginia Petitions, nos. 928a, 1076, 1084, 1300, 1330, 1410a, 1416,
1597a, 1605, 1610, 2162. One of these petitions is signed by the ancestors
of Abraham Lincoln and William Jennings Bryan.

both branches of the state legislature.[15] To be sure, much of the inequality had come from the growth of population in these frontier areas which was naturally more rapid than in the older sections, even during the war period. A heavier burden of taxation would, of course, tend to develop a grievance that had gone unnoticed or unfelt before.

The Tidewater had an advantage over the Valley in representation, in a ratio of three to one. The Southside had a like advantage, in the ratio of two to one, and the Piedmont in the ratio of three to two. Warwick County in the Tidewater had one representative in the legislature for every eighty-eight white males above sixteen years of age. At the same time Berkeley County in the Valley had only one representative for every 2,126 of the same population group. Seven Tidewater counties, with a total of less than 3,000 white males, were represented by as many delegates in the state Assembly as were the 19,000 in the seven Valley counties. The state Senate had an even greater disproportion of representation at the expense of the Valley. No matter which way the figures are com-

[15] Representation per white male population over sixteen years of age.

	White males 16 or over	Number of delegates	Males 16 or over per delegate	Number of senators	Males 16 or over per senator
Valley	19,708	14	1,408	$1\frac{1}{2}$	13,139
Tidewater	42,889	72	596	12	3,574
Piedmont	19,052	20	953	$3\frac{1}{2}$	5,444
Southside	21,291	30	709	$4\frac{1}{2}$	4,732
Seven Valley Counties	19,708	14	1,408		
Sevens Small Tidewater Counties	2,965	14	212		

Compiled from statistics furnished by the *Census of 1790*, Swem and Williams, *Register of the General Assembly of Virginia* and supported by the *Journals of the Virginia House of Delegates and Senate*. See also representation tables in Jefferson, *Notes on Virginia*, p. 172. Jefferson, of course, did not have access even to approximately accurate census data and used the militia return records which did not take into account the more rapid growth of population in the western part of the state. Nevertheless his proportions showed about the same variance as these.

puted there was discrimination against the Valley in varying degrees. Statistics based on the total population, including Negroes both slave and free, show more equal
proportions of population per representative. Nevertheless, the Valley still had a considerable deficiency of representation, far less indeed than had the eastern Virginia
sections, particularly the Tidewater and the Southside.

A reform in the state government was gaining adherents in the Valley even before Yorktown.[16] Early in 1781
Thomas Lewis of Augusta called a committee to meet in
Staunton to discuss ways and means, but nothing came of
it.[17] The most definite effort for a new constitution grew
out of an Augusta tax petition to the 1784 Assembly.
After stating their tax grievances and insisting that they
could get at the root of the trouble by a reformation of the
state government, the petitioners vigorously demanded
such a reform.[18] The Assembly was aroused to an unusual
interest and the preliminary response was favorable. The
Committee on Propositions and Grievances declared the
proposal reasonable and recommended it to the house.[19]

[16] Stephen Papers, no. 132. Stephen found his own county, Berkeley,
assessed at ten times that of the eastern Virginia county, Warwick, which
had an equal voice in the Assembly.

[17] Chalkley, *Records of Augusta County*, I, 518.

[18] *Journal, House of Delegates*, June 14, 1784.

[19] *Journal, House of Delegates*, June 14, 1784. The Committee reported:
"That the ordinance of Convention, commonly called the Constitution, does
not rest upon an authentic basis, and was no more than a temporary organization of government for preventing anarchy, and pointing out efforts
to the two important objects of war against our then invaders, and peace
and happiness among ourselves; but this, like all other acts of legislation,
being subject to change by subsequent legislatures possessing equal power
with themselves, should now receive those amendments which time and
trial have suggested, and be rendered permanent by a power superior to
that of the ordinary legislature.

Resolved that it is the opinion of this committee, that an ordinance
pass, recommending to the good people of this Commonwealth the choice
of delegates to meet in General Convention, with powers to form a constitution of government to which all laws present and future should be
subordinate; Providing, that the present government shall remain in every

The recommendation was referred to the Committee of the Whole House and was debated at sundry times for a week. Archibald Stuart, representative of Botetourt County at the time, who had introduced the resolution in the Committee, ably championed it in the Committee of the Whole House.[20] He had the warm support of Madison, but Zachariah Johnston, one of the ablest Valley leaders, was absent and thus missed an opportunity to support a measure in which he had an intense interest. The resolution met the "violent opposition"[21] of Henry, and after a bitter fight it was defeated in the Committee of the Whole.[22] There was, of course, no recorded vote. Henry's break with the Valley leaders was perhaps due to the rising controversy over paper money and over the question of paying British debts, on both of which they refused to follow Henry's leadership. During the same year Botetourt petitioners concluded their demand for the payment of British debts, and for the repudiation of paper money, with the statement that, "the representation of the people both in the Senate and in the House of Delegates, are very unequal."[23]

respect as it is now, until such constitution shall be finally settled and actually substituted."

[20] Madison, *Writings* (ed., Hunt), II, 53-58, Madison to Jefferson.

[21] Madison, *op. cit.*, pp. 53-58. In this letter to Jefferson, dated July 3, 1784, Madison stated the situation as follows: "A trial was made for a convention, but in a form not the most lucky. The adverse temper of the House & particular of Mr. Henry had determined me to be silent on the subject. But a Petition from Augusta having among other things touched on a reform of Gov^t—and R. H. L. arriving with favorable sentiments, we thought it might not be amiss to stir the matter. Mr. Stuart from Augusta accordingly proposed to the Committee of Propositions the Resolutions reported to the House as per Journal."

[22] *Journal, House of Delegates*, June 21, 1784.

[23] Virginia Petitions, no. 1501. A year later petitioners of the same county, protesting against unfair taxation, insisted that, while there was great need of preserving public faith and credit, there was a greater need of establishing and preserving equality of representation as "the soul of our government," because only thus could justice and fair taxation be maintained.—Virginia Petitions, no. 1933.

With the movement for a new federal constitution well under way in 1787, such Valley leaders as Stuart, Johnston, and White felt that the time was ripe for another effort to secure a fairer system of representation.[24] Johnston drew up the preliminary outline of an enabling act and worked out statistics of representation that would support the arguments for reform. Since Madison was recognized as the outstanding friend of the Valley in legislative circles, Stuart appealed to him for help.[25] Madison, however, persuaded him that it was not wise to mix federal and state reform movements. Representation reform therefore had to wait for another generation, while Valley taxpayers wrestled with their private as well as public debts.[26]

There is no lack of evidence of the seriousness of the post-war debtor problem in the Valley. Most of the outstanding leaders were debtors in varying degrees. Some were involved indirectly through suits against relatives. Among those heavily in debt were such men as William Fleming, Zachariah Johnston, Isaac Zane, Adam Stephen, Thomas Lewis, William Preston, and Alexander White.[27] General Gates engaged in a spirited correspondence with his creditors concerning obligations long past due.[28] His reason for not paying was his inability to collect from his own debtors. He insisted that if he sued, the long delay in the courts, in some instances as much as seven years, would be the same as the loss of the debt. He preferred therefore to await the convenience of his debtors as the best way out of the difficulty. In Rockbridge County,

[24] Johnston Papers, 1787.
[25] Ford, "Federal Constitution in Virginia," loc. cit., XVII, 478.
[26] Madison, Writings, V, 47-50.
[27] See Court Records, Valley counties; Johnston Papers; Stephen Papers; Etting Collection (Pennsylvania Historical Society).
[28] Gates Papers, Nos. 257, 807.

Joseph Moore was "sworn in as High Sheriff while in custody" for a debt of fifty pounds.[29]

The record of cases in the county courts, extant for most of the Valley counties, furnishes abundant proof of the debt burden borne by the rank and file of the people.[30] These compilations, for the period 1782-1788, show the amazingly large number of cases that were tried, or docketed, each year. For instance, the Berkeley County Court tried, or went through the formality of trying, 2,162 cases in 1783, and maintained an average of nearly 2,000 a year for the next two years. More than 90 per cent of these were for debts in one form or another. During these three years, then, the Berkeley court had an average of a case a year for every two of the adult male population of the county. The Augusta, Rockbridge, and Rockingham courts were not far behind Berkeley in this respect. The situation was as bad as in the Piedmont and Southside where there were actually fewer cases *per capita* of white population. The Valley had many more cases per county.[31]

The busiest years for the courts were from 1783 to

[29] Rockbridge Execution Book, II, 38.

[30] Cases in Court, Valley counties:

Year	Augusta	Berkeley	Frederick	Rockbridge	Rockingham	Shenandoah
1782	705	1,324	180	319	32	244
1783	818	2,162	461	661	213	346
1784	1,141	1,871	577	694	635	723
1785	1,202	1,821	475	547	838	516
1786	1,011	(1)	562	348	254(2)	(3)
1787	690	(1)	464	206	59(2)	(3)
1788	540	(1)	368	102	155(2)	(3)

(1) No record after 1785 except 359 cases to April court, 1786.

(2) Records incomplete and unsatisfactory after 1785.

(3) No record after 1785 except 236 cases to May court, 1786.

These statistics were gleaned from Order, Minute and Judgment Books of the various counties. The phrase "in debt" is appended to nearly all cases.

[31] See Order Books for such Piedmont and Southside counties as Amelia, Charlotte, Culpeper, Fluvanna, Halifax, Prince Edward, Spottsylvania, representative counties.

1786. In 1787 and 1788, especially the latter, there was a marked decrease in the number of cases. But before we conclude that the debtor problem had been solved and debtor discontent ended, we must examine the sheriff's executions of judgments for debt. The execution with its prospect of forced sale or imprisonment, was the real cause of debtor discontent. The seriousness of the problem in the Valley is indicated, not only by the increasing number of executions but particularly by the sheriff's appended notes, which record opposition by resort to firearms, clubs, axes, drawn swords, and "fixed" bayonets. The executions increased from 457 in Berkeley County in 1784 to 945 in 1788, while in Botetourt for the same years the increase was from 321 to 742. The incomplete records show 155 cases, in three counties, in which the sheriff noted that officers had been "kept off by force of arms."[82]

A crisis came in 1787, when one Black Matthews of Botetourt County refused to pay his debts and taxes and formed a band of a hundred and fifty or more men of like mind. They pledged themselves to resist by force the taking of property for the payment of debts and taxes. Matthews sent copies of the "resolutions" of his "association" to other Valley or back counties, but failed to secure many recruits. He was finally apprehended and placed in the Fincastle jail, and nothing further is known of him. His followers dispersed, and this embryonic Shays rebellion proved to be nothing more serious than a protest against an intolerable state of affairs. The majority of the Virginia frontiersmen undoubtedly sympathized with the grievances of Matthews' band, but most of them thought that there was a better way out than through an appeal to arms.[83]

[82] The Execution records are extant for only four counties and these are not complete.

[83] *Virginia Gazette*, Sept. 20, 1787. See also letter, James McClurg to

The Valley had naturally looked first to the Assembly for redress of its taxation grievances, and now it did the same in the matter of debts. The remedy which the great majority of its people sought was a reform in the court system, so that the administration of justice might be both fair and efficient. Through the speeding up of the wheels of justice many debtors could collect amounts due them and the vicious circle of indebtedness be eliminated. Thus might be accomplished both the payment of debts and the end of confiscatory forced sales. Such sales, and other evils that came from hurried and too frequently unfair decisions, could be prevented through making the courts function more smoothly.[34]

Archibald Stuart instructed a fellow attorney in the collection of a debt, "to get it if you can by fair means, if not sue." The context of the letter further indicates that Stuart felt strongly that the county court procedure and decisions were frequently unfair in result if not in intent. In the way of reform the plan sponsored by Alexander White and other Valley leaders called for a system of circuit courts with professional jurists, to supplement the work of the county courts. Several circuit court acts were passed prior to 1788, but they had, in each case, been amended beyond recognition and contained provisions that left the Valley little better off than under the county court system. The three outstanding proponents of court reform in Virginia, Alexander White, Archibald Stuart, and Zachariah Johnston, were all Valley legislators.[35]

Paper money was a popular remedy among debtors in this period of economic distress. A post-war movement

---

Madison, Aug. 22, 1787, in *Proceedings*, Mass. Hist. Society, XVII, 472-473. McClurg gives the number in Matthews' band as three hundred.

[34] See Breckinridge Papers, letter of Stuart to Breckinridge, March 7, 1788.

[35] Hening, *Statutes*, XI, 421-429; XII, 267, 464-474; *Journal, House of Delegates*, 1784-1788, *passim*.

for an "emission" of paper or fiat money had as one of its
sponsors no less a personage than Patrick Henry. The
Piedmont, and especially the Southside, rallied to his
leadership, but the Valley thought little of paper money
as a remedy. As early as 1780 Zachariah Johnston be-
wailed the use of paper money.[36] The Augusta Court
Martial meanwhile regarded its paper currency as a thing
contaminated and instructed its bursar to exchange it for
specie in any convenient way he could devise.[37] In 1786
Archibald Stuart wrote of a possible paper emission—"her
Evil genius haunts us."[38] He was fearful lest an emission
should now occur, since paper money had recently been
"brought forward in the pleasing garb of installments."[39]
This was a plan to amortize debt payment over a period
of years to ease the burden. It is interesting to note that
the leaders who were opposing paper were themselves
debtors though not as deeply involved as the rank and
file.[40] These adverse sentiments on paper money were
frequently echoed both directly and indirectly in the Winchester newspapers during the latter part of the period
of the Confederation. They were re-echoed in the promise to readers that the new federal constitution would be
a death blow to the long-feared evil of paper money.[41]

Sentiment against paper money is also to be found in
the petitions of 1786 and 1787. One of the first was presented to the Assembly early in the session of 1786 from
Botetourt County, which was the most definitely frontier
of the Valley counties, and the court records show that it

[36] Johnston Papers, 1781.
[37] Augusta Court Martial Record Book, p. 242. For this book see
Manuscripts under Bibliography. See also Chapter V.
[38] Breckinridge Papers, Stuart to Breckinridge, Nov. 24, 1786.
[39] Ibid.
[40] See Papers, Johnston, Stuart, White. See also court records of Augusta,
Botetourt and Frederick counties for debt cases against each of these
leaders.
[41] Winchester Advertiser, 1787-1788, passim.

was among those hardest pressed by debtor burdens. The journal of the House gave to it more than double the space usually allotted to such communications. Besides, it was referred to the committee of the Whole House rather than to the usual standing committee. The argument of the petition that appealed to the House, if we can reach a conclusion from the portion printed in the *Journal*, was that,

the emission of a sum of paper money at this period would prove greatly detrimental to the credit of the States, and be productive of innumerable inconvenience to its citizens who have, on a former occasion, experienced the fatal effects of such a measure.[42]

It further stated that paper money was dishonest in principle and a menace to the morals of the people, because it robbed the industrious of the fruits of their labors. The solution of the debtor problem lay not in a paper emission but in "Honest Industry and Parsimony," since only by the latter virtues could "the capital of individuals or a nation be increased." A few days after the Botetourt petition was read in the House, that body by a large majority passed a resolution repudiating paper money.[43] The Valley voted unanimously for the resolution.[44] Most of the votes for a paper emission came from the Southside portion of the Piedmont.

The overwhelming vote of the Assembly repudiating paper money did not crush but rather stimulated the movement for an emission. Henry's patronage of the

---

[42] *Journal, House of Delegates,* 1786; Virginia Petitions, no. 1501. The petition emphasized the complaint that eastern Virginia had already injured the credit of the state through its "flood of tobacco notes, civil list warrants, and certificates for militia pay and for supplies," all of which, the petitioners insisted were quasi-paper money.

[43] The resolution borrowed freely from the ideas and to some extent from the phraseology of the petition.

[44] *Journal, House of Delegates,* Nov. 1, 1786.

measure brought hope to its friends and new fears to its opponents; consequently the Valley petitioners were again pleading earnestly against it at the 1787 session of the Assembly.[45] They insisted that the experience with such currency during the Revolution had shown that instead of helping in the payment of debts it encouraged the contraction of more debts than it liquidated, "that the Rage for acquiring property on credit increased in proportion to the currency [paper money] itself." In addition they considered "every Departure from fundamental principles mere quackeries in politicks which tend to sap the foundations of our Constitution and corrupt the morals of the people." Public happiness must come through assuring rewards for industry, through encouraging economy by a "speedy execution of justice," and through maintaining a "Republican simplicity of manners." In so far as a second set of resolutions against paper could give it, the House of Delegates gave the assurance asked. These resolutions were again debated and decided in the Committee of the Whole House, hence there was no recorded vote in the House proper.[46]

[45] *Journal, House of Delegates,* Oct. 17, 1787. The following statements of these petitioners further explain the sentiment of the Valley people against paper money and their reasons for repudiating it as a solution to the debtor problem: "As every good citizen laments the Low Ebb of public credit which is visible in the Discount of all public securities how must he then abhor a measure which would procrastinate at least if not destroy the last hopes of relief from so great an Evil—The minds of men after being agitated so long during the late revolution and the subsequent state of confusion incident to new government naturally require some repose, some stability in public measures and a security for their property. This can only be effected by uniform and systematic exertions for the Restoration of public and private credit, the foundations of which must be laid in the strict observance of Contracts between individuals— No man can say paper money will have this tendency; we trust therefore no man will prescribe it as a remedy."—Virginia Petitions, no. 1673. The petitioners further suggested that paper money demands were like the hydra, which could grow new heads when its old ones were cut off.

[46] Virginia Petitions, no. 1673; *Journal, House of Delegates,* Nov. 3, 1787.

Thus the people of the Valley not only refused to join in the paper-money movement but vigorously opposed it, in spite of the fact that their debt problem was a serious one, in many senses more serious than in those areas that were demanding such currency. It is noteworthy that not a word approving a paper emission can be found in any Valley newspaper,[47] in any collection of private papers, in any petition to the Assembly, or in any vote of a Valley member in the Assembly. On the contrary, if such a remedy was mentioned, it was only in terms of spirited disapproval. There was, meanwhile, no lack of either petitions or votes for paper from the Piedmont.[48]

Since they were burdened with debts, why did the people of the Valley so vigorously repudiate paper money as a remedy? A careful search for motives, other than those given in their public and private utterances, as set forth in the preceding paragraphs, fails to reveal anything. Can we do better, then, than accept these statements of motive? They tell us that they had already experienced the evil effects of paper during the Revolution, and after, in such things as tobacco notes and military certificates. Instead of aiding in the payment of debts, paper money had encouraged the contraction of more debts, at least so it seemed to these pioneers, hence they repudiated it as a remedy.

Even the Treaty of Peace of 1783 had added to the economic troubles of the Valley. The fourth article provided for the removal of all impediments to the mutual collection of debts contracted at any time prior to the treaty. The Virginia legislature meanwhile had not only hindered by law the collection of the pre-war debts due to British merchants, but in addition had confiscated a

[47] The two Valley newspapers of the time were the *Winchester Advertiser* and the *Virginia Centinel*.
[48] See Virginia Petitions and *Journal, House of Delegates*, 1785-1787, *passim*.

large portion of the debts as a war measure. This simply meant that those indebted were to pay their accounts to the state treasury rather than to the normal creditor.

From the publication of the treaty until the controversy was, in a measure, settled by the ratification of the new federal constitution in 1788, one of the leading questions before the people and Assembly of Virginia was whether the debt clause of the treaty or the state laws came first; in short whether the British debts should or should not be paid. The party that insisted on payment was led by Madison and the opposition by Henry. Prior to the adoption of the federal constitution, the advocates of payment could clear the way only by the repeal of the state acts. This movement encountered a number of difficulties. In popular opinion the refusal to pay British creditors was a mark of patriotism. Added to this was the plausible argument that the debts represented unjust exploitation and that repudiation was a necessary and logical consequence of independence. It was further alleged that the armies of Arnold and Cornwallis had carried away some of the goods for which bills were being presented and had destroyed the crops which might have been used for the payment of other goods.[49]

Prevailing conditions and popular favor were on the side of those who led the fight against payment. But there were strong arguments for payment. Justice and business credit demanded that both public and private debts should be paid. National honor and public credit were at stake, and Virginia must join with the confederated states in carrying out the terms of the treaty in good faith. England would not surrender the Northwest posts until her

[49] *Journal*, Nicholas Cresswell, pp. 127-128; *Journal, House of Burgesses*, 1773-1776, p. 139. Since the Virginia state government had confiscated and collected a portion of these debts, some of the debtors feared that they might be compelled to pay a second time.

merchant creditors were assured that the debts owed them by Americans were in a fair way of being paid.[50]

The people of the Valley were almost as deeply indebted to these merchants as were eastern Virginians. In 1787-88 William Crow, prominent in the south Valley, made assignments of three tracts of land, comprising nearly 2,500 acres, in order that he might take care of his accounts with Nelson, Herron, and Company, late British merchants of Richmond, whom he "honestly desired" to pay.[51] Of the three referees designated by Crow for this transaction the most prominent was Archibald Stuart, ardent champion of the payment of British debts.[52] At Winchester, Joseph Holmes advertised land for sale to cover debts of about £350 owed to two British mercantile houses.[53] Also among these debtors were Isaac Zane, Alexander White, William Preston, Zachariah Johnston, Robert Breckinridge, Jacob Hite, and various others prominent in the affairs of the section. Even though the British debts in the Valley might not have been either so numerous or so heavy as in the eastern counties, they were sufficient to create a strong party against payment if personal interest had been the moving factor in the matter.

Sentiment for payment, however, was strong in the Valley. The argument that national honor demanded

[50] For a more thorough treatment of the subject of British debts in the state at large, see Isaac Samuel Harrell, *Loyalism in Virginia* (Durham, 1926); J. B. McMaster, *History of the People of the United States* (New York, 1897), I, 235-238. McMaster has the arguments pro and con which held good, particularly in Virginia. See also Armentrout, "A Political Study of Virginia Finance, 1781-1789."

[51] Botetourt Deed Book, IV, 46-47.

[52] See also Crow's proposals, Virginia Petitions, no. 1741; *Virginia Gazette, Supplement,* June 21, 1788; Hening, *op. cit.,* XII, 675-676.

[53] *Winchester Advertiser,* March 11, 1789. An examination of Valley court records and other sources shows additional large amounts due British merchants in Alexandria, Richmond, and other Tidewater ports. Simms Papers (Library of Congress), 1785-1788, *passim;* Allason Papers; Preston Papers; Valley court records for the period.

payment, whether Great Britain observed her obligations or not, appealed to its people. Its leaders so argued frequently and emphatically. The possibility that England would never relinquish the Northwest posts while the debts remained, threatened the economic and social welfare of Valley people in several ways. Facility of trade and settlement on the "Western Waters" would be enhanced in proportion as the Indians were friendly; and few expected Indian relations to be good while England held the posts. Furthermore, England was diverting the Indian trade to the St. Lawrence, by means of the posts, and the Virginia frontiersmen wanted this trade to follow their own river routes.[54]

As soon as the state legislature faced seriously the question of the payment of British debts, the representatives from the Valley were ready to play a prominent part. In the October Assembly of 1785 three of them, Stuart, Thruston and White, were placed on a special committee of five, headed by Madison, to draw up a bill to provide for repeal of the acts against payment. The bill was drawn up and passed its first reading, but was lost through postponements. This was partly because the more pressing religious questions were being fought out on close lines during the session, but more specifically, according to Madison, because the patrons of repeal legislation found that the only hope for passage was through amendments that would destroy the real purpose of the bill.[55]

[54] The frequent recurrence of these arguments in contemporary records makes their effect on public opinion more than a matter of inference. See *Winchester Advertiser*, 1787-1789, *passim*; *Winchester Mercury*, 1788, *passim*; Johnston Papers; Stuart Papers; Breckinridge Papers; Virginia Petitions, nos. 1493a, 1493b, 1493c, 1501, 1673, 1741, for examples.

[55] Madison, *op. cit.*, II, 206, 207, 210, 219. Proposals were made and even passed providing for such items as a seven years' delay in payment, safeguarding persons involved as securities, and forbidding the sending to prison of persons against whom judgments were obtained. *House Journal*, June 22-23, 1784; October, 1784-January, 1785, *passim*; Madison, *op. cit.*, II, 54-56.

In the summer and autumn of 1786 Valley petitions on the payment of British debts began to flow into the Assembly. These were the most numerously subscribed of all the Virginia petitions of the period, with the exception of those on religious matters. The petitioners remonstrated "against the policy of an Individual State opposing the mind of the Union." They considered the treaty on the whole as "not only advantageous but honorable, and the fourth article of it, inforcing the mutual discharge of debts, due individuals of the contracting parties, founded upon the immutable Laws of Justice." As long as the war continued they had aided freely in the efforts to defeat the common enemy, but they highly disapproved of the unjust measures still aimed at the same enemy, because such measures were "derogatory to the Federal Government in the Eyes of all mankind." Such an attitude was furnishing the British with a "pretext of retaining the Northern posts, to the great oppression of the citizens of the United States." They begged the Assembly, therefore, to comply with a treaty that "*alone* recognizes our existence as an Independent People."[56] Another petition argued that "the repeal of all the laws now in force in this state which prohibit the recovery of British debts, is essential to the national honor and justice."[57]

Backed by these petitions, the Valley delegation in the October, 1787, Assembly was solid for the payment of British debts.[58] Early in the session another Valley petition was read, demanding the payment of these debts,

[56] Virginia Petitions, nos. 1493a, 1493b, 1493c; *Journal, House of Delegates,* October 25, 1786.

[57] See *Journal, House of Delegates,* Oct. 26, 1786.

[58] In the meantime the 1786-1787 Assembly had been quiet on the subject, as far as resolutions were concerned. Madison wrote that this was a poor season for "positive efforts in favor of Justice. British debts have not been mentioned and probably will not." See Madison, *op. cit.,* II, 301-302. As Madison stated it, "The other evils" (paper, etc.) have been "parried."

along with the repudiation of paper money.[59] As in the preceding year, the emphasis of the petition was placed on the honor and justice involved, as well as on the expediency of payment. An installment plan of British debt payment, one of the pet artifices of the repudiators, was heatedly rejected by these petitioners. They argued: "Admit the policy of the measure when applied to Contracts between Citizen and Citizen, it will still be inadmissible in those with foreigners. It cannot fail to blast the reputation of any merchant who has foreign connections and put an end to our commerce. The measure would not only be subject to the change but the actual inconvenience of a retrospective law."[60] In answer to this plea a resolution of November 17, 1787, proposing repeal of all acts repugnant to the treaty of peace, was passed by a vote of seventy-two to forty-two. The Valley cast its entire vote in favor of the resolution.[61] The surrender of the Northwest posts, which the British were holding contrary to the terms of the treaty, continued to be closely related to the repeal of the acts repugnant to the payment of British debts, particularly in the minds of the north Valley people. When the Assembly passed the resolution for this repeal, the Winchester newspaper argued that now "the English government must invent some new excuse for refusing to deliver up to our Western Posts, or we may well complain of *Punica Fides Brittanica.*"[62]

[59] *Journal, House of Delegates*, Oct. 17, 1787.

[60] Virginia Petitions, no. 1673. Jefferson (*Writings*, ed. Bergh, VI, 226 and XVI, 228) says that the British merchants were definitely favorable to installment payment. However, this fact did not alleviate the fears of those who saw in the installment plan merely a program of evasion.

[61] *Journal, House of Delegates*, Nov. 17, 1787.

[62] *Winchester Advertiser*, February 8, 1788. A free translation of this uncertain Latin phrase is, "The British are as undependable as Carthaginians." A few weeks later the same newspaper suggested that the best solution of the British debt problem, and the consequent surrender of the posts, was to be found in the ratification of the new federal constitution. *Ibid.*, March 7, 1788.

The Valley, therefore, took a particularly active part in the movement for the payment of British debts, even though it felt the burden of those debts as did the rest of the state.[63] The desire for equal justice, the appeal to national honor, and the interest in the surrender of the Northwest posts in order to facilitate occupation of western lands, all had created a strong sentiment for payment.

The joy of victory in the War for Independence was marred for the Valley, as for other sections of the new republic, by economic troubles of various kinds. The burden of taxation was made more trying by the loss of markets and scarcity of specie, by the inequality of representation, by the evil consequences of debt both domestic and foreign, and by the conflicting proposals and distasteful remedies that were being advocated as a solution to such problems. The Ulster Scot and his German and English neighbors awaited a stable government and saw in it the chief reward of victory.

[63] A search of the *House Journal* and the state archives indicates that in those days of frequent petitions not a single one against repudiation reached the Assembly from a county outside the Valley.

≡☆≡ **8** ≡☆≡

Religious Liberty

THE WAR FOR INDEPENDENCE had carried the Valley dissenter well on his way toward realizing his hopes for full
religious freedom. He saw gains made in that direction
from the standpoint of both legislation and public opinion.
Religious *liberty* was substituted for *toleration* in the Virginia Bill of Rights. Quakers and Mennonites continued
to be allowed exemption from military service, since such
service was contrary to the tenets of their respective faiths.
Baptists and Methodists were allowed to serve under their
own officers in the Virginia militia, even to regimental
commanders, if there were enough men enlisted of a particular denomination to warrant a regimental organization.
All laws which provided punishment for religious opinion
were declared void by the legislature of the new state.
Dissenters were exempted from the tithe or tax paid to
the Anglican Church. Near the end of the war dissenting
ministers were accorded a limited right to perform marriage ceremonies.[1]

Yet despite the inclusion of religious liberty in the Bill
of Rights and despite much liberal legislation, the Treaty
of Peace found the Valley dissenter still laboring under
the laws of toleration rather than enjoying full religious

[1] Hening, *Statutes*, IX, 348; X, *passim*.

liberty. There were undoubtedly dissenters, groups as well as individuals, who had no clear distinction in their minds between toleration and freedom in religion. So far as these were concerned the state might have its established religion, provided it did not require the dissenter to subscribe to its doctrine or aid in its financing. But the Valley Presbyterians were not of this class, since most of their Ulster-Scot ministers had been well instructed in the principles of the separation of church and state. Then too, the Ulster-Scot Presbyterian laymen tended to dominate the political thought and action of the section. Since these Ulstermen were the most numerous of the dissenting sects and since they insisted on liberty rather than mere toleration, it was to be expected that they would lead the Valley in the movement for full religious liberty. Behind such a leadership, however, was a factor that cannot be ignored in any discussion of religious liberty in the Revolutionary period: the influence of the College of New Jersey and particularly of its able president, John Witherspoon.

The Scottish Presbyterians from North Ireland, who preceded Witherspoon by a generation in migrating to New Jersey and Pennsylvania, and subsequently to Virginia, had soon after their arrival in America attempted collegiate education of some kind in William Tennent's Log College at Neshaminy, Pennsylvania, in 1727. Twenty years later, in 1746, they had an important part in the establishment of the College of New Jersey at Princeton, and to this institution they devoted their efforts as a place for the training of their ministry. A score of years after its founding, the college was in need of a new president, and its trustees, for the first time since its establishment, turned to Scotland for a man to fill the position. The reason for the move is not hard to find.[2]

[2] See V. L. Collins, *President Witherspoon*, I, 70 ff.

The Ulster Scots in America had learned well the incompatibility of a state religion, if full religious liberty was to be accomplished. They had had their first lesson in this during their sojourn in North Ireland. In consequence, their conception of Presbyterianism and its relation to the state was different from that entertained by loyal members of the Established Church of Scotland. When these American Presbyterians needed a new leader for the training of their ministry, they found him in John Witherspoon, who for a number of years had been prominent in the revolt against the Established Church in Scotland. His theory of the relation between church and state is to be found in a sentence that he frequently used, "God alone is the Lord of the conscience."[3] His position is further explained in his various pamphlets and sermons, many of which have been assembled in the four volumes of his *Works*. In these we find such statements as, "No compulsion ought to be used to constrain men's choice in the matter of religion"; "Has not every man a natural right . . . to judge for himself in matters of religion?"[4]

Witherspoon continued his advocacy of the separation of church and state even more vigorously in America than in Scotland. He promised prospective students that in the College of New Jersey, "every religious denomination

[3] David Walker Woods, *John Witherspoon*, p. 36.

[4] Witherspoon, *Works*, IV, 324, 430. Ministers should "take care to avoid officiously intermeddling in civil matters . . . our blessed Savior . . . intimates to his disciples that they have no title to intermeddle with state affairs" (*ibid.*, II, 438). One may wonder, after reading the statements just noted, how Witherspoon reconciled his theory of the church's divorce from politics with his own political activity during the American Revolution. His explanation was that he must get into politics to get the church out of politics, or, if the state interfered in church affairs, the leaders of the church could interfere in state affairs, until interference by the state was ended (*ibid.*, III, 13-15, 36-37, 62). It can be said in his defense that, except for a keen interest in the making and ratifying of the new constitution, in which he seems to have realized his ideal of church and state separation, he did withdraw from politics when the success of the Revolution was assured.

may have free and equal advantages of education . . . any different sentiments in religion notwithstanding."[5] At the beginning of the Revolution he sent a pastoral letter to be read by the ministers of the Synod of New York and Philadelphia to their congregations. In the letter he reiterated his theory that there was no example in history in which civil liberty was destroyed and the rights of conscience preserved.[6] The theme of his Thanksgiving sermon for the year was a rejoicing at the prospect of civil and religious liberty. He concluded this sermon with his usual appeal for the separation of church and state.[7] As chairman of a committee so instructed he drew up, in 1786, a revision of church government entitled a "Draught of a Plan of Government and Discipline for the Presbyterian Church in North America." In the preamble of this revision he restated and clarified his theories on the relation of church and state, and argued that God alone is Lord of the conscience, which is free from the doctrines and commandments of men, that the rights of private judgment in religion are inalienable and that a religious organization needs no aid from the civil power except in keeping the peace.[8]

The Witherspoon theory can be summarized in three clauses: that God alone is Lord of the conscience, that freedom of conscience is an inalienable right, and that the state has no authority either to grant or to deny religious liberty. His greatest and most effective impression on politico-religious thought in Virginia was obviously in and through James Madison, who entered the College of New Jersey as a sophomore in 1769, the first year of Witherspoon's administration. Madison's attachment to him

[5] *Ibid.*, IV, 355-356.   [6] *Ibid.*, III, 13.
[7] *Ibid.*, III, 81-83.
[8] See John Witherspoon, "Draught of a Plan of Government and Discipline for the Presbyterian Church of North America". . . . Manuscript in Princeton University Library.

became so strong that after his graduation in 1771, he remained for a year of post-graduate work under Witherspoon's personal direction.[9]

It is not surprising then to find Madison a few years later demanding that religious *liberty* be substituted for religious *toleration* in George Mason's Virginia Bill of Rights.[10] In the controversies between 1784 and 1786, which resulted in the Virginia Statute for Religious Liberty, it was Madison and his lieutenant, the Scottish Presbyterian Zachariah Johnston, who bore the brunt of the fight for religious liberty and equality. It was Madison who, in the fight against assessment for religion, wrote the *Remonstrance*, probably the ablest paper ever penned by a Virginian on the separation of church and state.[11]

It is worthy of note that nearly every Presbyterian minister in Virginia, especially in the Valley, between 1785 and 1789 was a Witherspoon graduate or had been trained by a Witherspoon graduate.[12] For nearly twenty years

[9] Collins, *op. cit.*, II, 205. Some of Madison's associates at Princeton were "Light Horse Harry" Lee, Aaron Burr, and Philip Freneau.

[10] Gaillard Hunt, *Life of James Madison* (New York, 1902), p. 9; Madison, *Writings* (ed. Hunt), I, 24.

[11] Madison, *op. cit.*, II, 154, 163, 183-191; Eckenrode, *Separation of Church and State in Virginia*, esp. p. 83. This *Remonstrance* contains frequent echoes of the Witherspoon theories. His old teacher put the stamp of his approval on Madison's work at the Philadelphia Convention of 1787, with an honorary degree of Doctor of Laws, voted by the Trustees of the College of New Jersey within two weeks after the adjournment of the Convention. He also commended Madison's work in the Virginia Convention of 1788 with a letter of glowing praise. See William Cabell Rives, *History of the Life and Times of James Madison*, II, 517 ff.

[12] Others of the Witherspoon men in Virginia who undoubtedly influenced public opinion were: Caleb Wallace, who was an intimate associate of Madison and Jefferson in their earlier program for religious liberty; Samuel Stanhope and John Blair Smith, founders of Hampden-Sydney College; and David Witherspoon, son of John Witherspoon, who went to Hampden-Sydney as an instructor in 1776. Still others, some of whom have been noted in preceding chapters, were Samuel Doak, Thomas Craighead, Philip Vickers Fithian, Samuel McCorkle, John McMillan, Samuel Carrick, William Graham, James McConnell, James McRee, John Springer, Benjamin Erwin, Edward Crawford, Samuel Shannon, Abraham, Samuel,

there had been a steady stream of these graduates pouring into the Valley as well as into other parts of Virginia. Some came as itinerants and stayed only a short time, but if we can use Fithian as an example, even these lost no opportunity to set forth their views on the burning issues of civil and religious liberty. Their united voice in either religious or political matters undoubtedly was a great influence in molding public opinion, no matter how short the stay of some of them may have been. Of equal importance, however, was the fact that they found prepared and fertile soil in Virginia for the planting of their doctrines.[13] The Ulster Scot Presbyterians, as well as the German and Swiss Reformed Churchmen, were ready to receive the tenets that made for religious liberty.[14]

The three most popular and influential Witherspoon men in the Valley were John McKnight of Berkeley County, Archibald Scott of Augusta, and John Montgomery of Frederick.[15] All of them were ministers who had large congregations.[16] Archibald Scott wrote at least one of the petitions of Valley Presbyterians, which pleaded for

---

Richard, and Joseph Venable, Branch Giles, and Samuel Wilson. Minutes, Synod of Philadelphia; Minutes, Hanover and later Lexington Presbyteries, 1770-1789, *passim*; *Journal, House of Delegates*, November 19, 1776; Eckenrode, *op. cit.*, p. 51; Simms Papers, 1780-1788; S. D. Alexander, *Princeton College in the 18th Century*, pp. 127-219; Wm. B. Sprague, *Annals of the American Pulpit* (New York, 1858), III, 326-528.

[13] It may be of interest to note that the set of Witherspoon's *Works* used in the preparation of this chapter was the property of the Reverend James Waddell, known as the blind preacher, who, though a Presbyterian, preached in the Orange Episcopal Church for two years, 1786-1788. This was the church James Madison attended. Madison showed both interest in and enthusiasm for Waddell's preaching, and the admiration was evidently mutual. (The set of Witherspoon was presented to Reverend A. M. Fraser, D.D., Staunton, Virginia, by the grandson of James Waddell. Dr. Fraser in turn presented them to the writer.)

[14] Meade, *Old Churches, Ministers*, II, 95; Madison, Miscellaneous Papers (Library of Congress), Letter to George Nicholas, May 17, 1788.

[15] Princeton Catalogue, 1773-1775. These men, then, were of the classes of 1773-75.

[16] Minutes, Synod of Philadelphia, 1788.

separation of church and state.[17] The petition insisted that the best form of religious liberty was "a Temporal Legislature who have Temporal things as their sole and immediate object."[18]

No phase of the history of Virginia, with the possible exception of its founding and its several wars, has been as fully treated as the question of religious liberty.[19] The emphasis here will be on the influence and activities of the Presbyterians, particularly those who dominated the Valley, in the movement for the separation of church and state. The part played by other dissenters in the state at large was also important, as several accounts have emphasized. Of these the Baptists played the leading role, but their strength was chiefly in eastern Virginia.

Soon after the new state government was organized in 1776 the Virginia Anglicans, since they looked on the difference between toleration and liberty as of little importance, set in motion a plan to incorporate themselves as the Episcopal Church. It is not easy to determine the former Anglicans' purpose in this move for incorporation. Whatever their objective, the Presbyterian dissenters feared it was a plan to continue the Anglican Church in power

[17] Virginia Petitions, nos. 1736a, 1877. In this petition Scott restated the Witherspoon theory of the relation of church and state, almost as though that eminent educator had himself dictated it.

[18] *Ibid.*, no. 1877.

[19] Some of the more prominent of the treatises on the subject are: Johns Hopkins University *Studies in History and Political Science*, edited by Herbert B. Adams; see Henry R. McIlwaine, "The Struggle of the Protestant Dissenters for Religious Toleration in Virginia," XII, no. 4 (Baltimore, 1894), and Thom. W. Taylor, "The Struggles for Religious Freedom in Virginia: The Baptists," series XVIII, nos. 10, 11, 12 (Baltimore, 1900); Thomas Cary Johnson, *Virginia Presbyterianism and Religious Liberty in Colonial and Revolutionary Times*, Richmond, 1907; Jefferson, *Notes on Virginia*, "Query xvii"; H. J. Eckenrode, "Separation of Church and State in Virginia" in *Bulletin*, Virginia State Library, *Special Report of the Department of Archives and History*. The last is probably the best work that has been done in the field. It is based largely on the numerous religious petitions filed in the Archives of the Virginia State Library along with the resulting legislative action.

through a close alliance with the state as in the Colonial period. One of the Presbyterian spokesmen, John Blair Smith of the Witherspoon family, in a letter to Madison insisted that the proposed incorporation bill was "an express attempt to draw the state into an illicit connection and commerce with them, which is already the ground of that uneasiness which at present prevails thro' a greater part of the state."[20] Smith then reiterated the Presbyterian theory that the legislature of a state had nothing to do with religion, if the principles of the Revolution meant anything. The Valley dissenters with numerous petitions and resolutions, joined in a heated but unsuccessful campaign against incorporation. The incorporation bill was passed, but the Valley unanimously opposed it. The Tidewater was almost unanimously in favor of it, while the sentiment of the Piedmont was divided.[21]

Closely accompanying the movement for the incorporation of the Episcopal Church was what seemed a kindred one, the proposal to levy an assessment on the people of the state for the payment of teachers of religion.[22] This was to be a general tax to support all denominations and each taxpayer could designate the denomination to which his quota was to go. Whatever the motive behind the assessment plan, the dissenters saw in it a move to restore the hated tithe of Colonial days. One of the chief supporters of the assessment proposal was Patrick Henry[23] who was chairman of the committee to bring in the bill. The opposition to it was led by Madison, who had as his ablest lieutenants two Presbyterians, Zachariah Johnston of the Valley and John Blair Smith. As Madison stated it, "the Bill for a general assessment has produced some

[20] Madison Papers, XIII, 128.
[21] Journal, House of Delegates, December 22, 1784.
[22] Ibid., November 11, 1784; Madison, op. cit., II, 59, 94.
[23] See Journal, November 11, 1784.

fermentation below the Mountains and a violent one beyond them."

Madison had temporarily acquiesced in the movement
for incorporation, but his acquiescence was nearly disastrous. When the Valley Presbyterians learned that he
had not opposed incorporation, they rather hastily as-
sumed that he would likewise not oppose assessment.
Furthermore, the fact that Henry was a sponsor for assessment seemed to make its passage a foregone conclusion. These Valley dissenters, therefore, in their desire to
save something from the wreckage of their movement for
religious liberty, sent a memorial to the Assembly stating
that, if there was to be an assessment, they hoped that it
would be "on the most liberal plan," and further, that
they hoped the proponents of assessment had "no idea of
supporting religion as a spiritual system." In spite of the
fact that this Presbyterian memorial reiterated the Witherspoon theory of absolute divorce of church and state,
there were those including even Madison himself, who
were incensed by the premature rumor that the Presbyterian clergy favored assessment. Soon, however, any
misunderstanding between Madison and the Valley Presbyterians, in regard to the ways and means of achieving
religious liberty, cleared up, and they were in the thick
of the fight against assessment.[24]

The first test of the assessment measure on the floor of
the Assembly came late in 1784, in a resolution to prepare
a bill to that effect.[25] The resolution passed by a vote of
forty-seven to thirty-two, but the Valley vote was unani-

[24] Minutes, Hanover Presbytery (then included the southern end of the
Valley), 1784; Journal, House of Delegates, November 12, 1784; Madison, op. cit., II, 113, 131-132, 137, 146. The last reference is a letter to
Monroe, in which Madison stated that the back counties (the Valley)
were particularly opposed to assessment because it was an "alarming usur-
pation of their fundamental rights."

[25] Journal, House of Delegates, November 11, 1784.

mously against it. As in the case of incorporation the vote for assessment came largely from the Tidewater with some votes from the Piedmont. A short time afterward Henry was elected governor. This took the ablest champion of assessment from the floor of the Assembly, and left Madison and Johnston, the bitterest opponents of the measure, in a position to control that body. It is not known whether the election of Henry to the governorship was a part of Madison's strategy, but his next move proved a strategic one. With the continued unanimous backing of the Valley members in the Assembly as a nucleus, he rallied enough votes to postpone the final vote on the bill until the fall session of the following year.[26]

As soon as they had succeeded in postponing action on the assessment bill, the opponents of the measure set themselves to arouse the people of the state against it, and to educate them toward a demand for the full separation of church and state. In this movement Madison, as already noted, took the lead with his pamphlet, *A Memorial and Remonstrance*,[27] a statement of his own and the Witherspoon theory of religious liberty. Copies of the pamphlet were sent to the various counties of the state, particularly those in the Valley where many signatures were obtained, and were then forwarded to the Assembly in the form of petitions.[28] The Valley Presbyterians, at a general convention held in Augusta County in the late summer of 1785 issued a restatement of their ideal for religious liberty and opposition to the assessment, copies of which were also signed by large numbers as petitions to the Assembly.[29] The defeat of the assessment bill in the

[26] *Journal, House of Delegates*, December 24, 1784. The vote was forty-five to thirty-eight for postponement.
[27] Madison, *op. cit.*, II, 163. See pp. 183-191 for the text of the *Remonstrance*.
[28] *Ibid.*
[29] Rockbridge County petitioners added a touch of originality in the

next session of the Assembly was a foregone conclusion. The Presbyterians saw their leader from the Valley, Zachariah Johnston, made chairman of the all-important standing Committee on Religion.[30] After a final skirmish between Patrick Henry and John Blair Smith, both of whom were allowed to speak before the Committee of the Whole, the bill was defeated in the Committee.[31] This form of taxation was not to be added to the economic burdens of the Valley. The defeat of the assessment proposal was closely followed by the repeal of the incorporation act.[32]

Meanwhile, the defeat of assessment showed Madison and his following that they could muster enough strength in the Assembly to pass a statute providing full religious liberty. In fact, the two movements, the defeat of the assessment and the passing of such a statute, were practically identical.[33] Madison and his lieutenants, again with the unanimous support of the Valley legislators, along with the Piedmont dissenters and some Anglican sympathizers, simply took the provision for religious liberty out of the proposed Revised Code, or Revisal as it was

phrasing of their remonstrance, to the effect that, "Religion and all its duties being of devine original & of a nature wholly Distinct from the secular affairs of Public Society ought not to be made the object of Human Legislation." (See Virginia Petitions, nos. 1360, 1361, 1362, 1373, 1383, 1416, 1462, 1485, for copies of the *Remonstrance* and the Presbyterian address, no. 1283a.) Madison's *Remonstrance* gave the tone of the whole flood of petitions against assessment, which poured into the Assembly from the Valley as elsewhere. Such phrases as, "in matters of religion, no man's right is abridged by the institution of civil society"; and that "religion is wholly exempt from its cognizance"; "experience witnesseth, that ecclesiastical establishment, instead of maintaining the purity and efficacy of religion, have had a contrary operation"; "they have no authority to enact into law the Bill under consideration" (Madison, *op. cit.*, II, 183-191) found a ready echo in the hearts of Valley dissenters.

[30] *Journal, House of Delegates*, October 25, 1785.
[31] *Ibid.*
[32] *Ibid.*, 1786-1787 *passim*; Madison, *op. cit.*, II, 310.
[33] Madison, *op. cit.*, III, 216, Madison to Jefferson.

called, and after some slight amendment enacted it into the law.[34] The way of the Valley dissenter had been made smoother by the removal of possible interference in religious rites which he cherished as an important part of his way of life.

[34] Madison, *op. cit.*; *Journal, House of Burgesses*, 1785-1786, *passim*.

≡☆≡ **9** ≡☆≡

The End of an Era

THE GROWTH OF COMMERCE, the development of easier
trade routes, and the effects of expanding business enterprise undoubtedly improved living conditions during this
period of war and reorganization.

Even before the war, Valley trade routes were shifting
from Philadelphia and the other Pennsylvania centers to
the Tidewater ports of Virginia.[1] Alexandria, in particular, grew in importance as a port for the back country
commerce. But through all the growing popularity of the
East-West trade routes, there was the ever-present problem of crossing the Blue Ridge Mountains. Water routes,
if they could be opened up, promised one solution.

In connection with this East-West trade, attention has
already been called to the Valley business done by William Allason of Falmouth and Edward Johnson on the
James.[2] This commerce with the Tidewater continued to
grow. General Adam Stephen's accounts show that from
1780 his interests were almost entirely at Richmond and
Alexandria, expecially the latter.[3] He was trading with

[1] See Chapter I, *ante*.   [2] *Ibid*.

[3] Stephen Papers (Library of Congress), 1780-1790, *passim*, especially
nos. 128, 134-137. While the output of Stephen's armory was usually sent
to Richmond, his flour, whiskey, and cattle, all in considerable quantities,

not less than a half-dozen Alexandria merchants in the
seven years from 1781 to 1788.[4] General Horatio Gates,
Stephen's close neighbor, was buying at Baltimore as well
as Alexandria, but his letters show a growing interest in
the latter. Among his accounts is a paper summarizing
the exports and imports of Alexandria. The accounts of
Zachariah Johnston of Augusta were with Robert Gamble
of Richmond. In Botetourt, William Crow was trading
with another Richmond firm on a large scale.[5]

None of the private accounts extant for the period
1780-1790 mention Philadelphia[6] as a market, and few
of them refer to Baltimore, with the exception of those
of General Gates. There is, however, a definite interest in
Alexandria. One contemporary speaks of messages that
could be sent "by the Merchants who trade from Staunton to Alexandria."[7] Staunton, of course, is in the central
Valley and such a trade relation is of special note.

The Winchester newspapers are full of evidence that
the commercial eyes of the northern Valley were on Alexandria as the logical port for that section. These newspapers, more or less regularly during 1787-88, quoted
the prices and exchange rates of that port.[8] A number of

---

were hauled or driven to Alexandria. The quantity of the shipments is
seldom given, but for one year he leaves the memorandum of a hundred
and fifty-eight barrels of flour sent to one merchant in Alexandria. At
another time he noted that he had sent a drove of his cattle to the same
merchant.

[4] Stephen Papers, nos. 134-137. At times when there was no sale for
his products, his agents or merchants in Alexandria stored them for him.

[5] Gates Papers (New York Historical Society), 1782-1788, *passim*, especially no. 225; Johnston Papers, 1785-1790, *passim;* Virginia Petitions,
no. 1741; Botetourt Deed Book, IV, 46-47.

[6] The writer has gone through the account books of at least a score of
contemporary Philadelphia merchants but has failed to find a single reference to the Valley or a known Valley resident.

[7] Simms Papers (Library of Congress). John Stuart to Simms, Nov. 2,
1785.

[8] *Winchester Advertiser*, Sept. 21, 1787, *et passim*. The prices quoted
were on a great number of Valley products such as flour, wheat, corn,

Alexandria merchants regularly advertised in them and usually took up the major portion of the advertising space. In addition to listing merchants' wares and indicating the frontiersmen's products that would be taken in exchange, the advertisements generally listed the dates of arrival and departure of ships at Alexandria.[9] The impression one gets from these advertisements is that Alexandria had most of the Winchester trade, or that its merchants were engaging in an advertising campaign for the business of the northern Valley. A dominance of the trade would seem the logical conclusion, of which there is further corroborative evidence. As early as 1774 Nicholas Cresswell noted in his diary that "great quantities of wheat and flour were brought down from the back country in waggons" to Alexandria by way of Leesburg. Cresswell also has the significant note that, while the north-Valley-Alexandria road was full of wagons and a busy one, the north-south road through Leesburg was almost abandoned.[10]

---

ginseng, and beeswax, and on such Valley imports as clothing, hardware, salt and spirits. Furthermore, Alexandria prices were the only ones quoted, there being none from Philadelphia or Baltimore.

[9] *Ibid.* The merchants who advertised most frequently were W. Lowry and Company; Robinson, Sanderson and Company; Jonathan Swift and Company; and Daniel and Isaac McPherson. Even such a "captain of industry" as W. Baycock, "Soap-boiler and Tallow-Chandler" from Alexandria, did business in both Winchester and Alexandria.

[10] *Journal of Nicholas Cresswell*, ed. L. McVeagh (New York, 1924), pp. 47 ff. Leesburg is near the Potomac and east of the Blue Ridge. Soon after the Convention of 1788 we find the further evidence of an Alexandria dominance of this trade in the estimate that 132,000 barrels of flour were sent to Alexandria each year from the Valley. *Winchester Advertiser*, Sept. 22, 1790. Of a rather large amount of business that was done by Alexandria in the years 1786-1790, the major portion evidently came from the Valley. Some figures, furnished from the Gates Papers, show Alexandria in the lean year, 1786, as doing more than one-fourth as much export business as did the port of New York in 1788, when prosperity had partially returned. Gates Papers (New York Historical Society), no. 225; Trade Broadsides (Library of Congress), Port of New York, 1788. There is, to be sure, no way to determine whether these statistics are in any

The problem of opening roads to the eastern Virginia ports and market towns involved the choice of routes as well as the efforts at construction. Most of the trade with these ports was over three routes across the Blue Ridge Mountains. The first and most important from Winchester to Alexandria, by way of Leesburg, crossed the Blue Ridge at Snicker's Gap, a low pass with no appreciable grade. A Berkeley County petition in 1787 spoke of this route as "a very public road"[11] from the back country to Alexandria, and noted the rapid development of towns along it. Another petition termed it the "Great Road" leading from the "Eastern to the Western Waters."[12] The second route, from Staunton to eastern Virginia, led through Rockfish Gap to Fredericksburg, Dumfries, and Richmond, and was the route usually followed by European travelers. From their accounts this roadway was in a better condition than the one through the Valley from north to south. The third, or south Valley, route crossed the low divide between the headwaters of the James and the Roanoke and followed the upper Roanoke Valley to New London and thence through Southside Virginia to Richmond.[13]

The interest in improving the roads over these routes is nowhere better indicated than in the constant legislation of the period from 1775 to 1790. The importance of improving these roads is indicated in the legislative phraseology by such terms as: "a great advantage to Augusta and neighboring counties"; "a most convenient passage for extending their commerce"; "a considerable trade and commerce is carried on" over the route; "which will greatly shorten their distance to market"; and "to make

---

sense accurate, but they are illustrative of the importance of Alxandria at the time.

[11] Virginia Petitions, no. 1758, Nov. 6, 1787.

[12] Ibid., no. 1832, Nov. 19, 1787.

[13] See map in Jefferson, *Notes on Virginia*, for some of these roads.

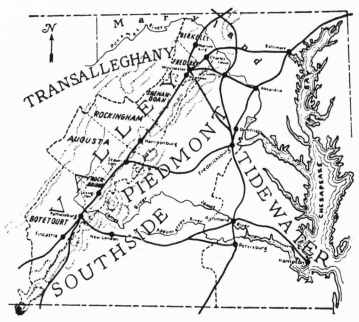

TRADE ROUTES OUT OF THE VALLEY, 1786

the great road" leading through Rockfish Gap "as easy and accessible as possible."[14]

Along with this legislation numerous petitions were sent the Assembly asking for better roads over the mountain passes.[15] One of the petitions had the significant statement that a particular road would benefit the "Great Body of People" living "beyond the Blue Ridge of Mountains, the Prosperity of which depends most materially on the cheapness of Carriage for their bulky Commodities to the trading towns on the navigable Waters of

[14] These phrases do not mean, of course, that the legislation referred to satisfied the needs of the Valley for better routes, or even attempted to do so in many cases. Hening, *op. cit.*, VIII, 16-17, 152, 252, 546, 548, 552; X, 367, 444; XI, 27, 28, 131, 294, 375, 429-430; XII, 72, 75, 174, 294, 297, 375, 513, 522, 729.

[15] Virginia Petitions, nos. 1440a, 1447, 1603, 1606a, 1758, 1823, 1928.

this State."[16] Sometimes the petitioners proposed additional ferries across the Shenandoah River on the Winchester-Alexandria road. They complained that because of the congestion at the existing ferries the wagoners often had to wait two or three days to be put over the river.[17] These petitions were signed by many of the leading farmers and merchants of the northern Valley, including Abram Shepherd, who lived by the Potomac Ferry on the Philadelphia road, Moses Hunter, William Darke, Charles Washington, brother of the General, Philip Pendleton, and Robert Stephen, all of whom lived near the Potomac and close to the Philadelphia road, but who evidently traded at Alexandria rather than at Philadelphia or Baltimore.

Closely allied with the demand for the improvement of roads to eastern Virginia ports and market towns was the keen interest in the development of navigation on the Potomac and James rivers. The moving spirit in the opening of these rivers to navigation was George Washington, whose activity in this direction began in the pre-Revolutionary period but was interrupted by the war.[18]

There were several problems closely related to the Potomac navigation project, such as the Northwest posts and the fur trade, Indian relations, and western lands. Washington and his associates, especially in the Potomac project, felt that they had reason to expect the fur trade of the Great Lakes to pass over the Potomac route, if the British evacuated the Northwest posts, and if that navigation route could be extended across the present state of Ohio. Indian relations were in turn closely connected with both the British occupation of the Northwest posts and the settlement of the West. Rapid settlement of the West and consequent trade development with that region

[16] *Ibid.*, no. 1447.   [17] *Ibid.*, nos. 1603, 1606a.
[18] Washington, *Writings* (ed. Ford), XI, 19.

would be affected favorably or adversely as Indian relations and facility of intercourse were good or bad. Western lands would increase in value, if Potomac navigation could be accomplished. Washington's chief motive was "to connect the Western Territory with the Atlantic States." His "object and aim" were "political," in that the West needed "to be bound by interest, by a commercial knot."[19]

Potomac navigation required the solving of such problems as interstate rights of way, interstate duties, the development of a port on the seaboard, and the collection of funds in a period of economic depression. In the Mount Vernon negotiations of 1784-85 Maryland agreed to coöperate,[20] but Pennsylvania's consent was necessary for that portion of the Potomac route which was to pass through her borders, since the Monongahela River was to be a part of the project. The problem of interstate duties had little promise of solution if left to the several state legislatures.[21]

The scarcity of specie made the collection of funds for the Potomac works difficult, but during the war Washington and his associates had solved more difficult financial problems than this one and were undaunted by it. By May, 1785, 403 shares in the Potomac Company had been

[19] See Washington, *Writings*, X, 407; XI, 26; Jefferson, *Writings* (ed. Bergh), VI, 273, 447; VII, 6, 347; *Maryland Journal* (Annapolis), May 9, 1788, letter from a Winchester correspondent. See also Washington, *op. cit.*, X, 487; XI, 32, 41, 105; Cora Bacon-Foster, "Early Chapters in the Development of the Potomac Route to the West," in *Records*, Columbia Historical Society, XV (Washington, 1912), 157.

[20] Bacon-Foster, *loc. cit.*, pp. 134-136; Washington, *op. cit.*, X, 437.

[21] Attempts to make Alexandria one of two designated ports in Virginia and thus develop that town into a great *entrepot* for Potomac trade, were blocked by no less a personage than George Mason. See Madison, *Writings* (ed. Hunt), II, 65-66, 151; Jefferson, *Writings* (ed. Bergh), V, 131. Was this from a Mason vs. Washington feud? Otherwise it is hard to see why Mason opposed. He lived almost as near to Alexandria as Washington did.

subscribed, a total of £40,300, and there was reasonable assurance that the scheme would succeed.[22]

The plans for Potomac navigation gradually took form and, following a trip by Washington over the route, a number of Valley leaders began to play active parts. Washington's long trip along the proposed route was made in 1784. He crossed the northern end of the Valley on his way out and traversed most of the region from Staunton to the northward on his return. While in the Valley, the General had conferences with such leaders as Daniel Morgan, Thomas Lewis, Gabriel Jones, and others, all of whom showed enthusiasm for the project, and promised coöperation. Lewis assured Washington that with little expenditure the Shenandoah River could be made navigable for 150 miles of its length and probably for thirty miles farther. Washington's fellow representative from Virginia, in a conference at Annapolis which followed his inspection of the route, was General Gates.[23] Alexander White served as the presiding officer at one of the annual meetings of the Potomac Company stockholders at Alexandria.[24] Thomas Lewis, Alexander White, John Shearman Woodcock, and Zachariah Johnston, were particularly active in carrying out the Potomac navigation program.

The Shenandoah River was to be one of the chief feeders for the trade of the Potomac route. In the movement for the opening of the Shenandoah, Zachariah Johnston was the leading spirit. He later played a prominent part in a mass meeting held at New Market, where representatives from the five northern counties gathered to discuss the opening of the Shenandoah. A commission of ten was

[22] Bacon-Foster, *loc. cit.*, pp. 147-150; excerpt from *Alexandria Gazette* in Pickell, *Early Life of George Washington*, p. 66.
[23] Bacon-Foster, *loc. cit.*, p. 147-151; *Winchester Advertiser*, October 27, 1790.
[24] Bacon-Foster, *loc. cit.*, p. 244.

appointed, with Johnston as chairman, to determine ways and means for the accomplishment of this enterprise.[25] The advantage to the Valley of Potomac navigation is presaged by a letter written by Washington in 1784, in which he says in part: "To describe the usefulness of water transportation would be a mere waste of time; every man who has considered the difference of expense between it and land transportation and the prodigious saving in the article of draft cattle, requires no argument in proof of it. And to point out the advantages which the back inhabitants of Virginia and Maryland would derive from an extension of the inland navigation of the river Potomack, even supposing our views did not extend beyond the Appalachian mountains, would be equally nugatory."[26]

Although the James River did not promise as much trade development as did the Potomac, plans for this waterway also were taking definite shape. In October, 1783, the Virginia House of Delegates appointed trustees and provided for subscriptions to be obtained for the extension of the navigation of the James to the mouth of the Cow Pasture River in the Valley. Subscriptions were receivable in hemp, tobacco, flour, or money. Tolls were provided for designated amounts of hemp, flour, and tobacco shipments. The new route was to supply transportation facilities to Botetourt and Rockbridge settlers, as well as to several Trans-Alleghany counties, if land routes could be improved and portage provided. Nine of the eleven trustees of this project to extend the navigation

[25] Johnston Papers, 1787-1790; *Winchester Advertiser*, July 24, August 21, Sept. 22, 1790. The name of William Darke of Berkeley is on the Potomac Company's book for a remittance of £300 sterling, on account, under date of August 6, 1787. Pickell, *op. cit.*, p. 104. Darke's neighbor from Berkeley, General Adam Stephen, was keenly interested in the canal project. Stephen Papers, 1785-1788, *passim*. Joseph Holmes was the Potomac Company's first agent in Winchester, and was usually active at the annual meetings of the company.

[26] Washington, *Writings* (ed. Ford), X, 404.

of the James were from the Valley. Most of the nine were prominent legislators, such as Zachariah Johnston, William McKee, Andrew Moore, and Archibald Stuart.[27] Two years later Valley petitioners asked that the amount required for subscription to the James River project be cut down, in order that a larger number might subscribe.[28]

Closely allied with the waterways project was the more ambitious one of bringing the federal capital to the banks of the Potomac, and preferably to the Valley. Agitation for the establishment of the federal capital in Virginia seems to have had its origin in a resolution of the Virginia Assembly on June 28, 1783. This resolution offered Williamsburg (the discarded Virginia capital) as a site, or any site on the Potomac, and proposed to donate £100,000 in addition for the erection of government buildings in the new federal city. By 1788 Madison was vigorously championing the Potomac site.[29] The interest of the Valley in locating the federal city on the Potomac route undoubtedly preceded by some time a Winchester newspaper's proposal of Shepherdstown as "the ideal and logical place" for the new capital.[30] Shortly afterwards it was reported that Washington, now President, had three Po-

[27] Hening, op. cit., XI, 341-42. George Washington's interest in the James was nearly as great as his interest in the Potomac. The shares in the James River Canal, which the Virginia Legislature vested in him, he turned over to Liberty Hall Academy in the Valley. This academy developed into Washington and Lee University.

[28] Journal, House of Delegates, Nov. 8, 1785; Virginia Petitions, Botetourt, 1785. At about the same time, Archibald Stuart wrote Jefferson of plans to connect the James River navigation with that of the Ohio by way of the Kanawha, and noted considerable progress on the enterprise. Land values, he reported, had already increased 50 per cent along the route.

[29] Papers of the Continental Congress (Library of Congress), nos. 46, 55-57; Journals of Congress, IV, 747; Madison, op. cit., V, 248, 252, 255, 256; Burnet, Letters, Members of the Continental Congress, I-VIII, passim.

[30] Winchester Advertiser, March 4, 1789. The article stressed the argument that Shepherdstown was the center of the new nation. The town was in Berkeley County on the banks of the Potomac.

tomac sites in mind, and liberal subscriptions were being
made in Shepherdstown for the erection of federal buildings,[31] provided the seat of government was located to
include that town. A total of nearly eight thousand dollars was raised among Valley people for the building of
the new capital.[32]

Meanwhile local interest in trading grew rapidly and
buying and selling was becoming much easier than in the
war period and earlier. The post-war depression was giving way to greater activity, and markets were being found
for Valley products. Winchester, the largest town in the
Valley, exhibited the greatest and most progressive activity of the time. The newspapers there carried advertisements of architects and builders from London and Dublin,
who had had "long experience in the first cities of Eu-
rope"; of an assayer of metals; of a rope factory; of a
staymaker who could make stays in "French, Italian, or
English fashions"; of two ladies who proposed to start a
millinery business, having served apprenticeships in Eu-
rope; as well as of sundry other shopkeepers.[33] The wares
usually listed by both Winchester and Alexandria merchants indicated that the backwoodsmen were beginning to
add some luxuries to soften the rigors of pioneer life. The
merchants, however, were still offering to take in exchange for goods such commodities as "hemp, ginseng,
furs, seeds, military certificates, and country produce."[34]

[31] *Winchester Advertiser*, Nov. 24, Dec. 22, 1790; Dandridge, Danske,
Historic Shepherdstown (Charlottesville, 1910), p. 280, letter Bedinger to
Washington.
[32] *Ibid.* Colonel William Darke of Berkeley was a leading spirit in the
movement.
[33] *Ibid.*, July 1, 1787, to June, 1788, *passim*.
[34] According to the same newspapers, the two hundred craftsmen were
in the line of march in the Winchester celebration of the ratification of the
federal Constitution. These marched in the following order: "Farmers
with sheaves, Bakers, Brewers, Butchers, Coppersmiths, White and Black-
smiths, Tanners, Saddlers, Shoemakers, Masons, Hatters, Tailors, Watch-
makers, Silversmiths, Wheelrights, Carpenters, and joiners, Painters, Pot-

At Shepherdstown, James Rumsey attempted to lead the way commercially by a distribution of broadsides which proposed the formation of a company to finance the building of a fleet of steamboats. These were to carry the increased volume of trade between the Valley and the Tidewater by way of the Potomac Canal.[35]

The inhabitants of Staunton in 1787 "erected a commodious bath" to accommodate "the traders who flocked" thither, as well as to take care of the numbers who were expected to come from far and near for the benefit of the mineral waters of those parts.[36] Peter Heiskell's tavern, "at the sign of General Washington, on Horseback," would help furnish entertainment with its billiard table for this expected increase of transients.[37]

In addition to the enterprises in Winchester, Shepherdstown, and Staunton, sporadic attempts were being made to develop such villages as Crowsville, Martinsburg, and Pattonsburg. There had certainly been progress during the thirty years since the Moravian missionaries found the Valley settlers crude frontiersmen in life and manners, without even a wagon road from Staunton (then called Augusta Court House) southward.[38]

One way to determine the economic progress of the Valley in this period is to compare it with the post-Revolution Piedmont, east of the Blue Ridge.[39] It must be

---

ters, Weavers, Barbers, Combmakers, Printers, Merchants, Doctors, Clergy and Bar." Both the list and the line were undoubtedly well padded, but they indicate a busy town. See *Pennsylvania Packet* (Library, University of Pennsylvania), July 22, 1788, Winchester Correspondent; *Winchester Mercury*, July 9, 1788.

[35] Draper Manuscripts, Virginia Collection (in Wisconsin Historical Society).

[36] *Winchester Advertiser*, October, 1787, *passim*.

[37] *Ibid.*

[38] "Moravian Diaries of Travel through Virginia," ed., William J. Hinke and Charles E. Kemper in the *Virginia Magazine of History and Biography*, XII (1904), 134-153.

[39] Statistics from inventories in will books, and also tax books, which

borne in mind that, while the Piedmont settlements had begun somewhat earlier, the two sections were developing simultaneously. According to the court records and the tax data, the average value of personal property per householder in the Valley was £212 while in the Piedmont the average was £509.[40] In productive property, the Piedmont again shows an advantage. Only 24 per cent of the Valley householders had slaves, as compared with 72 per cent in the Piedmont.[41] Only 19 per cent of the Valley people had looms, while 41 per cent in the Piedmont were so provided. Only in wagons did the Valley have an advantage, but the ratio was merely 43 to 32. The wagon, of course, was a vital possession for the Valley farmer, since he could not roll his product to market in hogsheads, or float it down streams with few or no rapids, as the eastern planters could. At the same time, the Valley showed a considerable increase, since the pre-war period, in the percentage of persons owning both looms and wagons. Another interesting comparison of the Valley with the Piedmont can be observed in the ownership of large num-

gave data on lands as well as personal property. The Piedmont counties from which statistics have been gathered were for the most part older than the Valley counties. For comparison of the data furnished by the inventories, the records of only five Valley counties are available, hence five counties from various parts of the Piedmont have been used. In the years 1786-88 the five Valley counties furnish a total of a hundred and two inventories, and the corresponding number of Piedmont counties a total of a hundred and thirteen for the same years. This material is illustrative, of course, rather than definitive.

[40] The inventories are gleaned from the following sources: Valley County Will Books: Augusta, VI, VII; Berkeley, I; Frederick, V; Rockbridge, I; Shenandoah, B; and Piedmont and Southside County Will Books: Amelia, III, IV; Culpeper, C; Fluvanna, I; Halifax, II; Spotsylvania, E. The pre-Revolutionary average for the Valley was £132, or a little over half what it was in the later period. This, however, can be accounted for in part by the higher price scale of the post-war period.

[41] This was an increase for the Valley of 50 per cent from the earlier period which had shown only 16 per cent owning slaves. Indentured servants decreased rapidly from the outbreak of the war, when trade in them ceased.

bers of slaves. For example we find that only twenty-
three persons in the entire Valley of seven counties owned
twenty or more slaves each, while in the seven Piedmont
counties there were a hundred and sixteen owners each
with that number or more.[42]

In the size and value of the farms, the comparison con-
tinues to be of interest. The land-tax books show that the
total number of holdings was nearly the same for the
seven counties in each section. The number of holdings of
over 500 acres, however, is only 487 for the Valley as
compared with nearly 1,000 for the Piedmont.[43]

[42] This comparison is further emphasized by two facts: the white population of the seven Valley counties was 50 per cent greater than that of
the seven in Piedmont; and six of the Valley counties had a total of only
eleven slave owners with more than twenty slaves each. The Valley total
of those who owned ten slaves or more per person was twenty-seven, as
compared with three hundred and eighty-nine in the Piedmont. These
statistics are taken from the Personal Tax Books for the Valley counties
and for the Piedmont and Southside counties: Culpeper, Fluvanna, Spottsylvania, Amelia, Bedford, Halifax, and Prince Edward.

[43] The data for such a comparison coming from the land tax books
should be more dependable than other economic data. The amounts are
more likely to have been given in accurately to the tax assessors, since the
latter had a ready check on the declarations in the form of deeds, land
grants, and quitrent rolls.

SIZE OF FARMS OR HOLDINGS

Valley	Holdings	500-1,000 acres	1,000-1,500 acres	1,500-2,500 acres	2,500-4,500 acres	over 4,500 acres
Augusta	1,980	43	9	2	0	0
Berkeley	1,100	74	9	3	5	0
Botetourt	622	56	9	8	4	3
Frederick	1,085	55	16	7	1	4
Rockbridge	691	49	4	4	0	1
Rockingham	1,049	59	6	1	0	0
Shenandoah	1,008	43	7	2	2	1
Totals	7,535	379	60	27	12	9
Piedmont	Holdings					
Amelia	1,225	159	34	15	3	2
Bedford	1,165	92	15	11	3	2
Culpeper	1,750	131	18	19	9	2
Fluvanna	537	44	10	6	3	2
Halifax	1,355	129	19	18	7	3
Prince Edward	745	85	20	7	2	1
Spotsylvania	720	76	20	9	2	1
Totals	7,497	716	136	85	29	13

Further statistics from the same source give the total value of land owned by each of the freeholders listed in the tax books, whose holdings amounted to £100 or more. According to these figures, 74 per cent of the Valley freeholders paid taxes on less than £100 value of land, as compared with 68 per cent of Piedmont freeholders in like circumstances. The percentages were about the same for the two sections in the valuations from £100 to £200. These statistics further show that the total valuation of lands in the Valley was only a little more than half of that in the seven Piedmont counties. They also indicate that average price per acre of Valley land was only 75 per cent of that in the Piedmont. The average size of the Valley farm was 229 acres, as compared with the Piedmont average of 284 acres. About the same ratio holds for the acreages owned by individuals of the two sections. Only about one third of the total acreage of lands had been taken up, while more than three fourths of that in the Piedmont was in the possession of freeholders. Mountain lands in the Valley would partly, but not wholly, explain the difference.

The Valley population had grown steadily during the war and the years that followed, partly because tidewater people were moving into the area in increasing numbers. For this and other reasons there had been a large increase in the Negro or slave population. Cutting off the supply of indentured servants undoubtedly had something to do with the increase of slaves. Population was still in a large measure transient, since the movement to the West and Southwest continued almost unabated during the war as well as after. A rather interesting illustration of this is to be found in the records of the Winchester Lodge of Free Masons for 1785. These records show that there had been a pre-war membership of about twenty-five. Of that number seven were present, six had been killed or died of wounds during the war while fighting the British or the Indians, one had died from natural causes, one had "gone to Ireland," and ten had moved to the West or Southwest.[44]

Winchester set the pace in educational as well as in economic development. The first Valley newspaper, *The Virginia Gazette*, or *Winchester Advertiser*, began to be published in that town in July, 1787. Extant copies show that, with its four pages devoted largely to politics, foreign news, and advertisements, it was nearly up to the standard of the time. Its motto is characteristic of the era: "Here TRUTH unlicensed reigns and dares accost e'en KINGS themselves or RULERS of the FREE!"[45] This journal was one of a "chain" of newspapers published by printers, who also had presses at York (town), Pennsylvania, and Frederick (town), Maryland.[46] These printers offered "the services of their rider" to those who wished to send mail to an enumerated list of places in Maryland and Virginia, including Valley towns as far south as Lexington, and parts of the Trans-Alleghany.[47] The places noted were probably subscription boundaries for the Winchester newspaper. In 1788 the printers of this first Winchester paper planned to establish a bi-weekly edition, and also to publish a newspaper in Staunton, but for the time being their plans failed to materialize.[48] Meanwhile, in April, 1788, a rival paper, *The Virginia Centinel* or *Winchester Mercury*, started in Winchester, with the characteristic and prophetic motto, *"Patria Cara, Carior Libertas."*[49] The extent of the circulation of these newspapers

[44] Minutes, Winchester Lodge, February 2, 1785, preserved in Minutes, Grand Lodge of Pennsylvania. The Lodge had been inactive during the war but was now being revived.
[45] *Virginia Gazette* or *Winchester Advertiser*. See Bibliography.
[46] *Ibid.*, January 4, 1788.
[47] *Ibid.*
[48] *Ibid.*, January 18, 1788.
[49] *Virginia Centinel* or *Winchester Mercury*. See Bibliography. Cf. Cal-

cannot be determined, other than in the offer of mail delivery noted above. Colonel William Fleming of Botetourt complained in February, 1788, that he had not seen the "public prints" for a long time.[50]

The grammar schools and academies, which were started in the various parts of the Valley not long after settlement, made progress in the post-Revolutionary period. Definite records of only three of these academies are available, and of the three only one, Liberty Hall Academy in the south Valley, is important. Through the aid of funds collected from as far away as New England[51] by its principal, William Graham, this Academy was rejuvenated in 1782, and soon afterward was incorporated by the Virginia Legislature.[52] Liberty Hall Academy became Washington Academy in 1798, Washington College in 1813 and Washington and Lee University in 1870. In 1788 John Carr proposed establishing a scientific school on the Potomac, which would instruct in surveying and navigation.[53]

Living conditions lacked many refinements. To General Washington in 1784 prosperous Berkeley County was still a "remote" country and "much out of the post road.[54] A few years later Bishop William Meade's family moved from the Tidewater to the vicinity of Winchester in Frederick County. This country, the Bishop tells us, was "then the backwoods of Virginia" and backward in manner of

houn's famous toast. A free translation is "One's country is dear, but liberty is dearer!"

[50] Draper Manuscripts, no. 5zz85.

[51] Minutes, Hanover Presbytery, 1776; Records of Washington and Lee University, I, nos. 2, 5, 15, 24.

[52] Journal, House of Delegates, December 18, 1782.

[53] Winchester Advertiser, February 12, 1788. Young men who went to college during these years usually attended William and Mary, Hampden-Sydney, or the College of New Jersey. The last two were Presbyterian institutions and thus appealed to the Valley dissenters.

[54] George Washington, Writings of George Washington, Sparks, ed., IX, 40.

life, which he saw exemplified in the four-horse wagons that the people used for conveyances. These wagons were "very different from the Vehicles" to which he was accustomed "in lower Virginia."[55] In 1789 James McHenry found Staunton a promising village, but he assured his correspondent that he would not like to make his home there, because of the frontier crudeness of the place.[56]

Foreign travelers to America, who were in the Valley during the period 1780-1796, corroborate these accounts. In 1786 Count Castiglione visited Staunton and Winchester, and his carriage, which had borne him safely through the Piedmont and across the Blue Ridge Mountains, found the going so rough on "the Great Road" between these two principal Valley towns, that it "broke into a hundred pieces and at the first smithy I determined to abandon the vehicle and proceed on horseback."[57] The Marquis de Chastellux, who was in the southern portion of the Valley a few years earlier, found no villages worthy of mention, but plain frontier homes, poor accommodations for travelers, trails instead of roads, no ferries, and nothing to admire except the Natural Bridge.[58]

In 1791 Captain Bayard visited the north Valley around Winchester; in 1796 Isaac Weld traversed the whole Valley; and in the same year the Duke de La Rochefoucauld-Liancourt[59] made the trip from Staunton to Winchester. Each described a rapid growth that had

[55] Bishop William Meade, *Old Churches, Ministers and Families of Virginia*, I, 19.
[56] Steiner, *op. cit.*, p. 118, letter from James McHenry to his wife, dated Staunton, July 17, 1789.
[57] *Travels in Virginia in Revolutionary Times*, ed., Alfred J. Morrison, pp. 61-69.
[58] Marquis de Chastellux, *Travels in America in the Years 1780, 1781, 1782* (Dublin, 1787), II, 71-110.
[59] Morrison, ed., *op. cit.*, pp. 81-122; Isaac Weld, *Travels through the States of North America . . . 1795, 1796, 1797* (London, 1799, 1807), *passim*; Duke de la Rochefoucauld-Liancourt, *Travels Through the United States of North America* (London, 1800), pp. 87-120.

taken place a few years previous to his travels, or was still in progress, but all had the impression that the region, with the exception of Winchester, was in a pioneer state.

These travel tales lead us usually through the Tidewater and the Piedmont or Southside, and then into the Valley. As the trip extends westward, more marked frontier conditions appear. To be sure, these descriptions must be taken as superficial observations of men passing through the country more or less hurriedly. But in their accounts of the Valley as the frontier or backwoods of Virginia they are supported to some extent by extant records of the counties of the Valley and Piedmont. Turning to the two sets of inventories already discussed in connection with the Valley's economic status, we find some enlightening, though to be sure uncertain, data on the relative cultural development of the two sections. For instance, only 44 per cent of the Valley homes had books, as compared with 63 per cent in the Piedmont. Likewise, in the matter of silver plate, the percentage was only four in the Valley to ten in the Piedmont. Unusual furniture, that is, furniture beyond the necessary beds, chairs and tables, was to be found in only thirty-four out of every hundred Valley homes, at a time when seventy-six out of every hundred Piedmont or Southside homes had such furniture.[60]

In the last years of the eighteenth century the possession of a carriage in the form of a chair,[61] a coach, a phae-

[60] In 39 per cent of the Valley inventories the appraisers had listed articles of wearing apparel. Such listing was very seldom done in the other sections. In the Valley lists, too, are to be found such phrases as "I silver sleeve button, 1 brass, ditto"; "a half dusan puter plaits"; "1 cross cut saw and 1 library of books" (as a single item with a value for the whole); "1 Bair skin and Tomahawk"; 1 Neagor named harry is of no value." Valley Will Books, 1785-1788, passim. This material is indicative only, of course, and cannot be regarded as an accurate picture of conditions.

[61] Early term for a simple two-wheeler.

ton, or a chaise, may be deemed a mark of luxury or of cultural superiority. The Valley had less than a score of these, as compared with a hundred and more in the Piedmont.[62] Thus, in the matter of riding, as the gentry were supposed to ride in some degree of style and luxury, the Piedmont and Southside peoples were several times better off than those of the Valley.

In spite of its backwardness as compared with the Piedmont across the Blue Ridge, the Valley was in no sense in a decline. It had suffered heavily in man power as well as in relative wealth during the war. Post-war tax and debtor troubles, along with a breakdown in the markets for its products, had exacted a considerable toll from the Valley's wealth-getting. The section was not prostrate, however, and in many cases it was already reviving.[63] This fact is nowhere better attested than in the interest in trade and in trade routes.

The Valley religious groups had prospered, despite any ill effects of post-war laxity. In 1786, at Timber Ridge, the Presbyterian churches of the section were formed into the Presbytery of Lexington.[64] They had grown strong enough to become themselves a parent body for churches in the new groups of settlements pushing into the Trans-Alleghany country, including Kentucky. Two years later representatives from all the Virginia Presbyterian churches came together in a large Valley church, New Providence, and were organized as the Synod of Virginia,[65] which placed them on a par with their brethren in Pennsylvania and New York as members of the new General Assembly of the Presbyterian Church in the United States. This

<hr/>

[62] See Personal Tax Books, Valley and Piedmont, 1783-1789, *passim*. Vehicles were assessed at so much per wheel.

[63] Cf. *ante*, Chapter VII.

[64] Minutes, Hanover Presbytery, 1785; Minutes, Lexington Presbytery, 1786.

[65] Minutes, Synod of Virginia (1788).

body had been organized almost simultaneously with the Philadelphia Convention of 1787 which drafted the Constitution of the United States.[66] The Anglicans were likewise gaining strength from the influx of Tidewater settlers. The Baptists were centering their efforts in the Southwest and in Kentucky where they were becoming strong.[67]

The Winchester Masonic Lodge was revived, with the leading citizens of the town in its membership.[68] In Staunton a similar lodge was started, which also appealed to the leaders of the town and county and was soon possessed of a substantial hall.[69] Philosophical or debating societies began to be formed, and several communities found more exalted interests than the humdrum of trading and making a living.[70]

There were still numerous marks of the frontier on most of the Valley counties in 1789, and the section was a generation or two from the ease and comforts of a well-established economy. Nevertheless, amazing progress had been made in the half century since John Caldwell had persuaded Governor Gooch that German and Scottish dissenters, even though they might "contaminate" his colony, were to be tolerated, if they would stay behind the mountains and keep back the red men, while they were getting a much better living than the Old World had ever furnished them.

[66] Minutes, General Assembly, May, 1787.
[67] See Asplund, *Register*, for the strength of the Baptists. They had about the same churches and membership in the Valley as in the pre-war period.
[68] Minutes, Winchester Lodge, February 2, 1785.
[69] Minutes, Staunton Lodge, 1785-1786, *passim*.
[70] Washington and Lee Records, 1783-1789, *passim*; *Winchester Advertiser*, 1787-1788, *passim*.

A New National Government

A NEW national government was in several ways a fitting culmination for the quarter-century of armed and economic conflict that had been the lot of the Valley pioneers. Soon after the Treaty of Peace was published, sentiment favorable to a reorganization of the federal government gathered strength in the Valley. The demand for reform became insistent before the Philadelphia Convention met. General Gates was not speaking entirely for himself when he wrote Washington in January, 1787, that anarchy must ensue if the Philadelphia Convention failed to work out a reform in the government of the Union. Gates wrote Madison on November 26, 1787, that the new government must be speedily adopted or "all must go to Ruin, and Anarchy, and Misrule, blast every Hope that so glorious a Revolution entitled us to expect."[1] Colonel William Fleming likewise spoke for his section and not for himself alone, when he wrote Jefferson in May, 1787, that "expectations are formed that this convention (Philadelphia) will lay a foundation for energy and stability in our Federal government, and for rendering us, as a na-

[1] Gates Papers; Madison Papers (Library of Congress), XV, 34.

tion, more respected abroad."[2] While the Philadelphia
Convention was in session, the same sentiment was voiced
indirectly in the central Valley by an assemblage of representatives of the Presbyterian church.[3]

At the same time, two groups, who were engaged in a
trade controversy in a Winchester newspaper, were agreed
on the one point, that a new Constitution would probably
furnish the best solution of the problem they were trying
to solve.[4] Four days after the Philadelphia Convention
adjourned, the same newspaper carried the statement:
"The impatience with which all classes of people wait to
receive the new federal constitution can only be equalled
by their zealous determination to support it."[5] A week
later a copy of the Constitution had reached Winchester
and the entire issue of the newspaper, except two of its
sixteen columns, was given over to the new plan.[6] Even
the advertisements were omitted, with a lone exception.
The printers excused themselves with the simple statement that the importance of getting the new document
before the people made unnecessary any apology for the
omission of all other matter.

Meanwhile, Berkeley County lost no time in its eager-
ness to show enthusiasm for the new Constitution. At a
mass meeting held on September 28, it was unanimously
resolved:

1st, that it is the opinion of the gentlemen now met, that the
United States are under the greatest obligation to the members of the late memorable Convention, for their assiduity
and perseverance in accomplishing a plan of federal government.

[2] Jefferson Papers (Library of Congress), William Fleming to Jefferson,
May, 1787.
[3] Minutes, Lexington Presbytery, August, 1787; *Journal, House of Delegates*, October, 1787. The Convention was spoken of as a "momentous
meeting" by the presbyters.
[4] *Winchester Advertiser*, August-September, 1787.
[5] *Ibid.*, September 21, 1787.   [6] *Ibid.*, September 28, 1787.

2nd, that two of the gentlemen now present do wait upon the clergymen of this county, of all persuasion, and request them to prepare a sermon, to be preached at their different places of worship, on a sabbath that they shall think proper to appoint, to return thanks in an especial manner, to Almighty God, for inspiring the members of the late Convention with wisdom, amity, and unanimity, to form a federal government with so great judgment and sound policy, under so many and various interests.

3rd, that it is the opinion of the meeting, that every friend of America ought, and will contribute all in his power, to establish and support the federal government proposed by the late Convention as it appears sufficient and well adapted to secure peace, liberty and safety to the citizens of the United States.[7]

The people of Winchester and Frederick County were not far behind in a similar action. Three issues of the *Winchester Advertiser* carried a notice summoning the first and second regiments of the Frederick County militia to a muster on October 22, at which time the freeholders passed a set of resolutions, which were "unanimously agreed to after mature deliberations."[8]

The resolutions emphasized not only the collapse of the powers of the Confederation but also the disregard of the several states for even the necessary recommendations made by Congress and their failure to comply with the "solemn compacts" entered into by that body, from which there had resulted a "breach of faith both with respect to foreign nations and our own citizens." A "direful state of anarchy and confusion" would have followed, according to these Frederick Resolves, if such a remedy as the new Constitution had not been found.

[7] *Ibid.*, October 12, 1787; *Maryland Chronicle* (Frederick), November 14, 1787.
[8] *Winchester Advertiser*, October 26, 1787; *Maryland Chronicle* (Frederick), November 7, 1787.

The concluding resolution stated that a "noble effort
has been made to reform, and an excellent plan proposed
for our acceptance." The question was not whether the
plan was perfect but whether it was an improvement over
the existing system. The main consideration was that it
secured both national independence and individual rights.[9]
Accordingly, the Frederick voters appealed to their representatives in the state legislature, not only to use every
effort toward providing for the earliest possible ratifying
convention but also to exert the "utmost influence in opposition to those (if any such there are) who may attempt
to frustrate a measure on which our peace, liberty, and
safety so essentially depend."

The Winchester newspaper made every effort to place
both sides of the question before the people of the north
Valley. The same issue which carried the Frederick Resolutions carried also a bitter attack on the Constitution from
a Philadelphia correspondent in which the writer enumerated the "blessings" that would accrue from the establishment of the new government—the abolition of the
liberty of the press, a standing army and Prussian militia,
no annual elections, fivefold taxes, excise laws and cus-
toms officers, a tax on the slave trade, general search warrants, a supreme court to which the rich could drag the
poor, and so on.[10] A week later the *Advertiser* began the
printing of the objections of "Centinel" to the new Constitution, and offered as an explanation that, "however
just or futile this writer's arguments may be, it is not our
business to determine; we present the following extract of
the most material passages to our readers that they may
judge of his merits themselves."[11]

In November, 1787, the prospects for adoption in the
south Valley seemed gloomy for a time, when it was

---

[9] *Winchester Advertiser*, October 26, 1787.
[10] *Ibid.*, October 26, 1787.   [11] *Ibid.*, November 2, 1787.

learned that William Graham, a prominent Presbyterian leader, had aligned himself with Patrick Henry and was trying to rally an anti-federalist party there. He even wrote Zachariah Johnston, who proved to be the outstanding federalist of the south and central Valley, suggesting that they get together on ways and means of opposing the Constitution.[12] Graham was the only Presbyterian leader of consequence among the anti-federalists. The irony of the situation was further accentuated by his proposal that Johnston associate himself with two other ardent federalists, one of whom was William McKee, opponent of Graham in the ensuing election of delegates to the Convention. Graham's plans for opposing the Constitution were to prove "it is inadequate to the end proposed." More cheerful news was coming to the federalists from Berkeley County, however, since we find one of General Gates' correspondents writing him, "We are glad you are so unanimous for the new government."[13]

The Winchester newspaper continued to give space to both sides of the discussion, and during November printed the objections of Richard Henry Lee and George Mason. An editorial defended the Constitution, giving as its reason, "The house divided against itself cannot stand," and in a later issue insisted that this was the last chance to adopt a government which gave protection to personal liberty and at the same time furnished all the advantages of a "sovereign empire." A mass meeting was called for Winchester, that the people might have a chance to learn more about the Constitution. There the enemies of the new plan were to state their objections and its friends would answer them.[14]

[12] Johnston Papers, Graham to Johnston, November 3, 1787.
[13] Gates Papers, no. 238, Carson to Gates, November 8, 1787.
[14] *Winchester Advertiser*, January 18, 1788. The typical frontier notice for the meeting was "Americans Attend! The fate of an empire may depend on the vote of a day!"

Alexander White, the dominant north Valley federalist, prepared the most comprehensive and forceful pre-Convention defense of the Constitution by a Valley leader, one indeed that ranks with the ablest in the state. It was published in the Winchester newspaper contemporaneously with "the Dissent of the Pennsylvania Minority."[15] White was answering the objections of the Pennsylvania minority as well as those of "Centinel"[16] and Richard Henry Lee. He was given the lion's share of the space in the *Advertiser* during January and February, 1788, his defense usually averaging one full page or more of the total four pages. When choice had to be made between White's defense and the objections of the Pennsylvania minority, the printers gave preference to White, especially as the elections drew near.[17] The anti-federalists attempted no reply to White, except for an anonymous personal attack, to which White made a vigorous reply.[18] One insinuation was that White expected an appointment to the federal bench. In his reply White charged one of the opposing anti-federalist candidates with having been responsible for the attack, in spite of his promise to keep personalities out of the campaign.

In Botetourt County William Fleming, a leading federalist, successfully stopped a rumor that he was against the Constitution.[19] In Rockbridge Graham's anti-federalist party did not gain many adherents. From Berkeley

[15] This was a statement or pamphlet, issued by those who had opposed the new Constitution in Pennsylvania. Many of the Scots in that state had been among the opponents, although many of them likewise had been supporters of the new plan. The situation in Pennsylvania was in a number of ways different from that in the Valley of Virginia, especially in state politics.

[16] Presumably a Pennsylvania anti-federalist.

[17] *Winchester Advertiser*, February 29, 1788. Several advertisements and local items were also omitted to make room for White's defense.

[18] *Ibid.*, February 15, 1788.

[19] Draper Manuscripts, no. 5zz85, Fleming to Thomas Madison, February 14, 1788.

it was reported that "federalist principles are so prevalent
. . . that all opposition has subsided,"[20] and it was expected that the "two veterans" would be elected without a
dissenting vote.[21] On the eve of the election, then, the
Valley federalists had every reason to be confident.

The election took place during the March court days of
the various counties. Results ranged from the approxi-
mate unanimity of such counties as Berkeley and Rockingham to the intense partisanship of Frederick and, in some
degree, Rockbridge. The federalists won in every county,
and secured a solid delegation with fourteen votes. John
Shearman Woodcock of Frederick reaped the benefit of
Alexander White's arguments, without suffering from any
of the calumny that was heaped on White, and led the
field by thirty votes. Both he and White had safe majorities over their anti-federalist opponents Colonel John
Smith and Colonel Charles Mynn Thruston.[22] Colonel
Thruston, who had failed but once in a number of years
to be elected to the House of Delegates, received the lowest vote, only about twenty-five per cent of the total.[23]
He never again represented Frederick in any capacity and
later joined the westward movement. In Rockbridge the
two federalist members of the legislature, Andrew Moore
and William McKee, were elected by safe majorities over
two anti-federalists,[24] William Graham, Rector or Principal of Liberty Hall Academy, and Major John Hayes,

[20] *Winchester Advertiser*, February 22, 1788.

[21] *Ibid.* The March 11 issue reported that the "two veterans" had been
elected without opposition. Generals Gates and Stephen were the two veterans usually mentioned, but another veteran, Colonel William Darke,
served in place of Gates, for some reason.

[22] *Ibid.*, March 7, 1788.

[23] *Ibid.*, March 7, 1788.

[24] It has been stated that the Rockbridge delegates were instructed to
oppose ratification. See for the correct and contemporary status of these
delegates *Winchester Advertiser*, April 9, 1788; David Henley to Samuel
Henley, April 28, 1788 (letter in Library of Congress); Madison to
Jefferson, April 22, 1788.

known only because of an excellent Revolutionary War record.[25]

The results of the election brought general rejoicing. In a short editorial the printers of the *Winchester Advertiser* expressed their pleasure over the unanimity in Berkeley and the success of the federalists elsewhere. They laid stress on a comparison of the Valley with the western frontier districts of Massachusetts, where the Shaysites were violently opposed to federalist measures.[26] They sensed the feeling that the people of the Valley, also, since they lived in a western or frontier district of Virginia, were expected to be violently opposed to the Constitution. The failure of the people there to do what was expected of them made the result the more agreeable.

Most of the Valley federalists were Ulster Scots and thus Presbyterian dissenters. A few were college men but the majority had limited education. Among them various interests and professions were represented, chiefly the law, but all were farmers, and most of them small farmers. Ten were veterans of the colonial wars or the War for Independence, in which they had served with distinction. Their economic interests centered in founding new towns, in the trusteeships of estates, and in western lands. Like their neighbors all had felt keenly the economic stress of the post-war period and had spent much time in court, suing and being sued for debts. Some of these federalists

---

[25] *Washington and Lee Historical Papers*, II, 29; Stephen Papers; Breckinridge Papers, Stuart to Breckinridge, March 7, 1788. Stuart was much worried lest Graham's sounding the "Bell of Sedition" would win him a seat. The Valley was to be represented in the Convention by the following:
Augusta: Zachariah Johnston and Archibald Stuart.
Berkeley: William Darke and Adam Stephen.
Botetourt: William Fleming and Martin McFerran.
Frederick: Alexander White and John Shearman Woodcock.
Rockbridge: William McKee and Andrew Moore.
Rockingham: Gabriel Jones and Thomas Lewis.
Shenandoah: Jacob Rinker and John Williams.
[26] *Winchester Advertiser*, February 22, 1788.

were large landowners whose unpretentious homesteads sometimes bore pretentious names. The rest had small estates, few or no slaves, and meager furnishings in homes that showed the frontier simplicity of life.

With a single exception, every member of the Valley delegation had been active in local or state politics. Most of them were, or had been, justices of the county courts. They had held or were holding such local civic offices as state's (formerly King's) attorney, clerk of the county court, sheriff, surveyor, and escheator. Eleven had served one or more terms in the state Assembly, two had been land or boundary commissioners. Jones had been elected a judge of the newly created system of general or district courts, but he had declined to serve.[27]

The political prestige and interests of these Valley members prior to 1788 can be partially determined by their activities in the state Assembly. With the possible exception of White, no Valley member received any notable recognition in the organization of the Assembly until 1785. In that session Johnston was made chairman of the Committee on Religion, which always came first on the list of committees during the period.[28] From this time Johnston and White were prominent in committee appointments, and we find increasing recognition for such younger Valley delegates as Moore and Stuart. There was something of added prestige for Johnston and Stuart, especially, in their close association and warm personal friendships with such dominant state leaders as Jefferson, and particularly Madison.

[27] Minute, Order, and Will Books, Valley Counties, 1745-1788; Swem and Williams, op. cit., passim; Augusta County Order Book, XVII, 326; Journal, House of Delegates, January 4, 1788; Fleming's service as acting governor has been noted. See Chapter VI.

[28] Journal, House of Burgesses, October 25, 1785 to January 16, 1787. This committee was particularly important during the 1785 session because of the contest over several phases of the problem of religious liberty.

Nearly all the Valley members of the ratifying Convention had participated in the sessions of the state Assembly that had struggled with such problems as taxation, debts and debtors, paper money, British debts, transportation and commerce, the state court system, and the persistent and hard-fought question of the relation of church and state. They would have liked representation reform, but the dominant eastern element refused a real hearing of the matter. On most of the acts and resolutions in the Assembly which dealt with taxation, paper money, British debts, and religious liberty, the Valley Convention members voted unanimously on the side of the question that the new Constitution favored.

On the floor of the Convention the delegates from the Valley had minor roles. Two of them, Jones and White, were among the twenty-six members of the important Committee of Privileges and Elections.[29] Stuart championed a petition that attempted unsuccessfully to seat a Southside federalist. White spoke briefly in favor of a parliamentary maneuver designed to block or postpone the discussion of Mississippi navigation.

Only three speeches of any length or consequence were made by Valley members, and two of these were delivered by General Stephen. The first of his speeches came two days before adjournment and was little more than a personal attack on Henry and a reply to Henry's arguments on taxation and the problems of the West.[30] A second and more substantial speech by Stephen, and a longer and much abler one by Johnston, were delivered in the closing hours of the Convention. Both speakers emphasized the demand of their people for speedy ratification without

[29] Robertson, *Debates*, pp. 13, 17, 36, 261.

[30] Robertson, *Debates*, pp. 414-415. He concluded with the suggestion that, if "the gentleman does not like this government, let him go and live among the Indians."

previous amendment. The importance of Johnston's speech is in the fact that he was reckoned the spokesman for the Valley, and had been saved for this strategic time.[31] From the standpoint of previous legislative and political experience, Johnston was the dominant figure in the delegation. His only possible rival for leadership was White, whose arguments in his pre-election defense of the Constitution, in some important particulars, closely paralleled those of Johnston's Convention speech.

As the Convention drew to a close and the lines tightened on the question of amendments to the Constitution, previous or subsequent to ratification, the delegation stood solidly against previous amendments.[32] No Valley member was considered interested enough to be appointed to the committee on subsequent amendments.[33]

For a better understanding of the part played by the Valley delegation in the final vote on ratification, it is necessary to review the situation in the state as a whole. Virginia at that time included the present states of West Virginia and Kentucky. It had seven generally recognized geographic sections, nearly all of them comparing favorably in both size and population with the smaller New England states. These were in order of extension toward the west, the Tidewater, Piedmont, Southside, Valley, Trans-Alleghany, Southwest, and Kentucky. Three were east of the Valley, then, and three west of it.

The Tidewater, like the other older and urban-minded areas of the new republic, gave a good majority of forty-nine to twenty-two for ratification. The Piedmont op-

[31] *Washington and Lee Historical Papers*, II, *passim*; A. J. Beveridge, *Life of John Marshall*, I, 474.

[32] Robertson, *Debates*, pp. 467-468.

[33] *Ibid.*, p. 469. One of the proposed subsequent amendments, which tended to weaken the federal power of taxation by allowing to the states the option of the old requisition system, was opposed by all except two of the Valley delegates. Prentis, *Debates*, III, 224-225.

posed ratification by a vote of twelve to eight and the Southside by a much larger majority, twenty-eight to two. These two sections are usually reckoned to have come under the head of the small-farmer, debt-ridden, up-country areas that opposed the Constitution in the United States generally.[34] They were likewise the stronghold of Baptist dissenters who feared that the original Constitution failed to furnish a proper safeguard for religious freedom.[35] The total vote of these three sections was sixty-two to fifty-nine against ratification.

The Trans-Alleghany, settled largely from the Valley and closely allied with it in trade and politics, voted thirteen to one for ratification. Prior to and during the War for Independence the Southwest had been filling up with Valley settlers, who, after the war had ended, moved on to Kentucky and Tennessee; their places were taken by people from Southside Virginia, who were largely Baptist dissenters.[36] The Southwest cast its six votes unanimously against ratification. Kentucky's fears that the new government would barter away the free navigation of the Mississippi River are usually given as the reason for the ten to three vote against ratification here. The total vote of these three sections were seventeen to sixteen against ratification.

The six sections of the state, other than the Valley, then, opposed ratification by a vote of seventy-nine to seventy-five. Moreover, the five up-country sections that were either frontier or semi-frontier in their economic and political outlook objected to the new Constitution fifty-seven to twenty-six. A mere majority of votes from the sixth semi-frontier section, the Valley, would not have

[34] See Libby, *Distribution of Vote on the Federal Constitution, passim.*
[35] The Virginia Baptist Association in March, 1788, voted this unanimously. See Semple, *History of the Baptists in Virginia,* p. 102.
[36] Johnston, *Middle New River Settlements,* pp. 84-86; Asplund, *Register of Baptists,* pp. 29-31.

been enough. It was necessary that it cast nearly all of its votes for ratification if the new government was to have the support of Virginia.

It is, then, of considerable importance that the Valley did cast its entire block of fourteen votes among the eighty-nine for ratification. From the speeches of the Valley members of the Convention, and from their legislative records and writings prior to ratification, several interests stand out. These may be reckoned as motives and may furnish reasons for this unanimity for the new Constitution. Among these were: taxation and its counterpart, inequality in representation; the debt problem and its paper-money panacea; the payment of British debts; the development of transportation routes; and religious liberty, or the separation of church and state. As preceding chapters have attempted to explain the attitude of the Valley people on each of these questions, it is unnecessary to do more here than show the possible relation of these questions to their unanimity for the Constitution.

In the matter of taxation and representation Zachariah Johnston in his Convention speech said:

As to the principle of representation, I find it attended to in this government in the fullest manner. It is founded on absolute equality. . . . As to the mode of taxation, the proportion of each state being known, cannot be exceeded. And such proportion will be raised in the most equitable manner of the people, according to their ability. There is nothing to warrant a supposition that the poor will be equally taxed with the wealthy and opulent.

He then proceeded to show by examples the weakness of the state government in its handling of both representation and taxation.[37] Reading over, in the light of

[37] Robertson, *Debates*, pp. 461-462. "I shall make a comparison to illustrate my observations between the state and general government. In our state government, so much admired by the gentleman over the way

Johnston's speech, the pages in a preceding chapter dealing with the Valley's problem of taxation and representation, one would gather that Johnston and his neighbors expected to find at least a partial solution in the new Constitution, in that it set the example of equal representation.[38]

As already noted, the people of the Valley were having as great difficulties with their burden of private debt as many other sections of the country.[39] Yet, contrary to other debtor areas, they not only refused to accept paper money as a remedy but opposed it vehemently in the state legislature. Therefore, when the Constitution offered a permanent prohibition of state issues of paper money they could be expected to give it their support.

With the same ardor that they had shown in their fight against paper money, the Valley pioneers had insisted on the payment of debts due British merchants, arguing that private integrity and national honor were at stake. They

---

(Henry), though there are 1700 militia in some counties and but 150 in others, yet every county sends two members to assist in legislating for the whole community. There is this disproportion between the respectable county of Augusta, which I have the honor to represent, and the circumscribed narrow county of Warwick. Will any gentleman tell us that this is more equal representation than is fixed in the Constitution, whereby 30,000 are to send one representative, in whatever place they may reside? By the same state system, the poor, in many instances, pay as much as the rich. Many laws occur to my mind, where I could show you, that the representation and taxation bears hard on those who live in large remote back counties. The mode of taxation is more oppressive to us than to the rest of the community. Last fall when the principle of taxation was debated, it was determined that tobacco should be received in discharge of taxes, but this did not relieve us, for it would not fetch what it cost us, as the distance is so great, and the carriage is so difficult.—Other specific articles were not received in payment of taxes. so that we had no other alternative than to pay specie, which was a peculiar hardship. I could point out many other disadvantages which we labor under, but I shall not fatigue the house."

[38] Cf. *ante*, Chapter VII. A republican form of government for each state might well be interpreted to mean equal representation after the manner of the federal government.

[39] *Ibid.*

had felt also that England would not surrender the Northwest posts until the United States was willing to carry out that part of the treaty of peace which provided for the payment of these debts. As long as England held the posts, they believed the Indians would be restless, the settlement of the West retarded, and land values continue at a standstill. The Constitution provided that treaties should be part of the supreme law of the land, thereby superseding any state law to the contrary. Ratification of the Constitution, then, would uphold the Valley's insistence on paying the debts.

One of the greatest trade problems of the section during this period was the matter of routes to the seaboard and to the "Western Waters." A water route that gave promise was the Potomac River, which might be made navigable nearly to the Ohio country by means of a canal system. However, interstate duties and consequent interstate rivalries and jealousies seemed to block its successful completion. The Constitution forbade interstate duties.

Valley dissenters believed that religion, or a man's relation with his God, was not a matter for legislation in any form. When the objection was raised that the omission of religious liberty from the new Constitution was dangerous for dissenters, the Valley leaders joined with the Witherspoon-trained Madison in denying that such was the case. In one of his Convention speeches Madison said of religion, "This subject is, for the honor of America, perfectly free and unshackled. The government has no jurisdiction over it. . . ."[40]

[40] Robertson, *Debates*, p. 75. A little later Madison wrote to Jefferson: "Experience proves the inefficacy of a bill of rights on those occasions when its control is most needed. Repeated violations of these parchment barriers have been committed by over-bearing majorities in every state. In Virginia I have seen the bill of rights violated in every instance where it has been opposed to a popular current. Notwithstanding the explicit provision contained in that instrument for the rights of Conscience, it is

Alexander White, in his defense of the Constitution printed in the Winchester newspapers, took the position that "There are other things so clearly out of the power of Congress that the bare recital of them is sufficient. I mean the rights of conscience or religious liberty." Such things as the demand for a bill of rights, he wrote, "seem to have been inserted among their objections merely to induce the ignorant to believe that Congress would have power over such objects and to infer from their being refused a place in the Constitution, their intention to exercise that power to the oppression of the people."[41] In free governments, such as America was establishing, bills of rights had no place, according to White in his concluding arguments just prior to the election, and, even under a monarch, such a statement of rights was "rather calculated to inform than to restrain. Paper chains are too feeble to bind the hands of tyranny or ambition." If under the Constitution "Congress attempts to exercise any powers which are not expressly delegated to them their acts would be considered void and disregarded. In America it is the governors and not the governed that must produce their bill of rights."[42]

It was left to Zachariah Johnston to defend this Valley ideal of religious liberty on the floor of the Convention. Johnston was Madison's second in command in the Assembly when the Virginia statute for religious liberty was passed. The fact that he was chairman of the all-impor-

---

well known that a religious establishment would have taken place in that state if the Legislative majority had found as they expected, a majority of the people in favor of the measure." Madison, *op. cit.*, V, 272, to Jefferson, October 17, 1788.

[41] *Winchester Advertiser*, February 22, 1788. He even argued that any single field of natural rights which was thrown open to legislation, in the very act of being thus thrown open, tended to "a swallowing up" of all natural rights. Therefore legislation must avoid any tendency whatever to invade those fields.

[42] *Ibid.*, February 29, 1788.

tant Committee on Religion in the 1785-1786 Assembly indicates his prestige in such matters. In addition, he was a typical Scotch Presbyterian of the uncompromising sort.[43] As spokesman for the Valley delegation, he replied vigorously to Henry's charge that the Constitution was a menace to religious liberty and this reply came at the strategic time, when the Convention was within a few hours of its decisive vote:

We are also told that religion is not secured—that religious tests are not required—You will find that the exclusion of tests will strongly tend to establish a religious freedom. If tests were required—if the church of England or any other were established, I might be excluded from any office under the government, because my conscience might not permit me to take the test required. The diversity of opinions and the variety of sects in the United States, have justly been reckoned a great security with respect to religious liberty. The difficulty of establishing an uniformity of religion in this country is immense—the extent of the country is very great. The multiplicity of sects is very great likewise. The people are not to be disarmed of their weapons—they are left in full possession of them. The government is administered by the representatives of the people voluntarily and freely chosen. Under these circumstances, should any one attempt to establish their own system, in prejudice of the rest, they would be universally detested and opposed, and easily frustrated . This is the principle which secures religious liberty most firmly.[44]

Thus without the erudition and without the grasp of political theory of Madison and White, but with a practical application understood by his own people in the Valley, Johnston stated for this group of dissenters why they preferred the Constitution and why they did not regard it as a menace to religious liberty.[45]

[43] See Archibald Alexander, "Zachariah Johnston," in the *Princeton Magazine*, I, 367-369, for a character sketch of Johnston.
[44] Robertson, *Debates*, p. 461.
[45] It is an interesting and significant fact that Presbyterian or Valley

It does not matter, then, whether this theory of religious liberty was sound; it does not matter to what extent it was original, but it is of considerable importance whether it appealed to the people of the Valley. To a marked degree it undoubtedly did. Certainly it appealed to the leaders of the section in the Convention, and they probably voiced public opinion not only on this issue but on the several others that created sentiment for ratification. It seems reasonable to conclude, then, that since religious freedom was an all-important factor in the period of the Confederation, these particular dissenters voted for the ratification of the Constitution largely because it measured up to their own theory of religious liberty or of the right relation of church and state.

Rejoicing over ratification was nearly universal in the Valley, according to the newspapers of the day. Winchester and Staunton vied with the most enthusiastic of the seaboard towns in the extent and nature of their celebrations. When the news reached Winchester a few days after ratification, there was a spontaneous outburst of enthusiasm, followed by a bonfire on Federal Hill and a banquet, with numerous toasts to the United States, the friends of the Constitution, the majority of the Virginia Convention, the spirit of manufacture and trade, peace and prosperity, and so on.[46] The newspapers reported that "Joy shone conspicuously on the countenances of all ranks and the greatest hilarity and good humor prevailed."[47] A week later Winchester had an elaborate parade, in which all the trades and professions were represented.[48]

There was a similar celebration in Staunton, with a

petitions pertaining to religion ceased entirely after ratification. See *Journal, House of Delegates*, 1788-1790, *passim*.

[46] *Winchester Mercury*, July 2, 1788; *Pennsylvania Packet* (Philadelphia), July 15, 1788.

[47] *Ibid.*

[48] *Ibid.*, July 9, 1788.

bonfire and "military evolutions," at which "the inhabitants of the town and many about gathered."[49] The Masonic Hall and the houses were "illuminated" and a "joy-
ful spirit of republicanism regardless of distinction," along
with the "utmost harmony" was the order of the day.[50]
One of the principal streets of the town was renamed
Federal Street. This enthusiasm was echoed at the polls
a few months later when all the members of the Convention of 1788 who could be prevailed upon to become candidates were elected to prominent state and federal offices.

Thus, from the time of the publication of the Constitution, the majority of the Valley people wanted its ratification without amendment. They continued in the same
mind in their election of delegates to the Convention, in
the Convention period, and even in the elections of state
and federal offices that followed ratification. Whatever
there was of opposition was defeated at the polls in
March, 1788, and any attempt of the anti-federalists to
change public opinion after that date proved futile.

The lot of these Ulster Scot and German pioneers had
not been happy in the Old World, and their life in the
new had been one beset with trials and dangers. Because
of this, or in spite of it, most of them, in their lives and
in their ideals, exemplified the influence of Calvinistic theology, which perchance developed for them an intangible
conscience motivation. Although this factor was varied
among them in its manifestations,[51] it is perhaps too little
appreciated as a motivating force in their history. They

[49] *Virginia Chronicle* (Richmond), July 12, 1788.
[50] *Ibid.*
[51] Many of the Scots in Pennsylvania had opposed ratification, but conditions there in many cases were different, and the cross currents of local
or state politics played an important part. Then, too, there was strong
support for the Constitution in that state as exemplified in the leadership
of James Wilson. It may be noted also that their Dickinson College was
a stronghold of federalism, as indicated by its commencement program of
1788.

seem to have derived from it not only their emphasis on religion and their interest in the advantages of education but likewise their insistence on the reward due individual effort. All of these factors caused them to see the importance of a stable government. Thus there was for them, at this the end of an important era, a happy conclusion in a government that promised "to form a more perfect Union, establish Justice, insure domestic Tranquillity, provide for the common defense, promote the general Welfare, and secure the Blessings of liberty to ourselves and our Posterity."

Bibliography

I. MANUSCRIPTS

A. Collected Papers

These are the collections, of Valley leaders and others, that have data dealing with the Valley. They are to be found for the most part in public libraries and historical societies, but some of them are in private hands and not readily accessible. Frequently the private collections, and sometimes those in the possession of libraries and societies, are not arranged in any sort of order.

Allason Papers. Include the correspondence, letter books, ledgers, day books, and journals of William Allason, a Scotch merchant of Falmouth, Virginia. In the Virginia State Library.

Bancroft Transcripts. The George Bancroft papers, Virginia section. In the New York Public Library.

Breckinridge Papers. Papers of John Breckinridge, 1753-1789. In Library of Congress.

Chalmers Papers. Virginia section of the papers of George Chalmers. In New York Public Library.

Cowpens Papers. Papers of General Daniel Morgan. In New York Public Library.

Dane Papers. The Papers of Nathan Dane. In Library of Congress.

Darke Papers. Correspondence and miscellaneous papers of Colonel William Darke. In the Briscoe home near Charles Town, West Virginia.

Draper Manuscripts. Virginia section of the papers of Lyman C. Draper. In the Wisconsin Historical Society Library, Madison, Wisconsin.

Dreer Collection. Papers of Ferdinand J. Dreer. Pennsylvania Historical Society, Philadelphia.

Emmet Collection. Papers of Thomas A. Emmet. In New York Public Library.

Etting Collection. Papers of Frank M. Etting. Pennsylvania Historical Society, Philadelphia.

Fleming Papers. Papers of William Fleming. In Washington and Lee University Library.

Gates Papers. Papers of Horatio Gates. New York Historical Society, New York City. Also in the New York Public Library.

Gratz Papers. Pennsylvania Historical Society, Philadelphia.

Henry Papers. Papers of Patrick Henry. In Library of Congress, William Wirt Collection.

Jefferson Papers. Papers of Thomas Jefferson. In Library of Congress.

Johnston Papers. Papers of Zachariah Johnston. In the possession of his descendants in the Zachariah Johnston home at Lexington, Virginia.

Madison Papers. Papers of James Madison. In Library of Congress.

Pemberton Family Papers. In Pennsylvania Historical Society, Philadelphia.

Preston Papers. Papers of William Preston. In the private collection of Preston Davie, New York City.

Simms Papers. Papers of Charles Simms. In Library of Congress.

Stephen Papers. Papers of Adam Stephen. In Library of Congress.

Stuart Papers. Papers of Archibald Stuart. In Virginia Historical Society.

Washington Papers. Papers of George Washington, Vols. ccxxxvii-ccxlii, 1787-1788 circ. In Library of Congress.

Wayne Papers. Papers of Anthony Wayne. Pennsylvania Historical Society, Philadelphia.

Williams Family Papers, including the Papers of Abraham Byrd. Loaned to the Virginia Historical Society by Dr. W. Twyman Williams of Hampden-Sydney, Virginia.

Witherspoon Papers. Papers of John Witherspoon. Library of Congress.

Wood Papers. Papers of James Wood. In the possession of Mrs. Katherine Glass Greene of Fort Loudon, Winchester, Virginia.

Zane Papers. Papers of Isaac Zane. Pennsylvania Historical Society, Philadelphia.

B. County Records

These records are to be found for the most part in the county courthouses of the respective counties. They are in various states of preservation and in varying degrees of accessibility, sometimes found in cellars and attics of the courthouses, piled together as rubbish. They are in the form of deeds, wills, minutes of the courts, court orders, executions of sheriffs, inventories, commissions, fees, dockets, marriage records. In counties like Augusta they are complete, but very incomplete in Rockingham and one or two others. They were used for some Piedmont counties, for purposes of comparison, as well as for all of those in the Valley. In so far as they could be found, the following records were used for each of the Valley counties:

Augusta County Court Martial Record Book, 1763-1786. In the City Clerk's Office, Staunton, Va.

Deed Books, 1763-1789.

District Court, Frederick, Will Book.

Execution Books, 1763-1789.

Marriage Record Books, 1782-1788.

Minute Books, 1763-1789.

Order Books, 1763-1789.

Will Books, 1763-1789.

C. Records of Religious Organizations

These are usually in the form of minutes of proceedings of the respective organizations, which include the list of churches and ministers:

Minutes, Donegal Presbytery, 1763-1788. In the Library of the Presbyterian Historical Society, Philadelphia.

Minutes, General Assembly of the Presbyterian Church, 1789-1793. Presbyterian Historical Society, Philadelphia.

Minutes, Hanover Presbytery, 1763-1788. In the Library of the Union Theological Seminary, Richmond.

Minutes of Lexington Presbytery, 1785-1788. In the Library of the Union Theological Seminary, Richmond.

Minutes, Linville (Smith) Creek (Rockingham County) Baptist Church, 1757-1775. In Baptist Historical Society, University of Richmond.

Minutes, Lutheran Ministerium of Pennsylvania, 1784-1793. In the Library of the Lutheran Theological Seminary at Mount Airy, or Germantown, Pa.

Minutes, Mill Creek (Berkeley County) Baptist Church, 1761-1789. Transcript in Baptist Historical Society, University of Richmond.

Minutes, Smith Creek (Rockingham County) Baptist Church, 1779-1789. In Baptist Historical Society, University of Richmond.

Minutes, Synod of New York and Philadelphia, 1785-1788. In Library, Presbyterian Historical Society, Philadelphia.

Minutes, Synod of Virginia, 1788-1789. In the Library of the Union Theological Seminary, Richmond.

Witherspoon Draught of a Plan of Government and Discipline for the Presbyterian Church in North America. In Princeton University Library, Princeton, N. J.

Records of the Church of Christ (Baptist) at Buck Marsh (in the north Valley). In the Baptist Historical Society, Richmond.

Records, Opecquon Presbyterian Church (Frederick County). In possession of church clerk at Kernstown, Va.

Parson Craig's Diary. Diary of John Craig, one of the earliest Presbyterian leaders in the south Valley. In Manse, Old Stone Church, Fort Defiance, Va.

Gordon, Mrs. Sarah Morgan. Notes on Cool Spring Presbyterian Church (Berkeley County). Transcripts of contemporary data. In possession of Mrs. Gordon at Gerrardstown, W. Va

Edwards, Morgan, "Material toward a history of the Baptists in the Province of Virginia." Transcript in Baptist Historical Society, University of Richmond. Original in possession of A. G. Furman, Greenville, S. C.

Subscription List of Congregation of Tuscarora, Falling Waters and Back Creek for salary of Rev. Hugh Vance, 1770. Transcripts in possession of Mrs. Sarah Morgan Gordon, Gerrardstown, W. Va.

Vestry Book, Christ Church (Anglican), Winchester, 1777-1804. In Handley Library, Winchester, Va.

D. State Papers and Records

Indicate local contacts and demands, and furnish property owning data, both real and personal, for persons and areas studied. They are in the Virginia Land Office and in the Archives Department of the Virginia State Library. Used for all of the Valley counties and a number of those in eastern Virginia.

Land Office Records.

Land Tax Books. The Berkeley County Books are in Archives Department, West Virginia State Capital, Charleston.

Personal Tax Books. Begin in 1782. Books for Berkeley County in Archives Department, West Virginia State Capital, Charleston.

Petitions.

Revolutionary Claims. In two sets, one of which is called Claims and Taxes.

E. Miscellaneous Papers

Alexandria Broadsides. Library of Congress.

Gilbert, Felix, Account Book.

Hampden-Sydney College Records, 1776-1819, vol. i. Minutes of the Board of Trustees of the Presbyterian College in the Virginia Piedmont. In Hampden-Sydney College Library.

Henly Letter. In Library of Congress.

Lamb Letters. Transcripts from the British Museum, numbers 6808, 6817. In Library of Congress.

Stephen Diary. In the Ridgway Branch of the Library Company of Philadelphia.

Stephen Transcripts. In the possession of Miss Nannie Spotswood Dandridge, Baltimore, Md.

Treasury Department Records. In United States Treasury Department.

United States Finance. In Library of Congress.

Virginia Broadsides. In Library of Congress.

Virginia Manuscripts. In the Manuscript section of the University of Virginia Library.

Washington and Lee University Records. In the Treasurer's Office at Washington and Lee University, Lexington, Va.

Whipple Papers. In Library of Congress.

White, Alexander, Letter. In Library of Congress.

II. PRINTED SOURCES

A. Debates and Journals

The Debates in the Several State Conventions on the Adoption of the Federal Constitution, as Recommended by the General Convention at Philadelphia in 1787. Edited by Jonathan Elliot. 4 v. Washington, 1836-1845.

Debates and other Proceedings of the Convention of Virginia convened at Richmond, on Monday the Second Day of June 1788, for the Purpose of Deliberating on the Constitution Recommended by the Grand Federal Convention. Taken in shorthand by David Robertson. Second edition, Richmond, 1805.

Journals of the Continental Congress, vols. i-xxv, edited by Worthington C. Ford and Gaillard Hunt. Washington, 1904-1922.

Journal of the Convention of Virginia Held in the City of Richmond, on the First Monday in June, in the Year of our Lord one Thousand Seven Hundred and Eighty-eight. Thomas W. White, ed. Richmond, 1827.

Journal of the Council of the State of Virginia, vols. i and ii, H. R. McIlwaine, ed. Richmond, 1931-1932.

Journal of the House of Burgesses of Virginia, 1727-1776. Edited by John Pendleton Kennedy and H. R. McIlwaine. Richmond, 1905-1915.

Journal of the House of Delegates of the Commonwealth of Virginia, 1776-1790. Thomas W. White, ed. Richmond, 1828.

Journal of the Senate of the Commonwealth of Virginia, Begun and Held in the City of Richmond, on Monday, the Seventeenth Day of October, in the Year of Our Lord Christ, 1776-1790. Thomas W. White, ed. Richmond, 1827.

Legislative Journals of the Council of Colonial Virginia, vols. i-iii, H. R. McIlwaine, ed. Richmond, 1918-1919.

Records of the Federal Convention of 1787, Edited by Max Farrand, 3 v. New Haven and London, 1911.

B. Documents, Essays, Pamphlets

American Archives, Peter Force, ed., 4th ser., vols. i-vi; 5th ser., vols. i-iii. Washington, 1837-1853.

American Husbandry, containing an account of the soil, climate, production and agriculture of the British Colonies in North America and the West Indies, vols. i-ii. London, 1775. By an American.

Calendar of Transcripts of the Virginia State Library, John P. Kennedy, ed. Richmond, 1905.

Calendar of Virginia State Papers and Other Manuscripts. Edited by William P. Palmer. Vol. iii, Richmond, 1883; vol. iv, Richmond, 1884.

Census, 1790, Return of the Whole Number of Persons within the Several Districts of the United States, per act Congress March 1, 1791 (i.e., 1790). Philadelphia, 1791.

Census, 1910, Thirteenth Census of the United States, taken in the year 1910, vol. iii. Hunt, William C., supervisor. Washington, 1913.

Chalmers, George. *Political Annals of the Present United Colonies from the Settlement to the Peace 1763; Introduction to the History of the Revolt of the American Colonies.*

Documentary History of the Constitution of the United States of America, 1786-1870. 2 v. Washington, 1894.

Essays on the Constitution of the United States, Published During its Discussion by the People, 1787-1788, ed. by Paul Leicester Ford. Brooklyn, 1892.

The Federalist and Other Constitutional Papers by Hamilton, Jay, Madison, and Other Statesmen of their Time. Edited by Erastus Howard Scott (Chicago, 1894).

MacDonald, William. *Documentary Source Book of American History,* 1606-1926, 3rd ed. New York, 1926.

Mercer, J. *Abridgment of the Virginia Laws.* London, 1759.

Pamphlets on the Constitution of the United States, Published During its Discussion by the People, 1787-1788. Edited with notes and a bibliography by Paul Leicester Ford. Brooklyn, 1888.

Sources and Documents Illustrating the American Revolution, 1764-1788 and the Formation of the Federal Constitution. S. E. Morison, ed. Oxford, 1923.

The Statutes at Large of all the Laws of Virginia, from the First Session of the Legislature in the Year 1619. William Waller Hening, ed. 13 v. Richmond, 1823.

C. Writings of Statesmen

Burnett, E. C. *Letters, Members of the Continental Congress,* vols. i-viii. Washington, 1921-1934.

Jefferson, Thomas. *Writings, Definitive Edition Containing His Autobiography, Notes on Virginia, Parliamentary Manual, Official Papers, Messages and Addresses, and other Writings, Official and Private.* Albert Ellery Bergh, ed., 20 v. Washington, 1907.

Madison, James. *The Papers of James Madison.* Published under supervision of Henry D. Gilpin, 3 v. New York, 1841.

Madison, James. *The Writings of James Madison.* Gaillard Hunt, ed., 9 v. New York and London, 1900-1910.

Monroe, James. *Writings.* Hamilton, S. M., ed., 7 v. New York and London, 1898-1903.

Official Letters, Governors of Virginia, vols. i-iii, 1776-1783, H. R. McIlwaine, ed. Richmond, 1926-1929.

The Preston and Virginia Papers in Wisconsin Historical Society *Publications,* Cal. Ser., vol. i. Madison, 1915.

Virginia Historical Register, vol. ii. Richmond, 1849.

Washington, George. *Letters to Washington, and Accompanying Papers;* published by the Society of Colonial Dames of
America, ed. by Stanislaus Murray Hamilton. 4 v. Boston
and New York, 1896-1902.

————. *The Diaries of George Washington,* 1748-1799. John
C. Fitzpatrick, ed. 4 v. Boston and New York, 1925.

————. *Writings of George Washington; Being his Correspondence, Addresses, Messages, and Other Papers, Official
and Private, Selected and Published from the Original Manuscripts with a Life of the Author.* Edited by Jared Sparks.
12 v. Boston, 1837.

————. *The Writings of George Washington.* Worthington
Ford, ed. 14 v. New York and London, 1889-1893.

————. *Writings,* J. C. Fitzpatrick, ed. Vols. i-xiv, in process.
Washington, 1931—.

D. Military and Indian Affairs

De Hass, Willis. *History of the Early Settlement and Indian
Wars of Western Virginia; Embracing an Account of the Various Expeditions in the West, Previous to 1795.* Philadelphia,
1851.

Dinwiddie, Robert. "Official Records," vols. i-ii, ed. by R. A.
Brock in *Virginia Historical Collections,* vols. iii-iv. Richmond,
1883-1884.

Doddridge, Joseph. *Notes on the Settlement and Indian Wars of
the Western Parts of Virginia.* 1769-1826.

*Historical Account of the Expedition against the Ohio Indians in
the year 1764 under command of Henry Bouquet, Esq. Colonel Foot.* Published by a Lover of his country. Philadelphia,
1766.

Johnson, Sir Wm. *Papers,* vols. i-vi, ed. by James Sullivan and
Alexander C. Flick. Albany, 1921-1929.

Lee, Charles. *Papers.* In New York Historical Society. Pub.
vols. iv-vii. New York, 1871-1874.

Lewis, General Andrew. *Orderly Book, March 18, 1776-Au-
gust 28, 1776,* while in command American Army in Virginia.
Charles Campbell, ed. Richmond, 1860.

"Orderly Book of the Company of Captain George Stubblefield, 1776" in Virginia Historical Society *Collections*, vol. vi. Richmond, 1887.

Stuart, John. "Memoir of Indian Wars and Other Occurrences." In Virginia Historical Society *Collections*, Old Series, vol. i. Richmond, 1833.

Thwaites, R. G., and Kellogg, Louise K. *Documentary History of Dunmore's War*. Madison, 1912.

————. *Frontier Defense on the Upper Ohio*. Madison, 1908.

Withers, Alexander Scott. *Chronicles of Border Warfare or A History of the Settlement by the Whites, of Northwestern Virginia, and of the Indian Wars and Massacres in that Section of the State*. Clarksburg, W. Va., 1891. New edition by Reuben Gold Thwaites, Cincinnati, 1920.

E. Religious Records and Treatises

Asplund, John. *The Annual Register of the Baptist Denomination, in North America; to the first of November, 1790. Containing an account of the Churches and their Constitutions, Ministers, Members, Association, their Plan and Sentiments*. Richmond, Philadelphia, 1791-1792.

Hopewell Meeting House Records, ed. by Walker M. Bond. Quaker records of the Winchester vicinity. Winchester, 1937.

Ireland, James. *Autobiography of James Ireland*. Winchester, Va., 1819.

"Journals of the Conventions of the Protestant Episcopal Church in the Diocese of Virginia 1785-1835." In Francis L. Hawks, *A Narrative of Events Connected with the Rise and Progress of the Protestant Episcopal Church*. New York, 1836.

Leland, John. *The Virginia Chronicle; with Judicious and Critical Remarks, under xxiv Heads*. Fredericksburg, Va., 1790.

"Memorials to the General Assembly of Virginia," 1776-1785. In *Literary and Evangelical Magazines*, vol. ix. Richmond, 1826.

Minutes and Letters of the Coetus of the German Reformed Congregations in Pennsylvania, 1747-1792. Philadelphia, 1903.

Minutes, Synod, New York and Philadelphia, ed. by W. M. Engels. Philadelphia, 1841.

Perry, Wm. Stephens, ed. *Historical Collections Relating to the American Colonial Church*. Vol. I: Virginia. Hartford, 1870.

Sweet, W. W. *Religion on the American Frontier*, vol. i—. New York, 1931—.

Wirt, William. *The Letters of a British Spy*, 10th ed. New York, 1832.

Witherspoon, John. *The Works of the Rev. John Witherspoon Late President of the College at Princeton, New Jersey*. Printed and published by William W. Woodward. 4 v. Philadelphia, 1801-1802.

F. Newspapers and Periodicals

Alexandria, Virginia:

Virginia Journal and Alexandria Advertiser. Some 1787-1788 numbers in the American Antiquarian Society, Worcester, Massachusetts; *ibid.*, August 30, October 18, 1787, January 18, March 28, May 29, 1788. Library of Congress.

The American Museum, or, Repository of Ancient and Modern Fugutive Pieces, &c. Prose and Poetical, 1787, 1788. Matthew Carey, ed. 3 v. Philadelphia, 1788-1790.

Annapolis, Maryland:

Maryland Gazette, June 12, 1788-July 31, 1788. Maryland Historical Society, Baltimore.

Baltimore, Maryland:

Maryland Gazette and Baltimore General Advertiser, March-April, 1788. University of Pennsylvania Library, Philadelphia.

Maryland Journal and Baltimore Advertiser, January 2-July 3, 1788, Maryland Historical Society, Baltimore.

Carlisle, Pennsylvania:

Carlisle Gazette and Western Repository of Knowledge, January 2-July 30, 1788. Library of Congress.

Frederick, Maryland:

Maryland Chronicle or Universal Advertiser, September 12, 1787-December 12, 1787. In Maryland Historical Society, Baltimore, Maryland; *ibid.,* June 27, 1787-December 5, 1787 and May 28, 1788. In American Antiquarian Society, Worcester, Massachusetts.

New York, New York:

New York Daily Advertiser, January-May, 1788. New York Public Library.

The New York Magazine, or Literary Repository. 6 v. January, 1790-December, 1795. Library of Congress.

New York Packet, January-June, 1788. New York Public Library.

Philadelphia, Pennsylvania:

The Pennsylvania Gazette, 1769-1775. In New York Public Library.

Pennsylvania Packet, July 1, 8, 15, 22, 1788. University of Pennsylvania Library.

Richmond, Virginia:

Virginia Gazette and Weekly Advertiser, 1763-1788. Virginia State Library, Richmond.

Virginia Independent Chronicle, July 18, 1787-May 21, 1788. Virginia State Library, Richmond. (Reference designation, Virginia Chronicle.)

Virginia Almanac for the Year 1787. Being the third Year after Bissextile for Leap Year. Richmond, 1787.

Winchester, Virginia:

Virginia Centinel and Winchester Mercury, April 2, 1788-July 18, 1788. Handley Memorial Library, Winchester, Va. (Reference designation, Winchester Mercury.)

Virginia Gazette and Winchester Advertiser, July 27, 1787-July 6, 1788. (Reference designation, Winchester, Virginia.) A few early numbers in the Library of Congress.

Virginia Gazette and Winchester Political Repository, January 7-August 26, 1789. Handley Library, Winchester, Va.

G. Travels in Virginia in the Revolutionary Period

Most of the travels listed included a visit to the Valley of varying durations within the period.

Anburey, Thomas. *Travels Through the Interior Parts of America.* London, 1791.

Chastellux, Marquis De. *Travels in North America in the Years 1780, 1781, and 1782.* Dublin, 1787.

Cresswell, Nicholas. *The Journal of Nicholas Cresswell, 1774-1777,* L. MacVeagh, ed. New York, 1924.

Fithian, Philip Vickers. *Journal,* 1775-1776. R. G. Albion and L. Dodson, eds. Princeton, 1924.

————. *Philip Vickers Fithian Journal and Letters,* 1767-1774. John Rogers Williams, ed. Princeton, 1900.

La Rochefoucault-Liancourt, Duke de. *Travels Through the United States of North America, the Country of the Iroquois and Upper Canada in the Years 1795, 1796, and 1797.* Vol. ii. Containing the tour through Virginia, Pennsylvania, the Jerseys, and New York. London, 1800.

Mereness, Newton D., ed. *Travels in the American Colonies,* 1690-1783. New York, 1916.

Monoghan, Frank. *French Travellers in the U. S., 1765-1932; a Bibliography.* New York, 1933.

"Moravian Diaries of Travels through Virginia," edited by Rev. William J. Hinke and Charles E. Kemper in *The Virginia Magazine of History and Biography,* vol. xii (October, 1904).

Morrison, A. J., ed. *Travels in Virginia in Revolutionary Times.* Lynchburg, Va., 1922.

"Records of the Moravians in North Carolina," Adelaide L. Fries, ed., 2 v. In North Carolina Historical Commission's *Publications,* Raleigh, 1925.

Pettengill, Ray W., ed. *Letters from America, 1776-1779.* Being Letters of Brunswick, Hessian and Waldeck officers with the British Armies during the Revolution. Houghton-Mifflin, Cambridge, 1924.

Schoepf, Johann David. *Travels in the Confederation* (1783-1784). Alfred J. Morrison, translator and editor. Philadelphia, 1911.

Stone, William L., translator, *Letters of Brunswick and Hessian Officers During the American Revolution.* Albany, 1891.

Washington, George. *Journal of My Journey Over the Mountains;* Edited by Joseph Meredith Toner. Albany, 1892.

Weld, Isaac. *Travels through the States of North America, and the Provinces of Upper and Lower Canada During the Years 1795, 1796, and 1797.* London, 1799.

H. Miscellaneous Writings

Alexander, Archibald. "Zachariah Johnston," *The Princeton Magazine,* vol. i. Princeton, 1805.

Ford, Worthington Chauncey. "The Federal Constitution in Virginia," Massachusetts Historical Society, *Proceedings,* vol. xvii, pp. 450-510.

Hutchins, Thomas. *Topographical Description of Virginia, Pennsylvania, Maryland, and North Carolina, Comprehending the Rivers Ohio, Kenhawa, Sioto, Cherokee, Wabash, Illinois, Mississippi, &c., the Climate, Soil and Produce . . . Mountains, Creeks, Roads, . . .* with map. London, 1778.

Jefferson, Thomas. *Notes on the State of Virginia, with an Appendix Relative to the Murder of Logan's Family.* Trenton, 1803.

Lewis, Margaret. "Commonplace Book of Me, Margaret Lewis, nee Lynn, of Loch Lynn Scotland," reprint in *Bulletin* 3, vol. B., Historical Society of Northwestern Ohio. Toledo, July, 1936. (Probably spurious.)

Lewis, Thomas. *The Fairfax Line; Thomas Lewis' Journal of 1746, etc.* Edited by John W. Wayland. New Market, Va., 1925.

Marshall, John. *The Life of George Washington, Commander-in-Chief of the American Forces during the War which Established the Independence of his Country, and the First President of the United States.* 4 v. Philadelphia, 1805-1807.

Phillips, U. B. *Plantation and Frontier Documents; 1649-1863.* Vols. i-ii. Cleveland, 1909.

Summers, Lewis P. *Annals of Southwest Virginia, 1769-1800.* Abingdon, Va., 1929.

III. Secondary Works Containing Source Material

Abernethy, Thomas P. *Western Lands in the American Revolution.* New York and London, 1937.

Aler, F. Vernon. *Aler's History of Martinsburg and Berkeley County, West Virginia.* Hagerstown, Maryland, 1888.

Alvord, C. W. and Bidgood, Lee, eds. *The First Explorations of the Trans-Alleghany Region by the Virginians, 1650-1674.* Cleveland, 1912.

Annals, Carnegie Museum, vols. i and iii., Boyd Crumrine, ed.

Bacon-Foster, Mrs. Cora. "Early Chapters in the Development of the Potomac Route to the West." In *Records* of the Columbia Historical Society, vol. xv. Washington, 1912.

Cartmell, T. K. *Shenandoah Valley Pioneers and Their Descendants, A History of Frederick County, Virginia.* Winchester, Va., 1909.

Chalkley, Lyman. *Chronicles of the Scotch-Irish Settlement in Virginia, Extracted from the Original Court Records of Augusta County 1745-1800,* 3 v. Rosslyn, Va., 1912.

Dandridge, Danske. *Historical Shepherdstown.* Charlottesville, Va., 1910.

Eckenrode, H. J. "Separation of Church and State in Virginia. A Study in this Development of the Revolution." *Bulletin,* Virginia State Library, Richmond, 1910.

Foote, William Henry. *Sketches of Virginia, Historical and Biographical.* Philadelphia, 1850.

Greene, E. B. and Harrington, Virginia D. *American Population Before the Federal Census of 1790.* New York, 1932.

Greene, Katherine Glass. *Winchester, Virginia and its Beginnings, 1734-1814.* Strasburg, Va., 1926.

Henry, William Wirt. *Patrick Henry, Life, Correspondence and Speeches.* 3 v. New York, 1891.

James, Charles Fenton. *Documentary History of the Struggle for Religious Liberty in Virginia.* Lynchburg, Va., 1900.

Morton, Oren F. *A History of Rockbridge County, Virginia.* Staunton, 1920.

Morton, Frederick. *The Story of Winchester in Virginia.* Strasburg, 1925.
Norris, J. E. *History of the Lower Shenandoah Valley.* Chicago, 1890.
Pennsylvania Archives, Third Series, Wm. H. Engle, ed., vol. iii, Harrisburg, 1894.
Peyton, J. Lewis. *History of Augusta County.* Staunton, Va., 1882.
Rives, William Cabell. *History of the Life and Times of James Madison.* 3 v. Boston, 1859-1868.
Rowland, Kate Mason. *The Life of George Mason,* 1725-1792. 2 v. New York and London, 1892.
Semple, Robert B. *A History of the Rise and Progress of the Baptists in Virginia.* Revised by J. W. Beals, Richmond, 1894.
Sprague, William B. *Annals of the American Pulpit or Distinguished American Clergymen of Various Denominations, from the Early Settlement of the Country to the Close of the Year 1855.* 8 v. New York, 1857-1861.
Swem, G. G. *Virginia Historical Index.* 2 v. Roanoke, Va., 1934-1936.
Tyler's Quarterly. Historical and Genealogical Magazine, vols. i-xv, Richmond, 1920-1935.
Virginia Historical Collections, vols. i-x, ed. by R. A. Brock. Richmond, 1882-1891.
Virginia Magazine of History and Biography. 43 v. Richmond, 1893-1935.
Waddell, Joseph A. *Annals of Augusta County, Virginia, from 1726-1871.* Staunton, Va., 1902.
Washington and Lee Historical Papers, nos. i-vi. Lexington, Va., 1890-1904.
Wayland, Jno. W. *History of Rockingham County, Virginia.* Dayton, Va., 1912.
———. *History of Shenandoah County.* Strasburg, Va., 1927.
William and Mary College Quarterly, 1st Series, 27 v. Richmond, 1892-1919. Second Series, 15 v. Williamsburg, 1921-1935.

206   BIBLIOGRAPHY

IV. SECONDARY WORKS

Alden, G. H. "New Governments West of the Alleghanies before 1780." In *University of Wisconsin Studies in Economics, Political Science and History*, vol. 3, no. 1. Madison, 1897.

Alexander, James W. *Life of Archibald Alexander, D.D., First Professor in the Theological Seminary at Princeton, New Jersey.* New York, 1854.

Alexander, Samuel Davies. *Princeton College During the Eighteenth Century.* New York, 1872.

Alvord, C. W. *Mississippi Valley in British Politics.* 2 v. Cleveland, 1917.

Ambler, Charles Henry. *Sectionalism in Virginia from 1776 to 1861.* Chicago, 1910.

Baker-Crothers, Hayes. *Virginia and the French and Indian War.* Chicago, 1928.

Bassett, John S. "The Regulator Movement in North Carolina." In American Historical Association *Reports*, 1894.

Beard, Charles A. *Economic Interpretation of the Constitution of the United States.* New York, 1913.

Beer, George L. *British Colonial Policy, 1754-1765.* New York, 1922.

Beveridge, Albert J. *The Life of John Marshall.* 4 v. Boston and New York, 1919.

"A Bibliography of Virginia," Parts I and II, *Bulletins*, Virginia State Library, vol. viii, nos. 2-4 and vol. x, nos. 1-4.

Bining, Arthur C. *British Regulation of the Colonial Iron Industry.* Philadelphia, 1933.

Bishop, Cortland F. "History of Elections in the American Colonies." In *Columbia College Studies in History, Economics and Public Law*, vol. iii, no. i. New York, 1893.

Bond, B. W. *Quit-rent System in the American Colonies.* New Haven, 1919.

Boogher, Wm. Fletcher. *Gleanings of Virginia History.* Washington, 1903.

Bruce, Kathleen. *Virginia Iron Manufacture in the Slave Era.* New York and London, 1931.

Channing, Edward. *The American Revolution, 1761-1789* (*A History of the United States*, vol. iii). New York, 1912.

Clark, Victor S. *A History of Manufactures in the United States*, vol. i, 1607-1860. Washington and New York, 1929.

Collins, Varnum Lansing. *President Witherspoon; A Biography.* Princeton, 1925.

Cross, Arthur Lyon. *The Anglican Episcopate and the American Colonies.* Cambridge, 1902.

Dictionary of American Biography. Allen Johnson and Dumas Malone, editors. 20 v. New York, 1928-1938.

Eckenrode, H. J. "List of the Revolutionary Soldiers in Virginia," Virginia State Library *Bulletins, Eighth and Ninth Annual Reports.* Special Reporter for the Department of Archives for 1911, 1912. Richmond, 1912-1913.

———. *The Revolution in Virginia.* Boston and New York, 1916.

Faust, Albert Bernhardt. *The German Element in the United States with Special Reference to its Political, Moral, Social, and Educational Influence.* Boston and New York, 1901.

Flippin, Percy S. "The Royal Government in Virginia, 1624-1775." In Columbia University *Studies in History*, etc., 1919. New York, 1919.

———. "Financial Administration of the Colony of Virginia." In Johns Hopkins *Studies in History*, etc., series 32, no. 2. Baltimore, 1915.

Ford, Paul Leicester. *Bibliography and Reference List of the History and Literature Relating to the Adoption of the Constitution of the United States, 1787-1788.* Brooklyn, 1888.

Frick, Bertha. "History of Printing in Virginia, 1750-1783." Columbia University *Theses*, 1933.

Gewehr, Wesley M. *The Great Awakening in Virginia.* Durham, 1930.

Goodwin, Edwin F. and others. *Colonial Churches in Virginia.* Richmond, 1908.

Gray, Lewis C. *History of Agriculture in the Southern United States to 1860.* 2 v. Carnegie Institute, 1933.

Green, Thomas Marshall. *Historic Families of Kentucky with Special Reference to Stocks Immediately Derived from the Valley of Virginia.* . . . Cincinnati, 1899.

Greene, Evarts Boutell. *The Foundation of American Nationality.* New York, etc., 1922.

Greene, E. B. and Morris, R. B. *Guide to the Principal Sources for Early American History (1600-1800) in the City of New York.* Columbia University Press, 1929.

Grigsby, Hugh Blair. "The History of the Virginia Federal Convention of 1788," Virginia Historical Society *Collections,* vols. ix and x. R. A. Brock, ed. Richmond, 1891.

Hanna, Charles Alonzo. *The Scotch-Irish, or the Scot in North Britain, North Ireland, and North America.* 2 v. New York and London, 1902.

————. *The Wilderness Trail.* New York and London, 1911.

Harrell, Isaac Samuel. *Loyalism in Virginia; Chapters in the Economic History of the Revolution.* Durham, N. C., 1926.

Harrison, Fairfax. *Proprietors of the Northern Neck.* Richmond, 1926.

————. *Virginia Land Grants.* Richmond, 1925.

Hawks, Francis L. *A Narrative of Events Connected with the Rise and Progress of the Protestant Episcopal Church in Virginia.* New York, 1836.

Heitman, Francis Bernard. *Historical Register of the United States Army, from its Organization September 29, 1789.* Washington, 1890.

————. *Historical Register of the Officers of the Continental Army, During the War of the Revolution, April, 1775, to December, 1783.* Washington, 1914.

Hunt, Gaillard. "James Madison and Religious Liberty." American Historical Association, *Reports,* 1901, vol. i, pp. 164-171.

————. *The Life of James Madison.* New York, 1902.

Jameson, John Franklin. "Studies in the History of the Federal Convention of 1787." *Annual Report of the American Historical Association* for 1902, pp. 163, 166. Statement of source material. Washington, 1903.

Johnson, Thomas Cary. *Virginia Presbyterianism and Religious Liberty in Colonial and Revolutionary Times.* Richmond, 1907.

Johnston, David E. *A History of Middle New River Settlement and Contiguous Territory.* Huntington, W. Va., 1906.

Kercheval, Samuel. *A History of the Valley of Virginia.* Second edition. Woodstock, Va., 1850.

Kieffer, G. L. "An Analysis of Colonial Enumerations—" in *Lutherans in Colonial Days,* published by the United Lutheran Church in America. Philadelphia, 1926.

Koontz, Louis K. "The Virginia Frontier, 1754-1763." Johns Hopkins University, *Studies in History and Political Science,* edited by Henry B. Adams, series xliii, no. 2. Baltimore, 1925.

Lancaster, Robert Alexander, Jr. *Historic Virginia Homes and Churches.* Philadelphia and London, 1915.

Lewis, Virgil Anson. *History of the Battle of Point Pleasant Fought Between White Men and Indians at the Mouth of the Great Kanawha River, (now Point Pleasant, West Virginia) Monday, October 10, 1774.* Charleston, W. Va., 1909.

Libby, Orin Grant. "The Geographical Distribution of the Vote of the Thirteen States on the Federal Constitution, 1787-1788." *Bulletin of the University of Wisconsin, Economics, Political Science, and History Series,* vol. i, no. 1, pp. 1-116.

Lingley, Charles R. "The Transition in Virginia from Colony to Commonwealth," Columbia University *Studies.* New York, 1910.

Malone, Miles S. "The Distribution of Population on the Virginia Frontier in 1776." Princeton Ph.D. thesis, 1935, in manuscript.

McAllister, J. T. *Virginia Militia in the Revolutionary War.* Hot Springs, Va., 1913.

McIlwaine, Henry R. "The Struggle of Protestant Dissenters for Religious Toleration in Virginia." In Johns Hopkins University *Studies in History and Political Science,* edited by Herbert B. Adams, series xii, no. 4. Baltimore, 1894.

Maxson, Charles H. *Great Awakening in the Middle Colonies.* Chicago, 1920.

Meade, Bishop William. *Old Churches, Ministers and Families of Virginia.* 2 v. Philadelphia, 1861.

Miller, Elmer I. "The Legislature of the Province of Virginia." In the Columbia University *Studies in History,* etc., vol. 28, 1907.

Muhlenberg, H. S. *The Life of Major-General Peter Muhlenberg, of the Revolutionary Army.* Philadelphia, 1849.

Peyton, J. Lewis. *History of Augusta County, Virginia.* Staunton, Va., 1882.

Phillips, Ulrich B. *Life and Labor in the Old South.* New York, 1929.

Princeton, *General Catalogue of Princeton University, 1746-1906.* Princeton, 1908.

Robinson, Morgan. *Virginia Counties: Those Resulting from Virginia Legislation.* Richmond, 1916.

Sabin, Joseph and Eames, W. *Dictionary of Books Relating to America; from its Discovery to the Present Time.* 20 v. New York, 1927.

Sabine, Lorenzo. *The American Loyalists or Biographical Sketches of Adherents to the British Crown in the War of the Revolution.* Boston, 1847.

Schaff, Philip. "Church and State in the United States; or the American idea of religious liberty and its practical effects, with official documents." American Historical Association *Papers,* vol. ii, pp. 385-543. New York, 1888.

Schuricht, Hermann. *History of the German Element in Virginia.* 2 v. Baltimore, 1898.

Semple, Robert B. *History of the Rise and Progress of the Baptists in Virginia,* rev. by G. W. Beale. Richmond, 1894.

Summers, Lewis Preston. *History of Southwest Virginia 1746-1786, Washington County, 1777-1870.* Abingdon, Va., 1929.

Swem, Earl G. "A Bibliography of the Convention and Constitutions of Virginia, Including References to Essays, Letters and Speeches in the Virginia Newspapers." *Bulletin,* Virginia State Library, vol. iii, no. 4, pp. 374-380.

Swem, Earl G., and Williams, John W. *A Register of the General Assembly of Virginia, 1776-1918 and of the Constitutional Conventions.* Richmond, 1918.

Thom, William Taylor. "The Struggle for Religious Freedom in Virginia: The Baptists." In Johns Hopkins University *Studies in History and Political Science,* edited by Herbert B. Adams, series xviii, nos. 10-11-12. Baltimore, 1900.

Turner, Frederick Jackson. *The Frontier in American History.* New York, 1920.

Tyler, Moses Coit. "President Witherspoon in the American Revolution," *American Historical Review,* vol. i, no. 4, July, 1896.

Wayland, John W. *The German Element in the Shenandoah Valley of Virginia.* Charlottesville, Virginia, 1907.

Wirt, William. *Sketches of the Life of Patrick Henry.* Richmond, 1817.

Index